Website Visibility

CHANDOS INTERNET SERIES

Chandos' new series of books are aimed at all those individuals interested in the internet. They have been specially commissioned to provide the reader with an authoritative view of current thinking. If you would like a full listing of current and forthcoming titles, please visit our web site www.chandospublishing.com or email info@chandospublishing.com or telephone +44 (0) 1223 891358.

New authors: we are always pleased to receive ideas for new titles; if you would like to write a book for Chandos, please contact Dr Glyn Jones on email gjones@chandospublishing.com or telephone number +44 (0) 1993 848726.

Bulk orders: some organisations buy a number of copies of our books. If you are interested in doing this, we would be pleased to discuss a discount. Please email info@chandospublishing.com or telephone number +44 (0) 1223 891358.

Website Visibility

The theory and practice of improving rankings

MELIUS WEIDEMAN

Chandos Publishing

Oxford • Cambridge • New Delhi

Chandos Publishing
TBAC Business Centre
Avenue 4
Station Lane
Witney
Oxford OX28 4BN
UK
Tel: +44 (0) 1993 848726
Email: info@chandospublishing.com
www.chandospublishing.com

Chandos Publishing is an imprint of Woodhead Publishing Limited

Woodhead Publishing Limited
Abington Hall
Granta Park
Great Abington
Cambridge CB21 6AH
UK
www.woodheadpublishing.com

First published in 2009

ISBN:
978 1 84334 473 5

British Library Cataloguing-in-Publication Data.
A catalogue record for this book is available from the British Library.

Typeset by Domex e-Data Pvt. Ltd.
Printed in the UK and USA.

Printed in the UK by 4edge Limited - www.4edge.co.uk

To Alta, who made this possible through her unwavering support, and Tanya and Oelof, for believing in me.

Contents

Foreword

Chris Sherman

Like the Oracle at Delphi, search engines are our contemporary portals into a world of knowledge that once seemed accessible only by the gods. And like the Oracle, search engines can often seem cryptic or enigmatic in the 'knowledge' they offer to us mortals seeking advice.

That needn't be the case. After all, search engines really are just software programs created by humans, helping us find nuggets of divine wisdom, but also subject to the biases and preferences of the programmers and engineers who create them.

In *Website Visibility*, Melius Weideman takes us behind the 'veils' of these oracles we consult for our information needs on the Web. It's the first book I've seen that combines an academic rigor with a practical view of how search engines work: how they scour the web for information and sift through billions of pages to bring us the most relevant information for our particular, and often very individual, needs.

It's also the first time I've seen a serious, scholarly treatment of the largely obscure techniques that web marketers use to influence search-engine rankings, for better or worse for us all.

And importantly, the book also looks at a crucial variable – one that's a huge factor in Google's dominance, in my opinion – user interface design. After all, even the 'smartest' search engine seems more like an idiot savant if we can't use it to quickly, efficiently – and with trust – find the information we're looking for.

Website Visibility offers a thorough introduction to anyone wanting to understand how search engines work. From this foundation, you can either progress to a higher level of skill as a searcher, able to cut through the chaff on the Web, or, if you're more technically or entrepreneurially inclined, build websites that will attract search engines and searchers alike, to drive your online business to a new level of success. And best of all, the book is grounded in serious science, research and pragmatism.

Chris Sherman is Executive Editor of SearchEngineLand.com *and President of Searchwise LLC, a web consulting firm based in Boulder Colorado. He is frequently quoted in the* Wall Street Journal, *the* New York Times, Business Week, USA Today *and other publications, and has appeared on CNN, NPR, CBS and other television and radio networks.*

Acknowledgements

As with any large project, writing a book of this nature is a team effort. Not only did many people contribute to the content – many others contributed in terms of support, advice, constructive criticism and in other, much appreciated ways. Forgive me for not mentioning all your names.

Large parts of my enthusiasm for the topic comes from listening to the big names in my field speak at conferences and reading their works: Chris Sherman, Danny Sullivan, Mike Thelwall, Shari Thurow and Jill Whalen. The five of you have laid the foundations, shaped my thinking, spurred me on and helped me to get to the point of finishing the big one of the academic world – a full-sized researched book. Thank you for that contribution.

The content of the book is based on all my research on website visibility of the past seven years, plus some new comparative analysis. This analysis was done to establish a standard in website design for visibility. For lack of a better word, this result is called the Weideman model. The book was reviewed extensively for accuracy, depth and academic value by a number of experts from three countries. This includes a cross section of both academics and practitioners, which I believe is the spirit of the way this book was written. Every chapter was reviewed individually by two different experts, another two industry web practitioners reviewed the book as a whole for technical accuracy and one editor finally did an overall review to ensure consistency.

These ten individuals spent a large amount of time performing a thankless but important task, and deserve more praise than just a short mention! The reviewers are, in alphabetical sequence:

Prof Matthew Adigun (SA)

Prof Andy Bytheway (SA)

Mr Wouter Kritzinger (SA)

Dr Theo Mandel (USA)

Ms Beth Martin (USA)

Ms Liesl Muller (SA)

Ms Avi Rappoport (USA)

Dr David Stuart (UK)

Prof Peter Underwood (SA)

Mr Eugene Visser (SA)

Furthermore, I spent a quarter in Germany during 2008, teaching at MUAS (Munich University of Applied Science). My two groups of students at MUAS (I remember them affectionately as MASE (Mathematical Applications: Search Engines) and WVIR (Website Visibility and Information Retrieval)) assisted me with small subsections of the book, and I want to thank each one of them for the part they played in getting it all together. They are: Alexander Heinemann, Andreas Weiß, Anton Kurz, Benedikt Zais, Christoph Pohl, Elena Gärtner, Fabian Hollunder, Florian Ullmann, Franz Marksteiner, Hans Gabriel, Jiang Lan, Johannes Borchardt, Johannes Schleehuber, Kilian Kreglinger, Lukas Lindqvist, Marc Möhner, Markus Baumgartner, Markus Grauer, Markus Grießenböck, Michael Fußeder, Nicolas Wyrwa, Pascal Ruß, Patrick Schulte-Middelich, Peter Seibt, Philipp Hämmer, Stefan Frena, Thomas Gierlinger and Zeljko Jeremic.

The initial front cover layout plus all the freehand drawings in the first chapter were done by a very capable graphic artist Steven Moseley, whom you should contact if you want similar good service (*steven.darkwater@gmail.com*). Excellent support and amazingly fast responses to numerous queries came from the publishers, notably Dr Glyn Jones and Peter Williams. Your patience and dedication to a complex task is much appreciated. A special mention has to go to Wouter Kritzinger, my research assistant, for his effort, time and expertise put into the support system to make this book happen.

Finally, I cannot thank my dear wife and children enough – Alta, Tanya and Oelof, for their belief in me and their love. No book can describe Alta's constant support during the painful three months of giving birth to the crux of this book in a strange country under pressure.

I wish the reader an exciting journey of discovery in the wonderful world of website visibility!

Melius Weideman
Cape Town
June 2009

List of figures and tables

Figures

Tables

About the author

Melius Weideman is currently a Head of Department in the Faculty of Informatics and Design, Cape Peninsula University of Technology (CPUT) in Cape Town. After working in the electronics and computer industries, he joined academia in 1984. In 2004 he was appointed Associate Professor at CPUT and gained full Professor in 2008. His research interests were initially focused on computer viruses, but after 1994 his attention turned to the Internet and specifically search engines.

Having graduated with a PhD in Information Science from the University of Cape Town in 2001, Melius concentrated on helping students to find study-related material easily through the correct application of search engine technology. He has also published widely since then on topics including website visibility, search engines and information retrieval.

In 2007 he was chosen to become the first Fellow at the Munich University of Applied Sciences where he spent three months teaching in mid-2008. Also in 2008 Campus02 in Graz, Austria invited him to conduct two workshop series on Internet Marketing through Websites.

Melius is highly respected internationally and has delivered a number of guest lectures over the years at many universities around the world, including Oxford in the UK and Columbia in the USA. He also actively manages two websites: one to support this book (*http://www.book-visibility.com*), and another to make research funding and resource information easily available to colleagues and students (*http://www.mwe.co.za*).

The author may be contacted via the publishers.

The trilogy: users, webpages and search engines

Introduction

Humans use the Internet mostly via interaction through a website. If a given website is mission-critical, or if the owner wants the website to be indexed by search engines, it should be visible to them. Users can then find this website through the use of a search engine. One way to make a website visible is to design it in such a way that search engine crawlers can easily find it and successfully index the contents. Some elements of website design have a positive and some a negative effect on website visibility.

The purpose of this book is to identify (Chapter 2), rate (Chapter 2) and describe (Chapters 3 and 4) both positive and negative factors which influence website visibility. The approach is non-technical, and no programming techniques or technologies are discussed in any detail.

Relationships

Computer users, websites and Internet search engines are three closely linked entities. Some of their relationships and interaction can be described as follows:

- Most computer *users* are also Internet users (Fontaine, 2002).
- Most of the time users spend online, they read or interact with *webpages* (SIQSS, 2000).
- Most Internet traffic is generated by *search engines* (Smith, 2006).

As a result, the *trilogy* can now be defined – the synergistic relationship between the *user*, a *webpage* and a *search engine*. When any one of the three is removed, the Internet as we know and use it will cease to exist.

If you are reading this book, the chances are high that you are already an Internet user. You have used search engines before, you have experienced frustration with badly designed websites, you have hunted for that perfect piece of information lurking out there somewhere. You have probably viewed many search engine result pages, and clicked on some results hoping they would fulfil your information need. This is one side of the coin – the Internet and websites as seen from the *user side*.

However, websites are also viewed in a different way for a different purpose – by *search engine crawlers*. These are the programs which traverse the web, visiting millions upon millions of webpages and saving them in the search engine index for later processing. It is important to understand how crawlers interpret webpages and what webpage content they can and cannot index. An understanding of this view could lead to high rankings of certain webpages.

This book is about the second part – webpages and their relationship with search engine crawlers. In the process it addresses some needs many users who are non-programmers have. This includes website owners and company CEOs. One of these needs is to ensure that a website is seen and listed by search engines, which in turn would lead to more human visitors.

The book is aimed at students, academics and practitioners who are motivated to improve the ranking of a website on search engine result pages. It could be used as a research resource, a course textbook, a how-to guide and an authority to guide decision-making on website design.

Figure 1.1 shows a concept map depicting the trilogy identified above, and their interrelationships. The three shadowed boxes in Figure 1.1 are the three elements of the trilogy. The other four are the

Figure 1.1 The trilogy – users, webpage and search engines

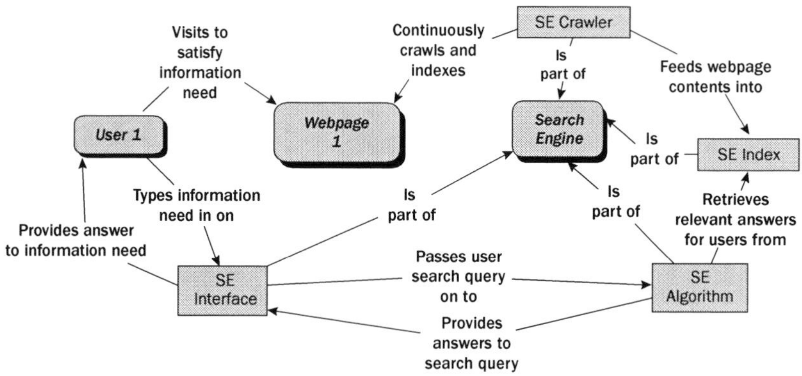

Source: Created with IHMC (2008).

components of a typical search engine. The arrows between the boxes are an indication of the relationships and interactions between the components.

The trilogy relationship includes every human who has ever used the Internet. Even if this user is new to search engines, he/she has viewed and interacted with a number of webpages as indicated in Figure 1.1 (top left). If there has been search engine interaction, the two relationships in the bottom left corner become relevant. As indicated, the user only really interacts with one of the four search engine components, namely the interface. The rest of the interactions are between the search engine components and the webpage.

Users

Arguably, the Internet user is the most important part of the Internet. Webpages are created for and read by this user. Search engines index webpages and provide extracts for the user. Advertisements are created for the user to respond to. It follows that webpages should be created with the user as consumer in mind and that software technology should be harnessed to improve the Internet experience for the user.

User versus coder and technology

One can draw another relationship diagram to illustrate how the webpage coder, the Internet user and the search engine are related to the webpage (see Figure 1.2). The user in the centre is the typical human Internet user. The search engine is a company which maintains programs that supply users with free answers to their information needs. The webpage box represents all the webpages on the Internet, collectively containing a vast array of information. And finally the coder represents the programmers who design and code webpages.

From this diagram, it appears that the user is the most important element in the relationship. The user supplies the finances by responding to advertisements to keep the search engine company going. Secondly, the user is the main reason why webpages are being designed. Thirdly, the search engine spends most of its time and energy providing for the information needs of the user. Finally, the coder creates webpages (using software technology), where these webpages are the staple food of both the user and the search engines.

Therefore it follows that the coder should focus on the needs of the user and aim to please the crawler at the same time. The role of technology – more specifically software tools – does not feature in this diagram.

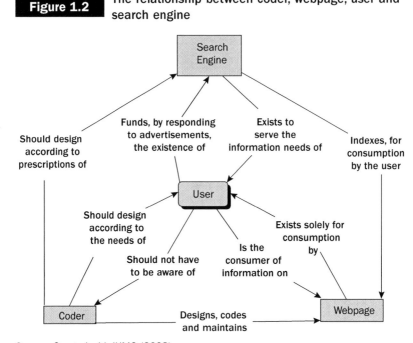

Figure 1.2 The relationship between coder, webpage, user and search engine

Source: Created with IHMC (2008).

In practice, this is often not the case. Numerous websites exist which were apparently designed to please neither the user nor the crawler, since they are both user- and crawler-unfriendly. At the same time, in some cases software technology has been used extensively to create a *good* website without considering the two main consumers.

Usability can be defined as the ease with which a particular tool can be used to achieve a given goal (Wikipedia, 2008c). The field of human–computer interaction includes research on the way humans interact with websites to achieve their goal.

Figure 1.3 is an example of a website feature considered to be user-unfriendly. Software technology has been used to create the drop-down menus, in this case to provide choices under the menu *Messaging* – see *a*. However, when the user tries to select *sms* (the leftmost option – just above *c*), the pointer cannot be moved from *a* directly to *c*, which is the most natural action. It must first be moved vertically downward from *a* to *b*, then horizontally to the left to *c*. If this is not done, other options to the left of *Messaging* are accidentally selected, with much user frustration as a result.

| Figure 1.3 | Example of technology use making life difficult for the user |

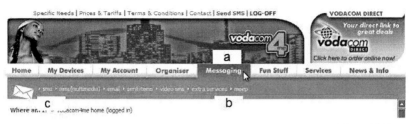

Source: https://www.vodacom4me.co.za/vodacom4me-personal/login.do (1 June 2009).

Searching success

As long ago as 1997 it was claimed that 71 per cent of Internet users access search engines to find websites with content which meet their information needs (CommerceNet/Nielsen Media, 1997). It has been proven that over 80 per cent of the traffic on the Internet is generated by search engine queries. This implies that Internet searching is an often-used pastime, and as such it deserves extra attention. Early research attempted to ease the path to searching success for students in the information systems world (Weideman, 1999). Other authors claim that Internet searching is second only to e-mail in the list of the top Internet applications (Vinson, 2007; Ashley, 2007).

Inherent in the Internet searching process is the expectation that there will be a successful conclusion. A user typing in a search phrase into a search engine search box is positive that the information need will be met within a short time. Sadly, this is not often the case. Research provides a range of numbers indicating searching success, mostly between 30 and 40 per cent. Weideman claims a 32 per cent success rate for searching for one topic under controlled circumstances (Weideman, 2001). Another author claims a figure of 33 per cent (Voorbij, 1999: 604). Some of the factors influencing searching success are investigated in the next section. A simple interface was designed after research into how successful queries are constructed, to increase searching success. This program was called Finder of Information on the Internet (FOIOTI) (Weideman, 2002b, 2005).

Number of results

Internet searching success is related to the number of results produced on a search engine result page (SERP). The concept of *more is better* does not seem to hold true for the number of search results. In fact, it is quite easy to produce a SERP with many millions of results. Simply type in a very common single-word term, like *news*, *sport* or *weather* on a big search engine, and the user is guaranteed to receive millions of answers.

Quite the opposite is true – once one manages to do a search on a very specific topic and receives a small number of results, the chances are much higher that one of them will lead to a relevant answer. The secret lies in focusing one's search in such a way that most of the irrelevant answers are filtered out, leaving only a small pool of relevant ones from which one good choice will mostly supply the information need.

One method of decreasing the number of results, i.e. focusing the search, is to increase the length of the keyphrase being used as the query. This technique could be termed *successive search focusing*. For example, a user needs to buy a Dell laptop in a computer shop. This user works in the Foreshore area of Cape Town. Table 1.1 lists the keyword, growing into a keyphrase which could be used in this search for the ideal shop. As the keyphrase grows in length and degree of *specificness*, the number of results decreases progressively. This indicates a sharpening of focus, which most likely will lead to a better chance of searching success.

This leads to the discussion: *How many keywords should I use to increase my chances of Internet searching success?*

Table 1.1 Successive search focusing

Keyphrase	Number of answers on SERP
computer	1,350,000,000
computer shop	35,900,000
computer shop cape town	2,230,000
computer shop cape town foreshore	21,400
computer shop cape town foreshore dell	457
computer shop cape town foreshore dell laptop	229

Number of keywords

At this point one should distinguish between two implied meanings of the term *keyword*. On the one hand it refers to the word or phrase a user types into a search box in an attempt to find relevant information on the Internet. This section is based on this first meaning.

Secondly, it could refer to the use of descriptive words in a certain way on a webpage in an attempt to increase its visibility. In fact, the correct use of keywords needs to be implemented in a number of ways, and collectively represents the second most important aspect of website visibility. The Weideman models in Chapter 2 will confirm this fact.

Research seems to indicate that most users specify around two words in the search box when starting a search. Spink produced results indicating typical query lengths of between 1.5 and 2.8 words per search, with an average of 2.21 during 1997 (Spink and Xu, 2000). During the same time Jansen indicated a peak at two words, with single-word queries being a close second – see Figure 1.4 (Jansen, 2000). These figures are for actual usage, not necessarily best practice.

Weideman reported that users specifying single-word queries have a 30.3 per cent chance of success, while those specifying two or more words weigh in at 42.3 per cent (Weideman et al., 2004). The experiments producing these results were done in a controlled environment, including the time spent on searching and the type of topic specified.

A top 50 search term summary for 2007 from a large search engine is given in Table 1.2. These are the most commonly used terms in searching, with no indication of the searching success resulting from their use. This table produces some alarming patterns. The number of searches using one, two, three and four search terms respectively were 26, 21, 2 and 1. The highest concentration is on single-term searching, which is unlikely to produce relevant results in general. Most of the two-word searches were name-surname combinations – some of them apparently celebrity names. Many of the single-term searches were for simplistic concepts, like *golf,*

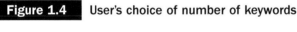

Figure 1.4   User's choice of number of keywords

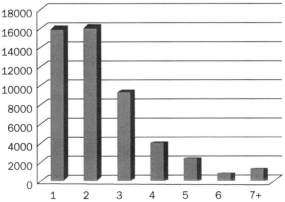

Source: Jansen (2000).

Table 1.2   Top search terms actually used

Top 50 Lycos Searches, 2007			
1	Poker	26	LimeWire
2	MySpace	27	Facebook
3	Britney Spears	28	Trish Stratus
4	Paris Hilton	29	Shakira
5	Golf	30	Christmas
6	YouTube	31	Jessica Alba
7	Naruto	32	Inuyasha
8	Disney	33	Angelina Jolie
9	Pokemon	34	Carmen Electra
10	WWE	35	Harry Potter
11	RuneScape	36	World Series
12	Pamela Anderson	37	South Beach Diet
13	Clay Aiken	38	Dancing with the Stars
14	Fashion	39	Wikipedia
15	Spyware	40	Jessica Simpson
16	Dragonball	41	Jennifer Aniston
17	Anna Nicole Smith	42	Stephanie McMahon
18	Vanessa Hudgens	43	Jennifer Lopez
19	Halloween	44	Hilary Duff
20	NFL	45	Webkinz
21	Antonella Barba	46	Thanksgiving
22	Apple	47	Valentine's Day
23	Beyonce	48	Barbie
24	Baseball	49	The Sims
25	Lindsay Lohan	50	Emma Watson

Source: *http://searchenginewatch.com/showPage.html?page=3627937* (1 August 2009).

Christmas and *Fashion*. Using a single word for searching has a good chance of success only if the term is very specific, as explained further in this chapter. Searches for general single terms are too vague to produce answers likely to satisfy an information need.

This trend seems to indicate a lack of sophistication in search query formulation, and a total lack of ability to focus a search to eliminate the thousands, often millions, of useless answers.

If these figures are linked to the rather low success rate of Internet searching in general, one cannot help but wonder about the relationship.

Is the low number of search terms not one of the reasons behind the low success rate in searching?

The author would like to present a simple model (see Figure 1.5) to demonstrate one way to searching success, based on excessive experience and many tests with users. If an Internet search query is too short (in general, one word is regarded as too short), the chances are that too many answers are produced on the SERPs. This mostly leads to searching failure – the search focus is too wide, trapping the user in GLUT – the mountain of too many answers. On the other hand, it is also possible to specify a search query which is too long – a full sentence for example. This is likely to produce no answers from the search engine, leaving the user in BARRENNESS, the valley of zero answers.

The ideal situation is that the user finds himself in EQUILIBRIUM – the flat and easy area of Internet Searching Success.

It is not possible to suggest a single figure as being the *best* number of keywords to use. Personal experience has proven that one and even two keywords are generally too few, and that the ideal lies somewhere between three and six keywords.

If the words in the query have any one or more of the following attributes, a shorter query will probably lead to success (example search queries are given in brackets):

- technical terms (e.g. *derailleur*);
- medical terms (e.g. *thrombophlebitis*);
- scientific or mathematical concepts (e.g. *differential equation examples*);

Figure 1.5   Query length suggestion

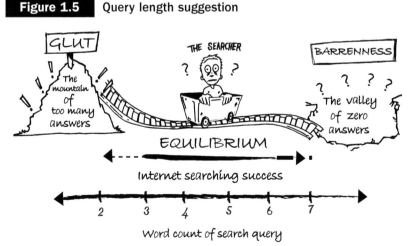

Artwork by S. Moseley, 2008.

- difficult to spell words (e.g. *curriculum vitae*);
- acronyms which are not generally used (e.g. *CAV disk mechanism*).

An exception here is when user experience dictates that a certain website ranks well for a certain keyword. In such a case using a simple single term as search query, for example, will produce searching success.

If the search query is general by nature, more terms will be required, for example:

- *accommodation london hotel tube station paddington*
- *7 day weather forecast new york*
- *tour de france 2008 stage winners*

Basic formula

The following sequence of steps has been identified during empirical experiments with learners in South Africa and Germany as producing a consistently high success rate in Internet searching:

- Express the information need as a single, keyword-rich English sentence.
- Remove all stop words from this sentence.
- Type the remaining string of keywords into a search engine search box.
- Using multiple simultaneous windows, open between one and ten windows of potential relevant answers.
- Filter these until one or more useful websites remain – the need has been met.

At this point the terms *keyword* and *stop word* should be defined. While considering the trilogy of user, webpage and search engine (see Figure 1.1), a keyword is any word which is descriptive and weight-carrying in a given context. A stop word, again, is an overused term which adds no value to the content of a website. Keywords could be: *dollar, university, mountain bike, Cape Town*, etc. Stop words could be: *me, search, find, and, this, that*, and in terms of Internet searching, even overused words such as *computer, system, information, Internet* and others. Unfortunately, users and search engines sometimes classify stop words differently. Figure 1.6 shows the difference between keywords and stop words from a user perspective. In this example, keywords are indicated in boxes, implying that for this specific website they are descriptive of the content.

| Figure 1.6 | Example of difference between keywords and stop words |

The Absa Cape Epic presented by adidas takes place every year around the last week of March and the first week of April. The race is held over 8 days and includes a time-trial prologue. The route changes every year, and leads aspiring amateur and professional mountain bikers from around the world through approximately 800 kilometres of the unspoilt nature of the Western Cape and up approximately 16 000m of climbing over some of the most magnificent passes in South Africa.

Source: http://www.cape-epic.com/content.php?page_id=23&title=/Introduction/
(1 June 2009).

It follows that what is a stop word in one context for one webpage could be a keyword for another. For example, the word *news* is probably of no consequence on a website which advertises second-hand furniture (*Our latest news is that we now also sell new desks ...*). However, it should appear with high density on websites like *http://www.cnn.com* and *http://www.bbc.co.uk*. No absolute categorisation can be done, although over-used, common and very short words have very little meaning in terms of Internet searching.

Webpages

Some might argue that a webpage is the most important element of the Internet. It is where the user finds information. It is what the designer spends large amounts of time and energy on designing. It is what search engines visit, index and present to users as answers to their queries. It is understandable that webpages evoke emotions, spawn discussions between users, create income and raise red flags with search engines and users alike. Webpage addresses are advertised on television, billboards and business cards, swopped via e-mail and SMS and they are used to boost egos. The text, graphics and videos filling millions of screens worldwide every day warrant some closer inspection. The relationships depicted in Figures 1.1 and 1.2 play a role in our interaction with the Internet, as described below.

Design

The world has not yet seen as powerful a mechanism to distribute information, coupled with such a wide degree of freedom, as webpage design and hosting. Just about any human with some very basic skills in design, access to the Internet and a message to convey can create and maintain a website. Lately even these basic design skills are no longer required – blog templates enable users to create websites without any design experience. The downside of this power and freedom is that a large number of badly designed, unethical, untrue and sometimes downright offensive websites exist on the Internet. Unfortunately there is no easy way of improving or removing these sites.

Assume for a moment that a user viewing a given webpage needs to interact with this page out of their own choice, i.e. there is a dependency on this webpage to provide certain information (for example, a user doing online banking). Further assume that the website has a non-intuitive navigation scheme, or a bad choice of colour, or has many grammatical errors. This will lead to user frustration, or even failure to achieve the basic objective, e.g. transferring money from one account to another.

Even more seriously, if the site had been an online shop, they would have lost a customer, who would simply click elsewhere and spend his/her online money at a competitor's site. It is therefore crucial that mission-critical websites are designed properly, after having considered the needs of the user. Fortunately, many guidelines towards *good webpage design* exist, and applying any tested one will result in an improvement in the user experience.

One trustworthy source lists the following five elements as being critical success factors for a good website. A well-designed website should be:

- easy to read;
- easy to navigate;
- consistent in layout;
- quick to download; and
- easy to find. (Thurow, 2003a: 34)

The first three can be collectively grouped as supporting website usability, the fourth one is a technical prerequisite to decrease user frustration and the last one is the basis of this book: website visibility.

A website is usable if it is easy to read and has been laid out to please the human reader, having been tested on different browser types and versions, different makes and sizes of monitor, using easy-to-read fonts, etc. If this has not been done, different users will experience the website in different ways, not all of them being classified as easy to use.

Navigation schemes used on modern websites are either text-based or graphic-based, or a mixture of both. The location of navigation controls is important, as well as the presence of a sitemap, help and a site search feature (Ngindana, 2005; Weideman et al., 2004).

Webpages can be coded directly in HTML, which provides the coder with the best understanding of the structure and of how the browser interprets and displays elements of the webpage. However, it would be extremely time-consuming to code in HTML only, and downright impossible when considering the modern technologies available and the complex websites required today.

When inspecting existing websites, it is preferable to have a very basic understanding of HTML code, without ever having to code in HTML. The following section provides some simple HTML examples, sufficient to enable the reader to understand the elements of HTML code needed to evaluate websites as it is done in this book. One can use the Notepad program in Windows to create the files used as examples below. As long as they are saved with an .htm or .html extension, they can be viewed on your screen as webpages through your browser (e.g. MS Internet Explorer).

HTML, short for HyperText Markup Language, is the language of the Web. One can easily view the HTML code for any webpage currently in the browser window. For MS Internet Explorer, select the *Page* menu and *View Source*. Alternatively one can simply right click on an unused area of the webpage and select *View Source* from the menu.

Figure 1.7 shows a very simple HTML program. The start and end of the coding is delimited by the <HTML> and </HTML> tags. Similarly, the header section, which can be empty, is marked by the <HEAD> and </HEAD> tags. The contents of the TITLE tag will be displayed in the user's browser window, at the top of the screen, but is not part of the main display inside the body. However, this (and other) tags play an important part in website visibility. Finally, the body, which contains whatever the designer wants to appear on the screen, is enclosed inside the <BODY> and </BODY> tags.

The contents of the HEAD section, although optional for the basic operation of the webpage, could have important effects on webpage

Figure 1.7   A simple HTML program

```
<HTML>
<HEAD>
<TITLE>This program explains the basics</TITLE>
</HEAD>
<BODY>
Hi there! This is a tutorial on webpage programming.
Everything coded between the two "body" tags will be displayed on the screen.
</BODY>
</HTML>
```

Figure 1.8   Expanding the HEADER section

```
HTML>
<HEAD>
        <TITLE>The Melius Weideman page on Internet Searching,
        Information Technology Research and Education at CPUT</TITLE>

        <META name="DESCRIPTION" content="This home page of Melius Weideman leads to
                        Internet Searching Assistance, a friendly
                        Internet Searching user interface called FOIOTI,
                        Information Technology Research Projects,
                        Information Technology Educational online
                        material">
        <META name="KEYWORDS" content="Internet search searching FOIOTI search engine
                        information technology research education degree
                        training FAQ reference tips evaluation cycling
                        site Melius Weideman">
</HEAD>
```

Source: *http://www.mwe.co.za* (1 July 2009).

visibility. One should add not only a TITLE tag as in Figure 1.7, but also a DESCRIPTION and a KEYWORDS tag, as in Figure 1.8. Details on how to write these tags follow later on in the book.

More detail about using the *H1* tag in the body – to make certain headings stand out more than others, for example – is discussed later in the book. A *perfect website* in terms of website visibility has been designed and hosted at *http://www.book-visibility.com*. Although the site is simple in design, it implements the elements identified and described in Chapters 2 and 3 of this book. Readers are urged to view the HTML code of some of these webpages as an example of simple but visible layout.

Visibility

This term is what this book is all about, and refers to a feature of a given webpage. This feature is defined by the degree of ease with which a search engine crawler can find the webpage. Once found, it is further defined by the degree of success the crawler has in indexing the page. A webpage with high visibility can be easily found and has been designed in such a way that a crawler will find a large amount of relevant, easy-to-index information on the page.

Both these factors can be manipulated by the website owner and/or coder. All important webpages should be submitted manually to the important search engines which will result in subsequent crawler visits. Secondly, if a webpage has been designed as suggested in this book, that page will present a rich harvest to the crawler.

Website visibility cannot be measured by simply viewing a webpage on the screen. Some inspection of the workings under the hood is required, although not on a highly technical level. See *http://www.book-visibility.com* for an example of a highly visible website.

Usability

Computer users have a natural expectation that websites will *behave* and respond to their prompts in a certain way. When this does not happen, user frustration increases, up to the point of users simply navigating away to another website. Sometimes, however, a user has no choice but to get to grips with a given website and fight through difficult menus, non-obvious selections, etc. One example is using a bank's website – users are unlikely to move all their accounts from one bank to another just because they have an unfriendly website. Website usability can loosely be defined as a *feeling* of being easy to use or not.

An obvious question could be: why not design all websites to be both visible and usable? This way the website would please both crawler and human visitors. The answer is that although it sounds like an ideal solution, it is not always possible. Sometimes, the use of a feature to make a webpage more user-friendly will make it more crawler-unfriendly (e.g. JavaScript and images). Thus the designer is caught between trying to serve two masters, where each has requirements opposite to the other. Research on human–computer interaction (HCI) in general and website usability specifically has been carried out for many years. Leaders in the field are Agarwal, Nielsen, Palmer and Zhang, among others.

One of the most basic but important results from this kind of research has been the identification of the most viewed areas from the user point of view on a typical computer screen. Consider this area to be prime real estate – website designers should locate the most important part of the website in this area. Enquiro (2008) has defined this prime area, the top left corner, as the 'golden triangle'. Figure 1.9 indicates heat maps of where the users' eyes will spend more time (the darker areas) and less time (the lighter areas) respectively.

Nielsen provided similar results with his *Capital F* heat maps – see Figure 1.10 (Nielsen, 2006). According to Nielsen, most users scan a webpage from the top left-hand corner towards the right, then return to the left side, move down and then to the right again. Continuing in this way, a capital F pattern is traced out, with most of the focus again in the top left-hand corner.

A study was done to compare the interfaces of a number of freeware virtual library products and found them to be lacking in many aspects (Weideman, 2004c). A comparison was made between user preferences for a concept map type interface (as used in Figures 1.1 and 1.2) and traditional hyperlink interfaces. It was found that male users from a European culture had a stronger preference for concept maps as opposed

Figure 1.9   Enquiro's golden triangle

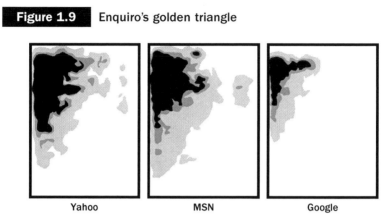

| Yahoo | MSN | Google |

Adapted from Enquiro (2008) (23 June 2009).

Figure 1.10   Nielsen's Capital F pattern

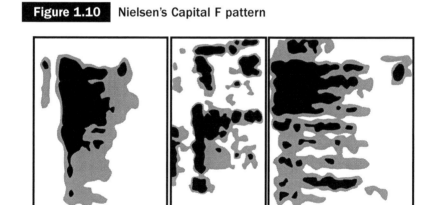

Adapted from Nielsen (2006) (23 June 2008).

to other users from an African culture and language groups (Weideman et al., 2003b).

Another study on a government website was done to determine how its visibility to search engines and usability for human users compared (Weideman, 2006). It was found that usability was higher than visibility, but that both needed to be improved. Research is currently underway which attempts to define and standardise the synergy between these two worlds. Can a model be built to prescribe website design in such a way that both usability and visibility can be implemented?

Popularity measures

A number of measures exist to express the popularity of a website. Some of them are useful, some not, and all have to be viewed in context to make sense. All of them have to be expressed as a function of time period, for example *page views per day* or *visitors per hour*.

Probably the most commonly used (and abused) measure is the notion of a *hit*. A hit is defined as a request for a file from a file server. If a user types in *www.book-visibility.com* into a browser and presses Enter, the file www.book-visibility.com/index.htm is loaded from a server and one hit is recorded. However, this one file may contain many other files embedded in the HTML coding, for example seven image files for navigation purposes, plus one JavaScript file. A further eight hits will therefore also be recorded. It follows that a claim such as *my website registered 100,000 hits per day* carries little value, since it is an indication of the complexity of webpages rather than popularity. Claims of popularity based on hits could be misleading and create a false impression of popularity.

A more conservative measure is that of a *page view*. One page view can be formulated as: *number of hits minus number of non-HTML pages*, or simply *number of HTML pages* downloaded. For the same webpage, a hit counter should be much higher than a page view counter for the same time period. Page views could also provide an inflated view of popularity, since refreshing a page will increment this counter. A user aimlessly navigating backwards and forwards through a number of webpages in the same website will have the same result.

Furthermore, some websites use only one page view counter for *all* the HTML pages on the website. If one webpage is viewed, the user might get the impression that the counter is an indication for only that one page. It is fairly easy to determine if this is the case. Simply view the counter for more than one webpage of the same website, and if it has the same value and both increment by one if any one page is refreshed, it is the same counter. Figure 1.11 indicates a page view counter before and after a refresh click on the webpage.

Another value in the use of page views as a metric is the determination of the *stickiness* of a website. Stickiness is an indication of how much time a visitor spends on one website (Li et al., 2006). If one visitor creates a large number of page views in one session for the same website, it can be assumed that the website was considered to be a useful resource.

A fourth popularity measure is that of the number of *visitors*. This figure should again be lower than the page view indicator, since one visitor can generate ten page views, which in turn could generate 100 hits

Figure 1.11	Page view counter before and after refreshing

Pages	578
Pag. today	9
Visits	437
Online	1

Pages	579
Pag. today	10
Visits	437
Online	1

Adapted from *http://www.mwe.co.za/hm.htm* (1 June 2009).

during the same session. One argument for the value of the visitor counter is that it is a better popularity indication than page views, since two visitors are worth more than one visitor generating two page views. This is because there is a better chance that x amount of visitors will spend money than one visitor visiting x webpages. At the same time, an opposing argument is that the same visitor returning to a site ten times per day is not worth as much as ten different visitors in one day, making the visitor counter less valuable. This, in turn, has led to further variations in the visitor counter as a measure of popularity.

At least four variations are known: *first visitor, repeat visitor, singleton visitor* and *unique visitor*. A first visitor is one who has not been recorded as a visitor to this website on any previous occasion. A repeat visitor is the opposite – a visit has been made to this website before. A singleton visitor is one who views only one webpage on the website before leaving. And finally, a unique visitor is a repeat visitor with a given time period having expired between successive visits. The length of this time period is debatable – do you count the same person as a repeat visitor if the visit frequency of a news website is twice per hour? Twice a week? Three times a month only?

In summary, some of these measures are difficult to quantify and of academic interest only. Hits, page views and unique visitors are the easiest to measure, and when used in context, most valuable to compare the popularity of different webpages. Many free counters are available on the Internet and an empirical experiment was carried out to determine which one of the measures above they implement. A random selection of

20 of these counters was made which were installed on a webpage and hosted. It was found that they all counted page views.

Visible and invisible web

The photograph of an iceberg in Figure 1.12 is an indication of the meaning of these two terms and the relation between their respective sizes. The visible web is the collection of indexable webpages – those which a search engine crawler can find and index. The invisible web (also called the deep web) is a collection of those webpages which are hidden from a crawler since they are behind a firewall. User login is required before access is granted to information behind the firewall. They could also be buried in a database, requiring a user query to be executed before they could surface.

Therefore human users can access the invisible web, but not through standard search engine queries. As a comparison, the visible and invisible

Figure 1.12   The visible and invisible web

Source: Google Image search (1 June 2009).

web was estimated to contain 19 and 7,500 terabytes of information respectively (Bergman, 2001). However, these figures have probably grown out of proportion since this estimate.

A very simple, text-only webpage is typically 5 kB in size. If all webpages on the visible web at this time had been this simple, it could be approximately:

19,000,000,000,000 / 5,000 = 3,800,000,000

webpages in size.

A more recent study made of the four biggest search engines (Google, Yahoo!, MSN and Ask Jeeves) lists the size of the visible web in 2007 as being approximately 47,000,000,000 webpages in size. The same author claims the number of webpages indexed by Yahoo! in May 2008 to be 45,500,000,000 (de Kunder, 2007). These two figures alone seem to indicate a steep growth in size of the indexable Internet.

One of the main reasons why certain webpages are inaccessible by crawlers is the format of their URLs. *Plain* URLs such as *http://www .cape-epic.com* are easy for a crawler to index. This URL refers to a simple HTML file, which is part of the visible web. However, if a certain menu selection on this same webpage is made (in this example, asking for more detail on the stages in this cycling event), a new webpage is displayed and this URL is generated: *http://www.cape-epic.com/ content.php?page_id=116&title=/The_Stages/*. Notice the *?* and *&* characters in this new URL. The first, simple URL above is that of a static webpage, the second, complex one is that of a dynamic webpage. These two kinds of webpages make up a large part of the visible and invisible web respectively. They are discussed in detail elsewhere in this book.

Search engines

It is probably safe to say that one of the areas of fiercest competition in the information wars taking place on the Internet is that of search engine dominance. It has also produced stories of amazing financial success and catastrophic failures.

Pecking order

During the late 1990s, AltaVista was the *biggest* search engine, at one stage claiming an index of around 250,000,000 webpages. Later, Yahoo!

Figure 1.13 Google's searching share

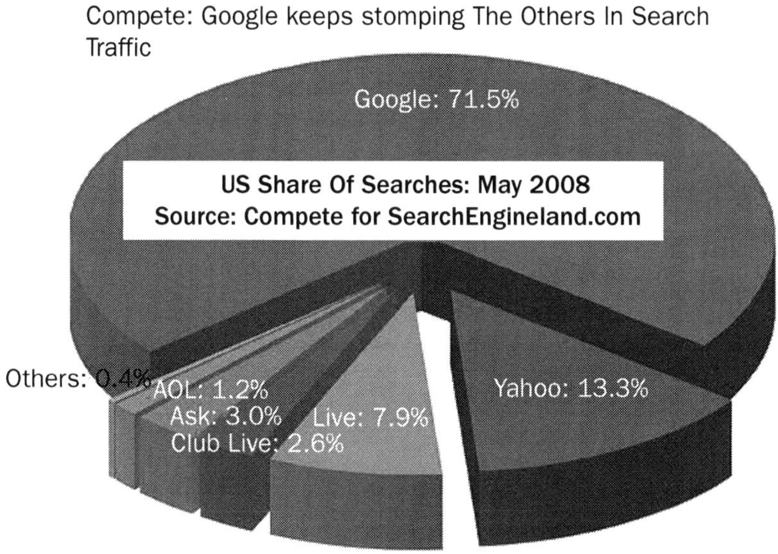

Compete: Google keeps stomping The Others In Search
Traffic

Google: 71.5%

US Share Of Searches: May 2008
Source: Compete for SearchEngineland.com

Others: 0.4%   AOL: 1.2%   Yahoo: 13.3%
              Ask: 3.0%   Live: 7.9%
              Club Live: 2.6%

Source: Sullivan (2008a) (1 June 2009).

took the lead, not in terms of index size, but in terms of user popularity. Soon afterwards, however, Google became the undisputed leader in terms of searches generated by a given search engine. At the time of writing, it is claimed that Google generated over 71 per cent of the searches that took place in the US during May 2008 (Sullivan, 2008a) – see Figure 1.13. Note how the means of measurement has changed over the years. Index size as an indication of superiority has given way to popularity, in turn succumbing to market share of searches having taken place.

There is no doubt that Google is currently the world leader in search, whichever measurement one wishes to choose. Love it or hate it, two out of three searches being done on the web in the US is channelled through Google. In terms of market share, it is twice as big as all the other search engines combined.

Components

There are many ways to describe search engines, their components and how they operate. One of them is to consider the four components identified in Figure 1.14 and discuss their interaction.

Two kinds of programs which assist users in finding relevant information on the Internet exist: search engines and directories. Search engines use automated programs to harvest the Internet for webpages to index. Directories use human editors for this purpose. Since humans can make intelligent decisions about webpage contents, they classify websites into directories and offer these directories to the user – hence the name. A combination of these two approaches is becoming more common – Mahalo claims to be the world's first human-powered search engine (see *http://www.mahalo.com*).

Both search engines and directories contain four components:

- an interface (which the user interacts with);
- an algorithm (a program used by the search engine to decide on rankings);
- an index (where large amounts of data about websites is stored); and
- a harvesting mechanism, often called a crawler.

Figure 1.14 shows a graphical presentation of the interaction between these four components.

Figure 1.14 The four components of a search engine

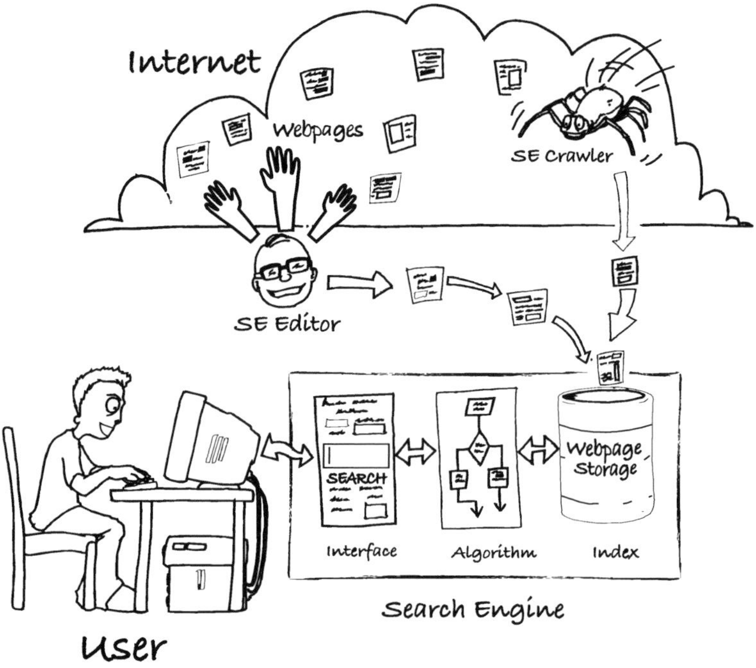

Artwork by S. Moseley, 2008.

Interface

Starting from the user's side, the interface is what the user sees on the screen while interacting with the search engine. It contains, among other things, a box where the user has to type in a search query, and a button named *Go* or *Search*. It appears to be no different from any other webpage when viewed on the screen. However, as with any other program user interface, it does have an effect on how users perceive the search engine.

Google is famous for its very sparse interface, which was introduced at a time when many Internet users were irritated by banner advertisements and other superfluous images on webpages (see Figure 1.15). Depending on which version you use, it could display as few as 36 words of text on a plain white background with no traditional advertisements. The search box is right in the centre of the screen and the *Search* button is highlighted by default. Some authors believe that this interface played a role in Google's success (Pouros, 2007; Elgin, 2005) while others disagree (Powazek, 2006; Norman, 2004). Powazek considers design ineptitude to be the reason for the sparse interface while Norman claims that it has been designed that way since it only offers one feature, namely search.

Figure 1.15   The central part of Google's interface

Source: *http://www.google.com* (20 December 2008).

Crawlers

The harvesting mechanism of a search engine is either an automated program called a crawler, robot or spider, or human editors. A crawler traverses the Internet 24/7 gathering the contents of webpages and sending them back to the search engine. In the case of directories, human editors spend their time reading and evaluating websites for possible inclusion in their index. Figure 1.16 provides a graphical representation of this process.

Each search engine uses its own crawler program and some have descriptive names. Crawler visits to a given webpage can often be traced in the logs of the server. Some common search engine crawler names are listed in Table 1.3.

Figure 1.16 How search engines crawl webpages

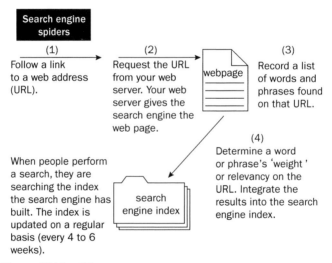

Source: Thurow (2003a: 15).

Table 1.3 Crawler names

Search engine	Crawler
AlltheWeb	fast-webcrawler
AltaVista	Scooter
Fast	Crawler
Google	Googlebot
MSN	MSNBot
Yahoo!	Slurp

Indices

During the early years of search engines (late 1990s), the size of a search engine's index was assumed to be an indication of its success. At one stage, when AltaVista was leading, they broke through the 250 million webpages barrier which was announced far and wide. Yahoo! was lagging behind, and Internet users were watching the growing numbers on search engine homepages with interest. Google also listed their index size on their sparse homepage and at one stage broke through the 4 billion webpage barrier. Again excited chattering in the search engine user community ensued.

Towards the end of 2005, rather unexpectedly, Google announced that they would be removing the index size counter from their homepage, since it had little value (Batelle, 2005). Most users agreed – more is not necessarily better in terms of search engine index size. In fact, Yahoo! have been claiming for many years that their index, although much smaller initially, is of much higher quality than Google's. Their claim was based on the fact that they used human beings to select webpages for their directory. Yahoo! offers both search engine and directory results, and this claim is based on the directory section.

It is debatable whether any user currently considers search engine index size as an indication of the quality of SERP content. Google's removal of this figure supports the belief that index size is not a determinant of quality. Furthermore, it has become virtually impossible to determine some index sizes, due to one company buying into part of or another's entire index. An established search engine optimisation (SEO) company has created a chart which graphically depicts these complex relationships (see Figure 1.17).

From this chart it appears that, in terms of indices, there are three kinds of search engine:

- those which only supply contents to others (Live Search, Google, Yahoo!);
- those which only receive contents from others (alltheweb, AltaVista, AOL Search, Netscape Search, Lycos, Hotbot, Iwon);
- those which do both (Ask).

However, some of those in the second category above also use crawlers to supplement their index.

It is interesting to note that the three search engines in the first category are the three biggest ones in the USA. Furthermore, their popularity is directly related to the number of other search engines they supply – Google, at number one on the popularity list, supplies the largest number of other companies.

Figure 1.17 How indices are related

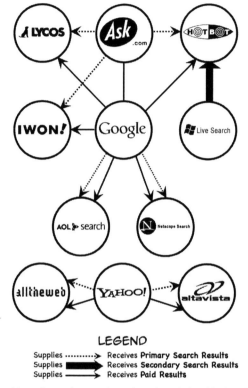

LEGEND

Supplies ··········> Receives **Primary Search Results**
Supplies ▬▬▬▬> Receives **Secondary Search Results**
Supplies ——————> Receives **Paid Results**

Adapted from *http://www.bruceclay.com/searchenginerelationshipchart.htm* (1 June 2009).

To summarise, it is debatable whether index size plays any role when a user decides which search engine to use, or even where the quality of the answers is at stake. Factors such as interface, response times and branding are probably the main factors which draw or repulse users.

Algorithms

The algorithm of a search engine is a program which decides, for every query, how to rank webpages on the resulting SERP. Understandably the detail of this program is considered to be a trade secret, since a successful search engine could find its algorithm copied by others if the detail were to become known. Developers could also create their websites in a way which would guarantee number one position for certain keywords, were this detail known. They could control the market in a sense, since they could sell the perfect SEO model. However, the basics of these programs are known, as well as the fact that these algorithms change over time.

The basic operation of search engine algorithms is important to webpage owners who need high rankings on SERPs, especially if they use SEO and no paid systems to improve their ranking. Algorithm operation could prescribe to a large extent how SEO is done to a website, in an attempt to entice search engine crawlers to visit and index these webpages.

Google uses the well-known *PageRank* algorithm, based to an extent on webpage popularity measured by number and weight of *inlinks* (hyperlinks from other webpages to this page). The argument is that, the more other webpages include a link to a given page, the higher value the content of this given page has. Furthermore, PageRank also weighs these inlinks themselves – a link from a webpage heavily referenced itself carries more weight than a link from an *unpopular* page.

Two of the current owners of Google described the operation of and formula used in PageRank in a seminal paper titled: 'The anatomy of a large-scale hypertextual web search engine', published in 1998 (Brin and Page, 1998). Currently Google uses a PageRank indicator on webpages to specify the PageRank figure for that given page, in the form of a horizontal green bar. This indicator will be visible if the user downloads and installs the Google Toolbar. PageRank uses a logarithmic scale, but the base of this scale has been the topic of many heated discussions. Some argue it is base 10, in which case a webpage with a PageRank of 5 would be 10 times as popular as one with a PageRank of 4. (Figure 1.18 shows three webpages with PageRank figures of 0, approximately 5 and 10 respectively.)

Spam

The term *spam* is probably most closely associated with batches of unsolicited e-mail arriving with frustrating regularity in millions of inboxes. This is understandably so, since this form of spam is highly visible to the average user and has been the first kind of *Internet harassment* earning this name. The name stems from a Monty Python comedy sketch from 1970, where customers trying to order breakfast in a restaurant found that almost every menu item contained a form of processed meat product. This product was branded Spam and actually exists (Wikipedia, 2008a). The common use of the term arises from the fact that a user seems to have no choice – if he/she uses the Internet, the inbox will receive spam. This form of spam will be referred to as *e-mail spam* from here on.

Figure 1.18 Sample PageRank figures for three websites with a PageRank of 0, 5 and 10

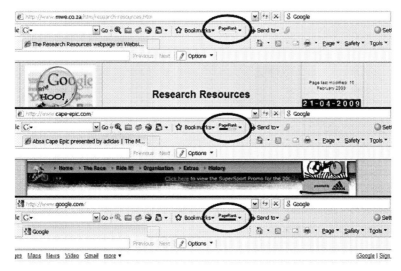

(Accessed 1 June 2009.)

Instead of the user, most search engines are also at the receiving end of unsolicited actions, also branded as spam. However, the average user is unaware of this form of spam being fired at its target. From here on it will be referred to as *spamdexing* (SPAMming the inDEXes of search engines).

Spamdexing is an attempt by unscrupulous website designers to present a webpage to a search engine in such a way that it receives a ranking much higher than it deserves by virtue of its content. This webpage normally has a strong commercial interest, and the purpose of spamdexing is normally to increase the number of visitors and as a result the income from the webpage. Search engine spamdexing is a deliberate attempt from a human to overcome the intelligence of a computer program, normally with the goal of ultimately making more money. Other authors have defined spamdexing as 'any attempt to deceive search engine relevancy rankings' (Machill et al., 2003: 54; Perkins, 2001). Yet another definition is: 'anything that constitutes unethical practices within SEO, and this includes manipulating search engine spiders and redirecting users to inappropriate content' (Wilkinson, 2004). However, a leader in the search engine industry claims that this form of spamdexing cannot be defined exactly (Sullivan, 2001).

If we refer back to Figure 1.1, it is clear that both the user and a search engine crawler regularly visit webpages. However, they have different intentions for doing so, and view them in rather different ways. The user is looking to satisfy an information need and is affected by the way the webpage appears on the screen and the use of colour, images, navigation and layout.

The crawler, on the other hand, is looking purely for indexable content (i.e. text), has no human intelligence and could be misled by the way information is offered to it. The result of what the crawler finds on its visit to a webpage determines to a large extent its subsequent ranking on a SERP. This ranking, if high (i.e. a low number like 1st or 2nd), can play a major role in the number of visitors to and the subsequent commercial success of this webpage.

Spamdexing can appear in many shapes, with descriptive names such as cloaking, doorway pages, hidden links, keyword stuffing, link farms and page redirects being bandied around. Fortunately for the user who is looking for quality content rather than webpages with a questionable ethical foundation, search engines are active in fighting spamdexing. For most of the known attempts at spamdexing, search engines have found a way of detecting it and penalising the guilty website.

For the user the dividing line between legitimate e-mail and e-mail spam is very clear – either you know the author and/or accept the e-mail message or you do not. With spamdexing, however, this dividing line is a lot more blurred. What one website author or search engine considers spamdexing, the next one might not. In fact, the dubious honour of being 1st and 2nd on the list of the 17 most unwanted elements in terms of website visibility goes to two different kinds of spamdexing: link and keyword spamdexing respectively. See Chapter 4 for more detail.

The presence of spamdexing, or what could be perceived as such, could result in one of two situations. Firstly, a webpage could be excluded from a search engine's index when it deserves to be there (since the search engine picked up what it considers to be spamdexing, unintended by the author). Secondly, a webpage could be indexed by a search engine when in fact it has used spamdexing successfully (instead of quality content) to earn a high placement in search engine rankings. Both these are undesirable situations. Furthermore, technical savvy (in creating skilful spamdexing techniques) could therefore earn one webpage a better rank than another (Introna and Nissenbaum, 2000: 57; Henzinger et al., 2002). To add to the confusion, Sullivan (2001) stated a number of years ago that not much guidance is offered by search engines themselves as to what can be considered as spamdexing. This is confirmed by Fusco, who claims that providing too much detail on spamdexing could reveal search engine algorithm secrets – a situation no search engine can afford (Goldsborough, 2005).

Search engine result pages

Probably one of the most often viewed types of screen on the Internet is a SERP. Users have grown used to the layout of and interaction with these webpages. Figure 1.19 shows a typical SERP layout.

When a user does a search for information via a search engine, the interface sends the query to the index where matches are made with the contents of the index. The user perception might be that the live Internet is being searched, but in fact the results produced are from the index of the search engine. The index is updated from time to time – the more often it is done, the *fresher* that specific search engine results are. These results are presented to the user on a SERP.

Research has proven over and over again that a webpage which is listed on the first SERP has a high chance of being read by the user. Very few users read anything past the third SERP. Even as early as in 2000, some authors stated: 'Many observe that to be noticed by a person doing a search, a Webpage needs to be ranked among the top 10–20 listed as hits' (Introna and Nissenbaum, 2000). A summary of extensive research spanning a decade on this issue is given in Table 1.4.

High rankings in search engine results (i.e. low numbered positions on the screen, where 1st is better than 2nd) are paramount if increased exposure to human visitors is required. The averages in Table 1.4 indicate a clear pattern as one reads from left to right. The further down in the ranking listing of a search engine a website appears, the smaller the chances that a user will see it. Using the extreme figures, 85 per cent of users read only the first SERP, which could be as few as the first 10 or 20 results. On the other side, 99 per cent of visitors will not look beyond the first three pages of results.

Regardless of the exact figures, there is agreement in general that the coveted top few ranking positions on any SERP is what matters. Any mission-critical website must aim to be seen in one of these top spots, for a given keyword or key phrase, if they want to draw traffic.

Figure 1.19 A typical SERP

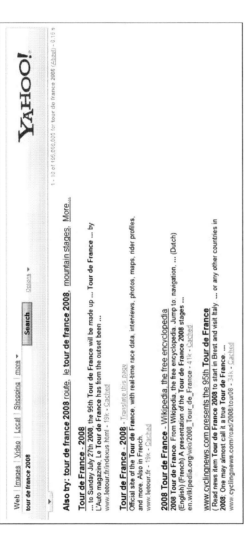

Source: *http://www.yahoo.com* (1 June 2009).

Table 1.4   Summary of research on SERP reading

What percentage of users read only the 1st SERP?	What percentage of users read only the 1st and 2nd SERP?	What percentage of users read only the 1st, 2nd and 3rd SERP?	Source
46.7%		83%	Neethling (2008)
	96%		Waganer (2008)
62%		90%	iProspect (2006)
	80%		George (2005)
		99%	Zhang and Dimitroff (2004)
85%			Henzinger et al. (2002)
58%			Jansen (2000)
85%			Silverstein et al. (1999)
67%	**88%**	**91%**	**Averages**

Ranking

Most owners of websites on the Internet have some motivation to see their website achieve high rankings in search engine result pages. Exceptions are children's/personal websites and others where there is no financial incentive or other motivation to get the crowds running to view a website.

No website will automatically draw customers *just because it's on the Web*. In fact, this is such a common misconception that a phrase is generally used to describe it – *Build it and they will come*, as adapted from the 1989 movie *Field of Dreams* ('If you build it, he will come'). A definite attempt has to be made to make the site visible and convince search engines to take an interest in it. This process is called search engine marketing (SEM), and can be subdivided into search engine optimisation (SEO) and paid placement (PP). These concepts will be discussed in more detail later in this book. At this stage, one should be aware of the difference between *free* results and *paid* results on a SERP. Free results have earned their position because of the relevance of their contents to the search query and the way the crawler interpreted the site. Although it is called free, money might have to be spent on SEO before it can earn a high ranking on a SERP. Paid results, in contrast, have achieved their

Figure 1.20 Free versus paid results

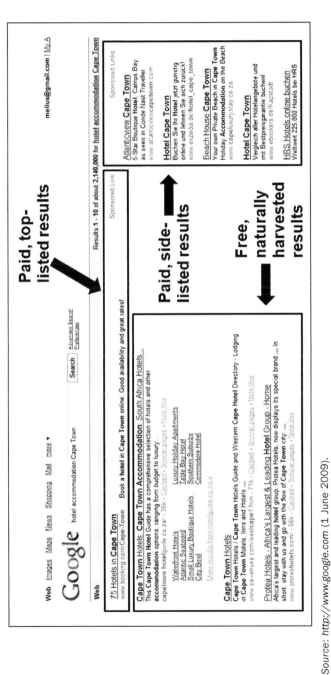

Source: *http://www.google.com* (1 June 2009).

position because the website owner has paid for a high position on a SERP, regardless of the actual content of that webpage. Google, for example, clearly separates these kinds of results – see Figure 1.20.

However, only one webpage can claim the top spot on one search engine for one search query at a time. Furthermore, this might change – a day later a different webpage might have claimed this top spot under the same conditions! This situation further fuels the continuous battle for top positions in SERPs. However, it is only true for so-called *naturally harvested results*. This refers to webpages which found their way into high rankings by virtue of their design, high-quality content and other ways of pleasing the crawlers. There is another method to achieve top rankings – paid inclusion, but even more so paid listings, discussed later.

Natural results – SEO

Search engine marketing refers to the overarching idea of doing something to achieve higher rankings for a given website and given keywords/phrases. SEO is the discipline of altering a website (or designing it that way in the first place) so as to please the crawlers and, once that has been done, achieve high rankings on search engine result pages. PP sounds simpler in principle than SEO in that somebody simply pays an amount to ensure top, second from the top, etc. listing for a given keyword, regardless of the content of the website. Figure 1.21 illustrates how these concepts are related.

Figure 1.21 The relationship between SEM, SEO and rankings

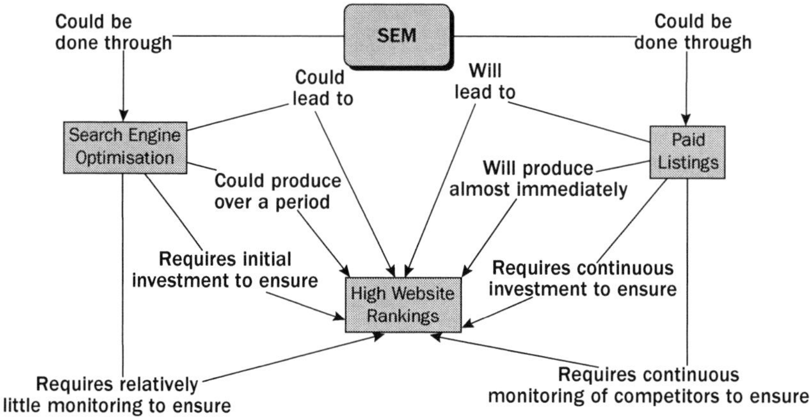

Source: Created with IHMC (2008).

SEO (also referred to as organic optimisation) involves tweaking the actual content of the website, i.e. a more *natural* process. This makes it easier for crawlers to index that webpage (Arnold, 2005). The overall goal is to increase the quantity and quality of traffic to the website, with the implied purpose of achieving higher sales and profits.

However, at the risk of oversimplifying a complex issue, there are two approaches to SEO: so-called *white hat* and *black hat* (also called spamdexing) techniques. The first refers to the use of above-board, ethically acceptable methods to increase ranking. Careful placement of keywords, manual submissions to search engines and correct use of metatags are some white hat techniques available. The second implies suspect methods which attempt to fool the search engine algorithm into allocating a higher rank to a webpage than the page deserves. Some of these are invisible text, doorway pages and spamdexing (Arnold, 2005; Mbikiwa and Weideman, 2006). These methods are discussed elsewhere in this book.

Theoretically white hat techniques are safe and will not lead to search engines penalising a website for using underhand techniques to gain higher rankings. Black hat techniques are more likely to cause a website to appear on a search engine's blacklist. However, there is a whole black hat industry out there, thriving by remaining close to the edge of what is acceptable in SEO practice and what is not and who are keeping their customers happy and paying.

Commercial ventures claiming to do SEO abound – Figure 1.22 provides a listing of some of those available. These services range widely, from plain optimisation of content, to search engine submissions, to the sale of specialised software. Often advice is supplied in generic terms but there is little evidence of research in this field being reported in academic literature (Kritzinger and Weideman, 2007).

A further distinction to be made within SEO as discussed refers to on-page and off-page optimisation. The elements identified above are on-page, since they are fully under the control of the webmaster and can be implemented with relative ease. Off-page optimisation involves factors not under control of the webmaster, such as the amount of links to a website, the quality of referring sites and search engine click-through data (Köhne, 2006).

Meta search engines

Standard search engines use crawlers to grow their own indices, an interface to communicate with users and an algorithm to make the best choices on behalf of the user. However, one *kind* of search engine has

Figure 1.22 Companies offering SEO services

MyTypes: **SEO** Tips - **SEO** Blog Templates - **SEO** Services Company ...
Learn the Secret Power of Blogs, SEO, Search & Social Marketing to grow your business.
mytypes.com/**seo**blogtemplates/ - 120k - Cached - Similar pages - Note this

SEO Guy Services Ltd
Professional Search Engine Optimization and Internet Marketing Services from the worlds
Leading SEO Company, SEO Guy Services Ltd. Call us for Search Engine ...
www.**seo**-guy.com/ - 15k - Cached - Similar pages - Note this

SEO Home
11/07/07, Purchase Andrew Golkin Benefit Tickets Here. 08/20/07, SEO Career Program 2008
Application Now Available Online! ...
www.**seo**-usa.org/ - 18k - Cached - Similar pages - Note this

SEO: Search Engine Optimisation. **SEO** advice and free keyword report.
Would you trust a SEO company that PAYS for their own Google listings? If they can't SEO
their own website - should you trust them to SEO yours?
www.ihaveawebsite-nowwhat.co.uk/ - 26k - Cached - Similar pages - Note this

Search Engine Marketing & Search Engine Optimisation **SEO** Australia
E-Web Marketing Australia's search engine optimisation & search engine marketing strategies
increase web traffic and market reach. Call 1300 785 122.
www.ewebmarketing.com.au/ - 25k - Cached - Similar pages - Note this

Google Optimization Search Engine Optimization - **SEO** WATCH
SEO marketing company specialized in search engine optimization and **seo** marketing for
google yahoo and msn.
www.**seo**-watch.com/ - 37k - Cached - Similar pages - Note this

SEO, Melbourne, Sydney, Australia, **SEO**
Exa is devoted to delivering our business partners an end-to-end web, IT & Marketing solution.
Our goal at Exa is to become your outsourced e-business and ...
www.exa.com.au/**seo**/ - 124k - Cached - Similar pages - Note this

Source: http://www.google.com (1 June 2009).

been developed which does not have its own index, thereby saving expenses. When it receives a query from a user, it simply redirects it to one or more indices of other, existing search engines. The results are combined, sorted according to (perceived) relevance and provided to the user. This kind of search engine is referred to as a meta search engine.

It is understandable that standard search engines are not eager to supply their hard-earned results to metas. When they do, they have to bear the brunt of overloading their own computers with the continuous queries they have to serve. Furthermore, the end user does not see the advertisements on the homepage of the standard search engine, thereby removing any potential benefit.

The most obvious benefit of metas appears to be access to a wider range of potential answers to user information needs. The question is: do

Figure 1.23   Mamma's search engine choices

Source: *http://www.mamma.com* (1 June 2009).

users want more answers? Are they not already overburdened with too many irrelevant answers on standard SERPs? Some experts prefer to stay with the likes of Google, Yahoo! and MSN (Sherman, 2007).

   Metas have been moderately successful but do not feature in the mainstream search engine exposure. There are no articles published in newspapers about takeovers while standard search engines often make the news in this regard. One of the oldest metas still around is mamma (*http://www.mamma.com*, claiming to be 'The Mother of All Search Engines'), which gives the user the option of which search engines to include, and whether or not to include paid listings (see Figure 1.23).

Conclusion – recommendations on the use of SEO

As is sometimes the case in the volatile Internet environment, direction is not clear and recommendations are to be carefully considered before implementation. However, there are a number of points considered to be not negotiable on the use of SEM in general. Sen (2005) proposes the following four options, with which this author concurs.

Do nothing

This option has zero cost implications and a good chance that the website of concern will remain at its current level of visibility – whether high or low.

This choice could be acceptable for a website whose ranking is of no concern to its owner, where there is no financial motivation to either spend money on SEM of whatever kind or to achieve high rankings and/or high volumes of visitors.

Invest in SEO only

Here the website owner would decide to invest only in natural content optimisation. It therefore implies that the text and keywords to be used in the SEO process are directly linked to the content of the relevant website. Using a competitor's brand name, for example, would not work to increase traffic, since it probably does not feature prominently on the website. However, it is still possible for the owner to go with either white or black hat techniques. This division is not always clear in practice – a black hat practitioner will probably not advertise services as such and might defend or totally disagree with any statements in this regard, if confronted.

Costs are impossible to estimate but are likely to be relatively high initially, assuming the existing site has not been optimised before and optimisation has to be done from scratch. Costs are likely to reduce drastically later.

The sample website for this book (*http://www.book-visibility.com*) has been optimised using the basic principles of SEO only.

Invest in PP only

This option will ensure high rankings as long as the search engine account is paid. Top spot for a given set of keyword(s) or keyphrases is assured, assuming that competitors' bids are constantly monitored and that one's own bid remains the highest and the content is relevant. It is possible to specify a fixed expenditure per month. When this amount is exhausted and not topped up, rankings in the PP section will disappear.

Problems with PP include relatively low user acceptance. Research has proven that many users prefer clicking on natural results above paid results (Neethling, 2008). In this case costs are easy to set for a given period, since a user account is managed by the search engine. However, in a complex situation (i.e. many keywords with simultaneous bids, fast-changing markets, many competitors, etc.), it will be necessary to constantly monitor one's bids to ensure an acceptable mix between expenditure and high rankings. Outside companies or expensive software could be used to continuously track rankings and update decisions on expenditure on regular intervals.

Invest in SEO and PP

Given the background above, this option could cost more but will cover both sets of audiences – those who (for whatever reason) prefer to click on natural results and those who prefer paid results. However, the complexity of managing both systems has to be considered in terms of not only financial outlay but also human involvement. Investing in both methods as the best methodology has been confirmed by Neethling (2008).

.

2

Elements of website visibility and research

Models

The aim of this book is to provide a balanced, tested approach to website design for visibility. Both the trustworthiness of the peer-reviewed academic world and the valued opinion of the experienced practitioner were considered in the process. Combining the respective weights of both these worlds and producing a balanced outcome is what the author is attempting to achieve in the rest of this book.

This author has read many references, documents and websites, and has never found a recorded attempt to:

- combine the results of academics' and practitioners' research and viewpoints on website visibility;
- create a point-scoring system which treats both sets of opinions equally; or
- produce a rating scale which indicates the relative importance of both positive and negative website visibility elements.

Much academic research has been done on attempting to determine what webpage designers should do to make websites visible to search engines. However, no evidence other than what is presented below could be found on attempts to not only classify but rank website visibility elements. These results are presented in the form of models to provide this type of guidance (Binnedell, 2003; Weideman and Chambers, 2005; Visser, 2007). At the same time, the tried and tested advice from practitioners was sought and incorporated. This includes the experience of 37 world-renowned SEO experts like Sullivan and Whalen (Fishkin and Pollard, 2007).

It was considered practical to combine the results of the three academic models, plus the SEO experts' opinions, to produce a fifth model – termed the Weideman model. A scoring system was designed where an arbitrary number of points was assigned to the oldest academic model, increasing with the next oldest and increasing again with the youngest. This would ensure that the continuously changing world of search engines would be represented more fairly, since more weight is given to more recent findings.

In an attempt to weigh the results of academic research and practitioner experience equally, it was considered prudent to allocate the same number of points to both these viewpoints. Since there were three academic but only one practitioner model, the total of the points allocated to all three academic models was also given to the single practitioner model, as described below.

The creation of the Weideman model is a piece of applied research based on the only four existing results found in academe and industry, rather than a selection from a large number of possibilities. The rigour in this research comes from the way that the academic experiments were peer reviewed and checked through the *before* and *after* comparisons. The contribution of what many consider to be some of the top SEO experts in the world is valued equally in this process.

The elements identified as being the most important for increasing and reducing website visibility in the Weideman model will be discussed in detail in the remainder of this book.

The Binnedell model

An early attempt at defining the elements of website visibility based on academic work was conducted in 2003. Binnedell carried out a detailed literature review to identify the elements that affect website visibility. Based on this review, a number of elements were identified as having either a positive or a negative effect on website visibility (Binnedell, 2003). No attempt was made to rank them as having a *more positive or negative effect* than the other, and no empirical work was done. However, this work laid the foundation for research to follow, and the classification of each element as having either one of two effects has been confirmed as correct in subsequent work. Figure 2.1 lists the respective elements of the Binnedell model and their classification. At this stage Binnedell included both organic optimisation, also termed SEO in the industry, and paid systems (like PPC).

Figure 2.1   The Binnedell model for website visibility

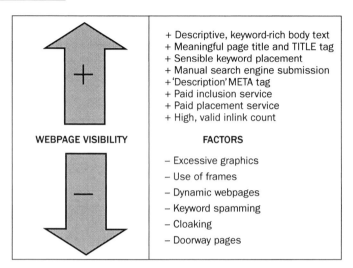

| WEBPAGE VISIBILITY | FACTORS |

+ Descriptive, keyword-rich body text
+ Meaningful page title and TITLE tag
+ Sensible keyword placement
+ Manual search engine submission
+ 'Description' META tag
+ Paid inclusion service
+ Paid placement service
+ High, valid inlink count

– Excessive graphics

– Use of frames

– Dynamic webpages

– Keyword spamming

– Cloaking

– Doorway pages

Source: Binnedell (2003).

Since this model is the oldest of the four considered, it was decided to allocate a (randomly selected) total of 40 × 2 credits to the Binnedell model, to be distributed evenly among each of the positive and the negative aspects.

The Chambers model

Chambers followed up the work done by Binnedell with initially a pilot study (Chambers and Weideman, 2005) and then a full research project in an attempt to correctly identify and quantify the important elements of website visibility based on empirical work (Chambers, 2005). Triangulation was done by comparing and combining results from a literature survey, an empirical experiment and a practitioner interview. The final results were summarised in table format, using a ranking figure to indicate the level of importance. A lower figure indicates higher importance. In this case positive and negative elements were mixed and had to be separated to enable the allocation of credits. Figure 2.2 provides a summary of the Chambers model (Weideman and Chambers, 2005, 2006; Chambers, 2005). The positive elements are numbers 1, 2, 5, 7, 8 and 10, leaving numbers 3, 4, 6 and 9 as the negative elements.

This model is the second oldest of the four considered, and a higher value of 50 credits was assigned to each of the two groups (positive and negative elements).

Figure 2.2   The Chambers model for website visibility

Number	Leading visibility elements	Rank
1	Inclusion of metatags	1.5
2	Hypertext/anchor text	2
3	No Flash or fewer than 50% of content	3
4	No visible link spamming	4
5	Prominent link popularity	4.5
6	No frames	5
7	Prominent domain names	7
8	Prominent headings	7
9	No banner advertising	8
10	Prominent HTML naming conventions	10

Source: Weideman and Chambers (2005) (2 June 2009).

The Visser model

A third study in this line was completed by Visser. This extended research project yielded a new model which grouped the elements of visibility into categories. In the final version four categories were identified, namely *Essentials, Extras, Cautions and Dangers*. Each title is an indication of whether or not a certain element should be included in website design. The Visser model is represented in Figure 2.3. The two categories marked *Implement* are positive elements, since their inclusion could have a positive effect on website visibility. The two marked *Avoid* are negative, since their inclusion in a website could be detrimental to its visibility.

The Visser model is the most recent of the three models, and a yet higher value of 60 × 2 credits was assigned to it. These credits would be distributed among each of the two types of elements.

The industry model

Extensive attempts were made to source a list of both positive and negative visibility elements that were supported by a number of experts and were ranked. Only one meeting these conditions was found. It is a summary of the opinions of 37 organic SEO experts on website visibility elements which are considered by the Google algorithm. A total of 200 questions were posed to this panel, and their answers and ratings of these elements were recorded (Fishkin and Pollard, 2007). Each panellist allocated a ranking out of five to each element, where, for the positive elements, five meant that this factor was *strongly weighted* in its determinacy of website

Figure 2.3 The Visser model for website visibility

```
                        ┌──────────────────┐
                        │ Website Visibility│
                        └──────────────────┘

    ┌──────────┐    ┌────────┐    ┌──────────┐    ┌─────────┐
    │Essentials│    │ Extras │    │ Cautions │    │ Dangers │
    └──────────┘    └────────┘    └──────────┘    └─────────┘
  Website content ┌───────────┐  ┌──────────┐  ┌──────────────┐
  ┌──────────────┐│Domain names│  │  Flash   │  │  Spamming    │
  │ Keywords     ││HTML naming │  │  Frames  │  │ • link spam  │
  │ • placement  ││ conventions│  │  Images  │  │ • text spam  │
  │ • proximity  │└───────────┘  │JavaScript│  └──────────────┘
  │ • frequency  │               │  Videos  │
  │ • metatags   │               └──────────┘
  │ • hypertext/ │
  │   anchor text│                       AVOID
  │ • link popularity│
  │ • headings   │
  └──────────────┘
        IMPLEMENT
```

Source: Adapted from Visser (2007).

visibility. For the negative factors, a ranking of five meant *strongly detrimental to crawling/rankings*. A summary was made of these factors. They were sorted by their score, and the 20 positive factors with the highest ranking were selected for this study (see Table 2.4 below). All nine negative elements were also included (see Table 2.5 below). One example of a highly weighted positive element, with a ranking of 4.9, is given in Figure 2.4. This whole process of ranking was executed by Fishkin and Pollard (2007).

Figure 2.4 Example of a highly weighted element from the industry model

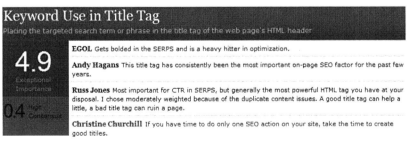

Keyword Use in Title Tag
Placing the targeted search term or phrase in the title tag of the web page's HTML header

4.9 Exceptional Importance

0.4 High Consensus

EGOL Gets bolded in the SERPS and is a heavy hitter in optimization.

Andy Hagans This title tag has consistently been the most important on-page SEO factor for the past few years.

Russ Jones Most important for CTR in SERPS, but generally the most powerful HTML tag you have at your disposal. I chose moderately weighted because of the duplicate content issues. A good title tag can help a little, a bad title tag can ruin a page.

Christine Churchill If you have time to do only one SEO action on your site, take the time to create good titles.

Source: Fishkin and Pollard (2007) (1 June 2009).

The Weideman model

The objective of the research done at this point was to allocate a score in terms of credits to each one of the elements of each one of the models discussed above. If no ranking was carried out (as with the Binnedell model), an equal score would be allocated to each element. If ranking was carried out, a score would be allocated according to the ranking. A higher score for a positive element indicates that it has a larger positive effect on website visibility, according to the original authors. A higher score for a negative element indicates that that element would have more of a negative effect on website visibility, according to the authors. Thus the ranking scales were normalised.

Once every element in every model had an associated score, the 43 positive and 26 negative elements were combined. Although different terminology is often used by different authors, some of these elements are duplicated in different models. Based on the author's experience these duplications were combined and their scores added, yielding the final list of elements in ranked order. The next two chapters (the main body of this book) contain a description of both these positive and negative elements.

Credit allocation: Binnedell model

This model lists eight positive and six negative elements, without any ranking, according to Figure 2.1. Each one of the eight positive factors therefore earns 40/8 = 5 credits. Each one of the six negative factors will earn 40/6 = 6.66 credits. The resultant credit list for the Binnedell model is summarised in Table 2.1, with an indication of the type of effect each element has on website visibility.

Credit allocation: Chambers model

The Chambers model lists six positive and four negative elements according to Figure 2.2. Both these categories of elements were ranked, so equal values could not be allocated. The six elements (numbered 6, 5, 4, 3, 2 and 1, where no. 6 is the one with the most positive effect) were then considered to have different weights, calculated as follows:

Total weight: 6 + 5 + 4 + 3 + 2 + 1 = 21

Element no. 6 would be allocated the highest weight, namely 6/21 × 50, which equals 14.3 credits. The second most important element would

Table 2.1   Binnedell model credit list (positive and negative)

Element	Effect	Credit earned
Descriptive, keyword-rich body text	Positive	5.0
Meaningful page title and TITLE tag	Positive	5.0
Sensible keyword placement	Positive	5.0
Manual search engine submission	Positive	5.0
'Description' META tag	Positive	5.0
Paid inclusion service	Positive	5.0
Paid placement service	Positive	5.0
High, valid inlink count	Positive	5.0
		(Total: 40)
Excessive graphics	Negative	6.66
Use of frames	Negative	6.66
Dynamic webpages	Negative	6.66
Keyword spamming	Negative	6.66
Cloaking	Negative	6.66
Doorway pages	Negative	6.66
		(Total: 40)

receive $5/21 \times 50 = 11.9$ credits. The four negative elements were scored in the same way. The *most negative* element earned $4/10 \times 50 = 20$ credits, down to $1/10 \times 50 = 5$ credits. Continuing in this way, the credit allocation for the Chambers model is given in Table 2.2.

Credit allocation: Visser model

The Visser model proposes nine positive and seven negative elements according to Figure 2.3. Both these categories of elements were ranked, but not inside each category. Therefore equal values had to be allocated to all those positive elements inside each category. The nine positive elements (numbered 9, 8, 7, 6, 5, 4, 3, 2 and 1, where no. 9 is the one with the *most positive effect*) were initially considered to have different weights, calculated as follows: $9 + 8 + 7 + 6 + 5 + 4 + 3 + 2 + 1 = 45$. Element no. 9 would be allocated the highest weight, namely $9/45 \times 60$, which equals 12 credits. The second most important element would receive $8/45 \times 60 = 10.7$ credits. Continuing in this way, the initial credit

| Table 2.2 | Chambers model credit list (positive and negative) |

Element	Effect	Credit earned
Inclusion of metatags	Most positive	14.3
Hypertext/anchor text	Positive	11.9
Prominent link popularity	Positive	9.5
Prominent domain names	Positive	7.1
Prominent headings	Positive	4.8
Prominent HTML naming conventions	Least positive	2.4
		(Total: 50)
Flash content	Most negative	20.0
Visible link spamming	Negative	15.0
Frames	Negative	10.0
Banner advertising	Least negative	5.0
		(Total: 50)

allocation for the seven *most positive* elements (labelled *Essentials* in Figure 2.3) were: 12, 10.7, 9.3, 8, 6.7, 5.3 and 4. Since these seven elements are equally ranked, their weightings were then added and divided equally again, yielding a value of 8 credits each.

Similarly, the two *less positive* elements (labelled *Extras* in Figure 2.3) produced the following calculation: (2.7 + 1.3) / 2 = 2 credits each. The seven negative elements were initially treated the same way, with allocations of 15, 12.9, 10.7, 8.6, 6.4, 4.3 and 2.1. Grouping the two *more negative* (labelled *Dangers* in Figure 2.3) and the other five *less negative* elements (labelled *Cautions* in Figure 2.3) and averaging their credits again produced a credit score of 14 for each *more negative* element and 6.4 for each *less negative* element. The final Visser model credit allocation is given in Table 2.3.

Credit allocation: industry model

The three academic models considered were allocated scores of 40, 50 and 60 respectively (per category), based on their age. An older model was considered to be slightly less relevant and received fewer credits to divide. Thus a total of 150 credits were assigned to these three cumulatively. The industry model was then assigned an equal weighting, namely 150 credits. This would ensure that the elements included in the

Table 2.3 Visser model credit list (positive and negative)

Element	Effect	Credit earned
Keyword placement	More positive	8.0
Keyword proximity	More positive	8.0
Keyword frequency	More positive	8.0
Keyword used in metatags	More positive	8.0
Keyword used in hypertext/anchor text	More positive	8.0
Keyword used in links	More positive	8.0
Keyword used in headings	More positive	8.0
Keyword used in domain names	Less positive	2.0
Keyword used in HTML naming conventions	Less positive	2.0
		(Total: 60)
Link spam	More negative	14.0
Text spam	More negative	14.0
Flash	Less negative	6.4
Frames	Less negative	6.4
Images	Less negative	6.4
JavaScript	Less negative	6.4
Videos	Less negative	6.4
		(Total: 60)

industry and academic models had an equal chance of making it to the final list. Tables 2.4 and 2.5 list the 20 positive and nine negative elements of the industry model respectively. The *Ranking* column lists the rank allocated by the 37 panellists to each element, while the *Credit earned* column contains the score calculated by this author.

Element no. 1 would be allocated the highest weight, namely $20/210 \times 150 = 14.3$ credits. The second most important element would receive $19/210 \times 150 = 13.6$ credits. Continuing in this way, the credit allocation for the 20 positive factors of the industry model is listed in Table 2.4.

In the same way, scoring was carried out for the nine negative elements. Element no. 1 was allocated the highest weight, namely $9/45 \times 150 = 30$ credits. The second most important element would receive $8/45 \times 150 = 26.7$ credits. Continuing in this way, the credit allocation for the nine negative factors of the industry model is listed in Table 2.5.

	Element	Ranking	Credit earned
	Table 2.4 Industry model credit list (positive elements)		
1	Keyword use in TITLE tag	4.9	14.3
2	Global link popularity of site	4.4	13.6
3	Anchor text of inbound link	4.4	12.9
4	Age of site	4.1	12.1
5	Link popularity within internal link structure	4.0	11.4
6	Topical relevance of inbound links	3.9	10.7
7	Link popularity of site in topical community	3.9	10.0
8	Keyword use in body text	3.7	9.3
9	Global link popularity of linking site	3.6	8.6
10	Quality/relevance of links to external sites	3.5	7.9
11	Topical relationship of linking page	3.5	7.1
12	Rate of new inbound links to site	3.5	6.4
13	Relationship of body text content to keywords	3.4	5.7
14	Age of document	3.4	5.0
15	Keyword use in H1 tag	3.3	4.3
16	Amount of indexable text content	3.2	3.6
17	Age of link	3.2	2.9
18	Topical relationship of linking site	3.1	2.1
19	Text surrounding the link	3.1	1.4
20	Relevance of site's primary subject matter to query	3.1	0.7
			(Total: 150)

Credit summary: Weideman model

At this point the results of the credit allocations had to be combined to produce the final ranking. To the author's knowledge, this kind of *marriage* between the rigour of academic peer review and the technical expertise of the SEO practitioner has not been done before.

After combining the 43 positive and 26 negative elements listed in Tables 2.1 to 2.5, the expected duplicates were identified and combined in separate tables. The cumulative score for each table was calculated, and the tables were then sorted from highest to lowest score. A total of nine

Table 2.5   Industry model credit list (negative elements)

	Element	Ranking	Credit earned
1	Server is often inaccessible to bots	3.8	30.0
2	Content is very similar or duplicate	3.6	26.7
3	External links to low-quality/spamdexing sites	3.6	23.3
4	Duplicate title/metatags on many pages	3.3	20.0
5	Keyword stuffing	3.3	16.7
6	Participation in link schemes	3.3	13.3
7	Very slow server response times	2.8	10.0
8	Inbound links from spamdexing sites	2.1	6.7
9	Low levels of visitors	2.1	3.3

tables, i.e. nine elements, were created in this way (see Tables 2.6 to 2.14). A single title which correctly and cumulatively describes the elements listed in each table was allocated per table. When listing the elements inside each table, a prefix is used to indicate each element's source (b = Binnedell; c = Chambers; v = Visser; and i = industry).

Furthermore, those elements which had no duplicates were grouped collectively in a table titled *Singles*. Another eight elements are listed here (see Table 2.15). Finally, another table was created with only the names of the 17 elements having made it this far, again sorted from highest to lowest score. Those elements originating from a combined table no longer have a prefix indicating its source, since they stem from more than one model. Their names are listed without a prefix. The *Singles* elements are still listed with their original prefix.

Table 2.16 summarises the result (positive elements) of this research. It provides a ranked list of elements to be considered when designing a website for search engine crawler visibility. Figure 2.5 provides a graphical presentation of the relative magnitudes of the cumulative score per element.

The process described above was then repeated for the negative elements. *Table 2.23 summarises the result (negative elements) of this research.*

Tables 2.16 and 2.23 represent the total sum of this research, namely a validated, ranked series of website visibility elements to be considered in website design. This research is best summarised in Figures 2.5 and 2.6.

Table 2.6 Cumulative score: inlinks (82.3)

Inlinks – cumulative score = 82.3	Score
b – High, valid inlink count	5.0
c – Prominent link popularity	9.5
i – Global link popularity of linking site	8.6
i – Global link popularity of site	13.6
i – Link popularity of site in topical community	10.0
i – Link popularity within internal link structure	11.4
i – Rate of new inbound links to site	6.4
i – Topical relationship of linking page	7.1
i – Topical relevance of inbound links	10.7

Table 2.7 Cumulative score: body keywords (54.0)

Body keywords – cumulative score = 54.0	Score
b – Descriptive, keyword-rich body text	5.0
b – Sensible keyword placement	5.0
i – Amount of indexable text content	3.6
i – Keyword use in body text	9.3
i – Relationship of body text content to keywords	5.7
i – Text surrounding the link	1.4
v – Keyword frequency	8.0
v – Keyword placement	8.0
v – Keyword proximity	8.0

Table 2.8 Cumulative score: hypertext/anchor text (32.8)

Hypertext/anchor text – cumulative score = 32.8	Score
c – Hypertext/anchor text	11.9
i – Anchor text of inbound link	12.9
v – Keyword used in hypertext/anchor text	8.0

Table 2.9 Cumulative score: metatags (27.3)

Metatags – cumulative score = 27.3	Score
b – 'Description' META tag	5.0
c – Inclusion of metatags	14.3
v – Keyword used in metatags	8.0

Table 2.10 Cumulative score: H1 tag (17.1)

H1 tag – cumulative score = 17.1	Score
c – Prominent headings (H1)	4.8
i – Keyword use in H1 tag	4.3
v – Keyword used in headings (H1)	8.0

Table 2.11 Cumulative score: TITLE tag (19.3)

Title tag – cumulative score = 19.3	Score
b – Meaningful page title and TITLE tag	5.0
i – Keyword use in TITLE tag	14.3

Table 2.12 Cumulative score: outlinks (15.9)

Outlinks – cumulative score = 15.9	Score
i – Quality/relevance of links to external sites	7.9
v – Keyword used in links	8.0

Table 2.13 Cumulative score: domain names (9.1)

Domain names – cumulative score = 9.1	Score
c – Prominent domain names	7.1
v – Keyword used in domain names	2.0

Table 2.14 Cumulative score: HTML naming conventions (4.4)

HTML naming conventions – cumulative score = 4.4	Score
c – Prominent HTML naming conventions	2.4
v – Keyword used in HTML naming conventions	2.0

Table 2.15 Singles (positive)

Singles	Score
b – Manual search engine submission	5.0
b – Paid inclusion service	5.0
b – Paid placement service	5.0
i – Age of document	5.0
i – Age of link	2.9
i – Age of site	12.1
i – Relevance of site's primary subject matter to query	0.7
i – Topical relationship of linking site	2.1

Table 2.16 The Weideman model: final positive element summary

Elements	Score
Inlinks	82.3
Body keywords	54.0
Hypertext/anchor text	32.8
Metatags	27.3
TITLE tag	19.3
H1 tag	17.1
Outlinks	15.9
i – Age of site	12.1
Domain names	9.1
b – Manual search engine submission	5.0
b – Paid inclusion service	5.0
b – Paid placement service	5.0
i – Age of document	5.0
HTML naming conventions	4.4
i – Age of link	2.9
i – Topical relationship of linking site	2.1
i – Relevance of site's primary subject matter to query	0.7

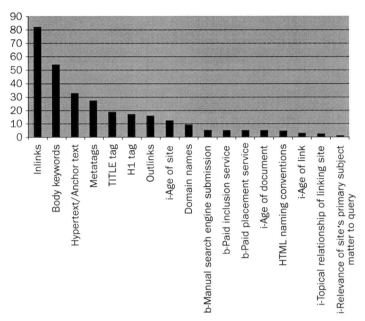

Figure 2.5 The Weideman model: relative magnitude of positive elements' scores

For the positive results, the ranking elements of Figure 2.5 will be discussed in detail in the next chapter.

The negative elements will now be quantified and summarised in the same way that the positive results were. The highest scoring element is listed first.

Table 2.17 Cumulative score: link spamdexing (42.3)

Link spamdexing – cumulative score = 42.3	Score
c – Visible link spamdexing	15.0
i – Participation in link schemes	13.3
v – Link spamdexing	14.0

Table 2.18 Cumulative score: keyword spamdexing (37.36)

Keyword spamdexing – cumulative score = 37.36	Score
b – Keyword spamdexing	6.66
i – Keyword stuffing	16.7
v – Text spamdexing	14.0

Table 2.19 Cumulative score: Flash (26.4)

Flash – cumulative score = 26.4	Score
c – Flash content	20.0
v – Flash	6.4

Table 2.20 Cumulative score: frames (23.04)

Frames – cumulative score = 23.04	Score
b – Use of frames	6.66
c – Frames	10.0
v – Frames	6.4

Table 2.21 Cumulative score: graphics (19.46)

Graphics – cumulative score = 19.46	Score
b – Excessive graphics	6.66
v – Images	6.4
v – Videos	6.4

Table 2.22 Singles (negative)

Singles	Score
b – Cloaking	6.66
b – Doorway pages	6.66
b – Dynamic webpages	6.66
c – Banner advertising	5.0
i – Content is very similar or duplicate	26.7
i – Duplicate title/metatags on many pages	20.0
i – External links to low-quality/spamdexing sites	23.3
i – Inbound links from spamdexing sites	6.7
i – Low levels of visitors	3.3
i – Server is often inaccessible to bots	30.0
i – Very slow server response times	10.0
v – JavaScript	6.4

| Table 2.23 | The Weideman model: final negative element summary |

Elements	Score
Link spamdexing	42.3
Keyword spamdexing	37.36
i – Server is often inaccessible to bots	30.0
i – Content is very similar or duplicate	26.7
Flash	26.4
i – External links to low-quality/spamdexing sites	23.3
Frames	23.04
i – Duplicate title/metatags on many pages	20.0
Graphics	19.46
i – Very slow server response times	10.0
i – Inbound links from spamdexing sites	6.7
b – Cloaking	6.66
b – Doorway pages	6.66
b – Dynamic webpages	6.66
v – JavaScript	6.4
c – Banner advertising	5.0
i – Low levels of visitors	3.3

For the negative results, the ranking elements in Figure 2.6 will be discussed in detail in Chapter 4. The eight lowest ranking elements will be grouped and discussed under one heading.

Model result comparison

The two graphs indicating the relative weights of both positive and negative elements (Figures 2.5 and 2.6) constitute an important contribution to the body of knowledge on website visibility.

A comparison of these two result sets produces a further confirmation of its validity. *The first element on the positive scale, when applied in the way discussed in this book under spamdexing, is also the first element on the negative scale!* The same holds true for the second highest value on both graphs. To summarise from Figures 2.5 and 2.6: *inlinks* earned the highest score as the most positive element (82.3) while *link spamdexing*

Figure 2.6 The Weideman model: relative magnitude of negative elements' scores

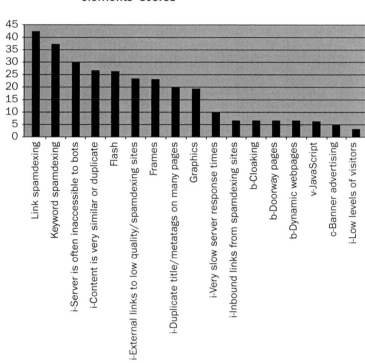

earned the highest score (42.3) on the negative scale. When an attempt is made to increase the quality and/or quantity of inlinks to a website using, for example, link farms, this element is in effect transformed from being the most positive to the most negative. Similarly, the correct use of keywords in a number of areas occupies position number two on the positive list. However, if keywords on a webpage are used to misrepresent the value of a webpage (e.g. by resorting to keyword stuffing), this second most positive element is transformed into the second most negative one.

This implies that spammers and other designers have chosen the correct elements to apply in an underhand fashion to achieve higher rankings for their webpages. Unfortunately, the search engines have been equally active in countering these moves, to strive towards higher result quality. The sample website (*http://www.book-visibility.com*) has been designed, as far as possible, to implement the positive and omit the negative elements.

The good ones

Introduction

An important ranking was carried out in Chapter 2 – that of deciding which elements affecting website visibility (both positively and negatively) were most and least important (see Tables 2.16 and 2.23). In this chapter, the list of positive elements is discussed in more detail. They are covered in order of importance, with the most important – inlinks – first. First, however, a few words on website content.

Content is king

The most important factor which will cause Internet users to remain at a website for a period of time, and probably to contribute to its goal, is content of value. This could vary widely with the type of website – it could be affordable, high-quality products for an online shop, pertinent information for an information seeker or relevant results on a SERP. The phrase *content is king* has a deeper meaning indeed (Csutoras, 2008; Pi, 2006; Sack, 2005). Advertisers in the SEO industry are very aware of this fact – see Figure 3.1.

When considering the 17 elements listed in Figure 2.5 it is clear that the use of keywords plays a role in eight of the nine top elements contributing to website visibility. Walking the thin line of using keywords as much as possible without raising the spamdexing flag will receive much attention in the following sections.

Inlinks

Inlinks refer to hyperlinks on websites outside of the one under consideration but pointing to it. This most important website visibility factor is one which is not easy for the website owner to control. Among

Figure 3.1 'Content is King' – a banner at a search engine conference

Photo taken by M. Weideman at the Search Engine Strategy Conference, Chicago, December 2005.

other things, they have to publish high-quality content and then wait for other website owners to recognise the value of the content of their website and link to it. However, there are more aspects to inlinks than just hyperlinks from other sites, as discussed further in this section. If we refer to Table 2.6, it can be seen that nine different headings have been combined under the one title of *Inlinks*, at the risk of oversimplifying the issue.

One reason why this factor occupies the top position is that the same system has been proven and in operation for many years as the citation system in the academic world (Thelwall, 2007). Authors who produce and publish research of high quality should receive many citations from other authors. These other authors should find their work relevant and useful, and will then quote them more often than others. This phenomenon is quantified in academic journals, where each journal is allocated an impact factor (IF). These calculations are done by a US publisher, Thomson Scientific, for the journals it lists. The IF is based on a simple calculation spanning a three-year period, and is an approximation of the average number of citations per year. The previous two years' values are incorporated in the calculation.

As an example, the 2009 IF for a journal (calculated after 2009 only) is expressed as x/y:

- x is the amount of times that articles published in 2007 and 2008 were cited in journals in 2009 (only journals indexed by Thomson are considered);

- y is the total number of *objects* of value which can be cited (mostly peer-reviewed research articles), also published in 2007 and 2008.

A journal with a high impact factor is considered to contain high-quality research publications, and academics often aim their submissions at high-IF journals. However, this system is not free of criticism. The English language is very strongly represented, and so are journals from certain countries and certain fields of study (see *http://scientific .thomsonreuters.com/products/jcr/* for more detail).

The term *impact factor* as used in academia has been transferred with the same meaning when referring to inlinks from and to websites. Many authors have done research on the value of these inlinks to the target website, and the term *web impact factor* (WIF) was born. Some of these studies are listed here:

- Gan and Suel (2007) attempted to find ways to overcome the incidence of link spamdexing, which has been identified as one of the top challenges in the web industry.

- Aguillo et al. (2006) proved the value of cybermetric indicators, including inlinks, in determining the value of technologically oriented institutions.

- Noruzi (2005) studied web impact factors for Iranian universities, and found that the language barrier prevents some websites from earning a WIF which they deserve.

- Vaughan and Thelwall (2004) confirmed that search engine coverage bias does exist, and that the number of inlinks to a website does affect its ranking.

- Noruzi (2004) did an in-depth study of the WIF, and suggested that it is useful for intra-country comparisons but should not be used across country borders.

A second reason why this website visibility element has made it to the top of the list is the fact that most popular search engines use inlinks as one of the main ranking factors in their algorithms. Not much is known about search engine algorithms, since that would enable competitors to copy successful algorithms in their own implementations. However, one thing that is known about Google's PageRank algorithm is that it does consider the quality and quantity of the inlinks to a website as an indication of its value or ranking. Every hyperlink to a given website is treated as a vote of confidence in that website, and therefore supposedly an indication of the quality of its content. PageRank not only assigns weight to the quantity, but also to the quality of these inlinks. It uses its own valuation of the webpage containing the hyperlink, namely its PageRank, as a measure of quality. The ideal is therefore to have many hyperlinks pointing from other webpages to one's own webpage. These webpages should all have a high PageRank, i.e. they should be viewed as being of high quality themselves.

As an example, Travelocity (PageRank approximately 8) and Expedia (PageRank approximately 7) are considered to be two of the top travel booking portals. EasyJet (PageRank approximately 4) is a low-cost airline (see Figure 3.2).

The two travel portals are well established in the tourism industry, and have built up trust with both human clients and search engines over the years. If easyJet wants to increase its ranking on SERPs, it should attempt to convince these two travel portals to link to the easyJet homepage. These links would be rated as high-quality inlinks and some search engines, including Google, will attach a high value to these links. The ranking of the easyJet website should increase as a result. This is of course assuming that all other factors remain the same and no black hat techniques are used. At the same time easyJet should attempt to increase the quantity of inlinks to its homepage.

On referring to Table 2.6, it is clear that the two major contributors to the winning score for this category, eventually renamed to just *Inlinks*, are *Global link popularity of site* and *Link popularity within internal link structure* respectively. Probably the easiest to implement is the second.

The creation of a so-called *site map* is an important addition for even a simple website. If done properly, this would not only aid the user in finding their way around the website (i.e. website usability), but it will also increase the internal link popularity (i.e. website visibility) of the website. Part of the sitemap for an Internet research website is given in Figure 3.3.

Every hyperlink on an internal sitemap normally points to a webpage on the same website. Since the contents on these pages are probably related, this will increase the value of these links and have a positive effect on the website visibility. It will also ensure that every single webpage in the website will be found by crawlers.

Figure 3.2 Hyperlinks between webpages

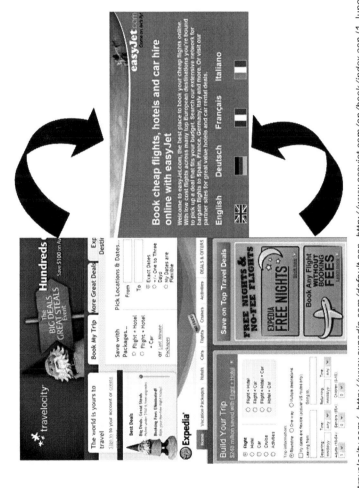

| Figure 3.3 | Example sitemap |

SITEMAP - www.mwe.co.za	
Sitemap	
Homepage	
- Book on Website Visibility	An external website with detail about a book on SE optimization
- Contact Book Author	How to contact the book author
- Target Market	What is the target market of this book?
- Buy book now	How to order this book now
- Book Content	What is the content of this book?
- Other Books	Which other similar books on this topic are available?
- Similar Publications	A database with academic publications (journal articles, conference papers, etc) on this topic
- What's Different	What makes this book different from other, similar books?
- Research Resources	A collection of Research Resources for young researchers in this field
- Cape Peninsula University of Technology	An external website - the official starting point for CPUT
- Research Funding One Stop Shop	A summary of opportunities for research funding for members of FID
- URF (University Research Funding)	Detail on the CPUT URF research funding opportunity

Source: *http://www.mwe.co.za* (22 April 2009).

Another approach would be to simply contact other websites with content similar to yours, after checking out their trustworthiness. Request them to add a link to your site. However, doing this on a large scale, or even worse, using an automated system or program to do this, will most certainly be classified as spamdexing. This is discussed in detail elsewhere in this book.

It would be worth the effort to create a Wikipedia entry for the webpage as one more step towards a high inlink count. However, a Wikipedia entry created by one person, not edited and unsupported by printed sources is likely to raise eyebrows. Wikipedia pages rank well on Google, to the point where this fact has been queried by some bloggers.

Body keywords

Body keywords can be defined as descriptive words which carry weight in terms of their value for a specific webpage. The following sentence (taken from *http://www.cape-epic.com/content.php?page_id=118& title=/Company_Ethos/*) shows keywords in italics, to indicate those words which carry weight in the context of the specific webpage: 'The *Absa Cape Epic* will promote the culture and beauty of *South Africa* and introduce the *South African mountainbike* scene to the world.' The remaining words are necessary to complete the sentence, but they do not contribute to the description of the page.

There is no question in the industry that the correct use of keywords in the body text of a webpage is of paramount importance. Initial research should be done on keywords used in the relevant industry. This factor has been identified as the second most important element determining website visibility, and goes hand in hand with *Content is King* (see Figure 2.5). Having the right amount of well-written text on a webpage, with keywords used correctly, is important. It keeps the user on the webpage for longer (a factor called *stickiness*), and it provides a rich harvest for the search engine crawler. If this balance between satisfying both the human user and the search engine crawler can be achieved, the webpage is highly likely to achieve its goal.

The keywords and key phrases which are important for each specific webpage must be identified by the website owner. If the metatags have been written, this task has already been done. If not, it should be done before the body text is generated. Some empirical studies have confirmed the importance of the correct usage of keywords in the webpage body (Kritzinger and Weideman, 2004, 2005).

The assistance of a professional writer should be sought to create and/or alter this text according to the guidelines given below (placement, frequency/density and proximity). This process evolves into a play with words. Text has to be generated which:

- is true and correct according to the website owner;
- is grammatically and technically superior;
- makes extensive use of the keywords defined earlier, as discussed below;
- does not exceed the proposed 6–12 per cent keyword density;
- reads well; and
- does not approach the look and feel of spamdexing, i.e. appears to be gibberish overflowing with keywords.

This task should not be underestimated, as it requires a blend of:

- content knowledge (provided by the website owner or their business experts);
- writing expertise (best done by a technical journalist or copywriter); and
- insight into the correct use of keywords (provided in this chapter).

Keyword placement

Some authors claim that the placement and frequency of keywords on a webpage are some of the most important determinants of search engine ranking algorithms (Wong, 2004; Sullivan, 2003). This is referred to as the *location/frequency* method. It is also claimed that keywords appearing towards the top of the body text carry more weight than those lower down. Kritzinger did some extensive experimentation to test this claim (Kritzinger, 2007).

In this study it was proven that keywords should be focused towards the top and diluted towards the centre or bottom of a webpage. It was measured by using the top four search engines in the USA at the time, singly and in combination, for a given search. The keywords found in each of the top, centre or bottom of each result webpage in the top 10 were counted, and a relationship between location and ranking was determined. The results of one of these experiments are listed in Table 3.1.

Table 3.1 Results of keyword placement experiment

Search engine	Top	Middle	Bottom
Yahoo!	–	–	Negative
Google	–	–	–
MSN	–	–	–
AskJeeves	–	–	Negative
Yahoo! and Google	Positive	–	–
Yahoo! and MSN	–	–	–
Yahoo! and AskJeeves	Positive	–	Negative
Google and MSN	–	–	–
Google and AskJeeves	–	–	–
MSN and AskJeeves	–	–	–
Yahoo!, Google and MSN	Positive	–	–
Yahoo!, Google and AskJeeves	Positive	–	Negative
Yahoo!, MSN and AskJeeves	Positive	–	Negative
Google, MSN and AskJeeves	–	–	–
Yahoo!, Google, MSN and AskJeeves	Positive	–	–

Source: Kritzinger (2007: 48).

The positive relationships (all are in the *Top* column) indicate that, for that search engine (or combination), there is a strong relationship between placing keywords at the top of the body text and high ranking. Similarly, the negative relationships (all are in the *Bottom* column) indicate that there is a strong relationship between placing keywords towards the bottom of the body text and low rankings. The dashes represent those cases where no significant relationship existed.

An example of a complete section of a homepage body text (*http://www.uvasys.com*), written by adhering to the specification of *keywords closer to the top*, is given below. The keyword optimised for is *Uvasys*, which is a brand name of a chemical rot-retardant sheet used in the fruit export industry. Notice how this keyword (in bold to allow the reader to see the pattern) appears more frequently towards the top of the document, but less and less towards the bottom. Also take note of the high ratio of keywords versus stop words. An attempt was made to include as many keywords as possible, while still retaining the basic rules of grammar and stopping short of irritating the user with nonsensical wording. For example, in the first sentence of 21 words, there are 13 keywords, producing a density figure of 13:8 = 62 per cent. This density is considered to be rather high and difficult to achieve without resorting to spamdexing (keyword stuffing).

> **UVASYS** is the pioneer laminated plastic sulphur dioxide generating sheet and is patented in all the major table grape exporting countries.
>
> The **UVASYS** brand name is known all over the world and it is used in every country where table grapes are produced or exported from, as the premium product to protect grapes from post harvest fungal decay. This is particularly true of the devastation that the *Botrytis cinerea* fungus (grey mould/mold) wreaks on grapes that need to be transported and stored for longer periods. Not only does **UVASYS** gently protect against fungal decay, but it also results in the superior appearance of stems and berries after weeks and even months of storage.
>
> **UVASYS** is the sulphur dioxide generating sheet prescribed or preferred by more prominent British supermarket groups and European vendors than any other. It is also the sheet used by more producers and packers of table grapes than any other sheet in the world.
>
> The **UVASYS** sulphur dioxide generating sheet produces a predictable and consistent emission of sulphur dioxide over a very

long period. This has the benefit of maximum fungal decay control combined with minimum sulphur dioxide burn damage. These major advantages are in part owing to its unique plastic and wax/sodium metabisulphite matrix laminating process and in part owing to the precise and stringent quality control procedures in conjunction with manufacturing processes within the narrowest parameters of accuracy.

This may well be the reason why the **UVASYS** laminated plastic sulphur dioxide (SO_2) generator is also the most copied or imitated sheet in the world. It is often to the detriment and regret of the unwary purchaser of look-alike sulphur dioxide sheets or packers of table grapes who may buy on the basis of price only. **UVASYS** is of such high standing that our competitors often buy our sheets to meet their own customers' needs.

These factors, combined with the extended shelf life that is obtained, make this invention/innovation the single most significant economic and marketing aid to table grape industries of the world since the introduction of basic sulphur dioxide pads thirty years ago.

Older technology sheets such as the plastic/paper granular sodium metabisulphate combination sulphur dioxide generating sheets lack the precise nature of the **UVASYS** laminated sheet's technology.

These three features of the **UVASYS** SO_2 gas-generating sheet have found favour with table grape exporters everywhere. Our sheet has earned the respect and loyalty of thousands of users worldwide as the best foil to counter the *Botrytis cinerea* fungus on fresh fruit. Those who recognise that there is no alternative for good quality, and those who understand that the calculation of real cost goes well beyond the purchase price of the protective SO_2 sheet that they choose to buy, are our clients.

Every small batch of generator sheets is uniquely numbered and its materials, manufacturing processes, manufacturing dates and quality test results can be traced and recalled down to the minutest detail.

This brand has become, in every grape producing country, synonymous with unparalleled quality and performance.

- It is simple to use.
- It is cost effective.
- It is reliable.

This SO_2 sheet remains the best way of ensuring that table grapes arrive at their destination in peak edible condition.

Keyword frequency/density

The number of occurrences of a certain word in one sentence or paragraph is referred to as its frequency. If this number is expressed as a percentage of the total number of words, this percentage is referred to as the keyword density. (Look again at Figure 1.6 and surrounding text for an explanation of stop words and keywords.)

Although keywords should have a strong presence on any important webpage to enhance its visibility, one cannot write a proper sentence in any language without using stop words. If all the stop words are removed from a full sentence, what remains could appear to be gibberish. Some search engines would recognise this kind of gibberish and flag that webpage as containing spamdexing. Furthermore, if the same keyword has a density of above around 12 per cent, it could also appear to be spamdexing. Keyword densities of about 6–12 per cent are suggested as being safe and efficient.

A simple calculation will produce the keyword density. It expresses the number of times one word appears in a sentence (or a paragraph etc.) as a percentage of the total number of words. For example, the keyword *mountain* appears three times in the following sentence of 33 words, giving it a 9.1 per cent density ($3 \times 100 / 33 = 9.1$):

> *The Cape Epic mountain bike event is awarded UCI status as the first ever team mountain bike stage race and the only mountain bike race in Africa to appear on the UCI calendar.*

Although this example sentence reads well, the reader will probably agree that another instance of the word *mountain* (resulting in a density of: $4 \times 100 / 34 = 11.8$ per cent) will probably push the sentence over the limit of acceptability.

As the density figure increases, the tendency of the text to become overbearing, repetitive – in short, appearing more and more like spamdexing – also increases. The example above is (arguably) on the verge of irritating the reader with too many repetitions. To reach the suggested maximum of 12 per cent keyword density without irritating the reader is a challenge, and often requires expert intervention to achieve.

Be aware that these suggested percentages are only there to guide the reader towards creating good content and protect him or her against spamdexing. It is not as if search engines have a built-in calculator which continuously measures the keyword density of each sentence, then gives a webpage a high rank if it is between 6 and 12 per cent and red flags it if not. Use this guideline purely to assist in writing good body content while using the important keywords (defined earlier by the website owner) judiciously.

Keyword proximity

Keyword proximity refers to the *distance* (normally expressed in words) between two strongly related keywords. In this sense the distance is a numerical presentation of how far objects are apart. Academic research has been done on the proximity of related keywords and a basic proximity score was defined as being the size of the smallest range which contains all the keywords of a query (Sung-Ryul et al., 2004).

The claim is that the first sentence below is better than the second in terms of the way crawlers will read it. The two important keywords in this case (*mountain* and *bike*) are closer to each other in the first example.

> *Buy a new <u>mountain</u> <u>bike</u> at Cycle Lab shop and get lifelong free service.*

> *Ride your favourite <u>mountain</u> paths with a new <u>bike</u> from the Cycle Lab shop.*

Again this implies careful writing of body text for important webpages. Keywords need to be identified – probably different keywords for different webpages, even on the same website. Once body text has been created, every sentence should be checked: can the keywords be moved closer to each other without changing meaning or resorting to keyword stuffing?

Hypertext/anchor text

A hyperlink is a piece of HTML code which produces a clickable area on the screen. This area in turn provides a way to jump directly to a point on another webpage. The other webpage can be on the same website or on a website halfway around the world. Anchor text is defined as 'The text in the clickable part of a URL' (Ramos and Cota, 2004: 101). Inside the body part of a webpage's coding, this hyperlink code has to be set up to prepare for a hyperlink to operate as a link and to display text of the designer's choice. It is the content of this anchor text field which has earned this element the third spot from the top in the list of important website elements in website visibility (see Table 2.16).

The importance of anchor text in website visibility is confirmed by the *Google bomb* episodes which made the headlines during the early 2000s. More detail follows later. The general HTML format of a hypertext link with anchor text is as follows:

> <a href='http://www.book-visibility.com'>Book on improving website visibility</a>

- The *<a* component is an indication of the start of the hypertext link.
- The *href=* is the attribute of the link (href is short for Hypertext Reference).
- The URL supplied is the landing page address – the webpage where the user will find him or herself after clicking on the hyperlink.
- *Book on improving website visibility* is the actual anchor text, to be displayed on the screen.
- The *</a>* component is the closing part of the anchor tag (Thurow, 2003a: 91).

Figure 3.4 shows part of a webpage, with one of the hyperlinks indicated inside the ellipse.

Figure 3.5 indicates part of the source code of this same webpage. The whole hyperlink is located inside the box, while the anchor text is shown in reverse text. The URL coded inside the quotes is the address of the landing page. In this case it provides a path through various levels of subdirectories (indicated by the slashes) down to the relevant page:

- subdirectory 1: *2008*
- subdirectory 2: Tour de France (*TDF*) website
- subdirectory 3: details about the *COURSE*
- subdirectory 4: English version (*US*) and
- the landing page's name (le_parcours.html) – *the course* when translated from French to English.

Figure 3.4 Location of a hyperlink on the screen

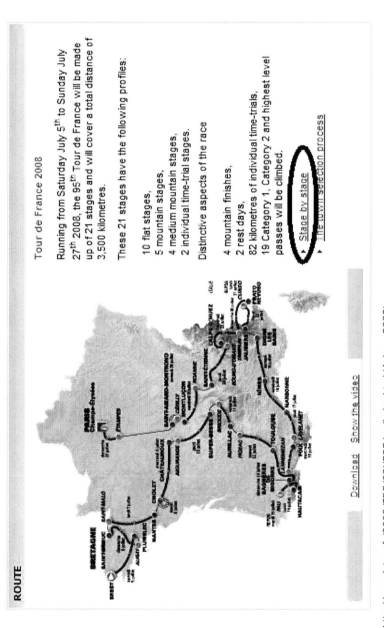

ROUTE

Tour de France 2008

Running from Saturday July 5th to Sunday July 27th 2008, the 95th Tour de France will be made up of 21 stages and will cover a total distance of 3,500 kilometres.

These 21 stages have the following profiles:

10 flat stages,
5 mountain stages,
4 medium mountain stages,
2 individual time-trial stages.

Distinctive aspects of the race

4 mountain finishes,
2 rest days,
82 kilometres of individual time-trials,
19 Category 1, Category 2 and highest level passes will be climbed.

▲ Stage by stage
▲ The town selection process

Download   Show the video

Source: http://www.letour.fr/2008/TDF/COURSE/us/index.html (1 June 2009).

Figure 3.5   Location of the anchor text inside the source code

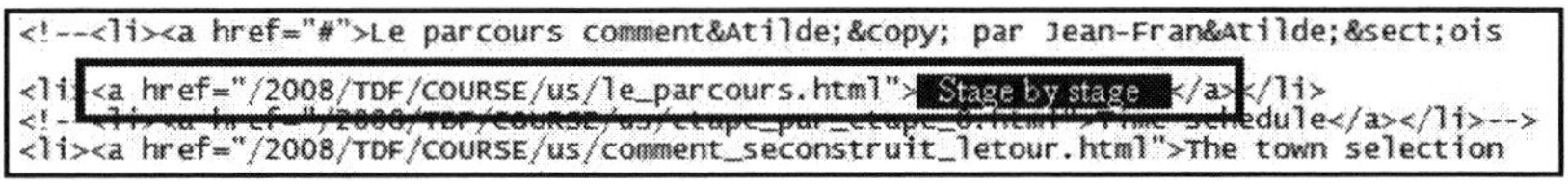

```
<!--<li><a href="#">Le parcours comment&Atilde;&copy; par Jean-Fran&Atilde;&sect;ois
<li><a href="/2008/TDF/COURSE/us/le_parcours.html">Stage by stage</a></li>
<!--<li><a href="/2008/TDF/COURSE/us/etape_par_etape_6.html">Time schedule</a></li>-->
<li><a href="/2008/TDF/COURSE/us/comment_seconstruit_letour.html">The town selection
```

Source: http://www.letour.fr/2008/TDF/COURSE/us/index.html (1 June 2009).

Guideline

The anchor text can be anything the designer wishes and technically does not have to relate to the hyperlink it is associated with. However, that is the whole point of anchor text and website visibility. The anchor text *should* be very closely related to the landing page and describe its contents as clearly as possible.

Examples abound of using keyword-rich anchor text to add weight to a hyperlink webpage element. See Figure 3.6 for some keyword-rich sets of anchor text leading to landing pages which hold no surprise for the user. The anchor text describes their contents accurately, and as such assisted the user in making a choice of which hyperlink to click on.

Figure 3.6   Typical use of information-rich anchor text

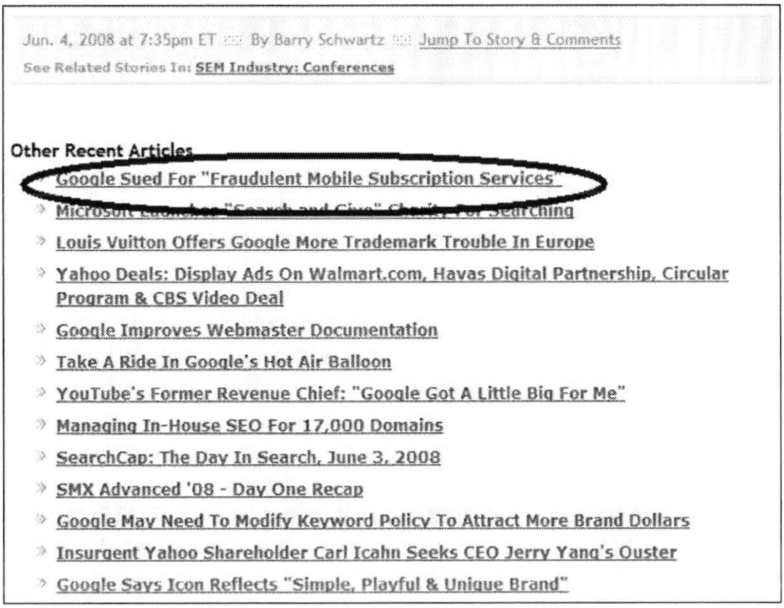

Jun. 4, 2008 at 7:35pm ET ::: By Barry Schwartz ::: Jump To Story & Comments
See Related Stories In: **SEM Industry: Conferences**

Other Recent Articles

- Google Sued For "Fraudulent Mobile Subscription Services"
- Microsoft Launches "Search and Give" Charity For Searching
- Louis Vuitton Offers Google More Trademark Trouble In Europe
- Yahoo Deals: Display Ads On Walmart.com, Havas Digital Partnership, Circular Program & CBS Video Deal
- Google Improves Webmaster Documentation
- Take A Ride In Google's Hot Air Balloon
- YouTube's Former Revenue Chief: "Google Got A Little Big For Me"
- Managing In-House SEO For 17,000 Domains
- SearchCap: The Day In Search, June 3, 2008
- SMX Advanced '08 - Day One Recap
- Google May Need To Modify Keyword Policy To Attract More Brand Dollars
- Insurgent Yahoo Shareholder Carl Icahn Seeks CEO Jerry Yang's Ouster
- Google Says Icon Reflects "Simple, Playful & Unique Brand"

Source: http://searchengineland.com/ (5 June 2008).

| Figure 3.7 | Typical use of non-informational anchor text |

Since 1996, DoubleClick has empowered the original thinkers and leaders in the digital advertising industry to deliver on the promise of the rich possibilities of our medium. Today, the company's DART and Performics divisions power the online advertising marketplace. Tomorrow, we will continue to enable clients to profit from opportunities across all digital advertising channels as consumers worldwide embrace them.

Click here for more information about our products and services.

DoubleClick is a member of the Network Advertising Initiative and has been reviewed for compliance with NAI principles.

MEMBER
NAI
Self-Regulatory
Compliance Program

Source: *http://www.doubleclick.com/privacy/index.aspx* (23 June 2008).

In contrast to the anchor text of Figure 3.6, one way to lose an opportunity to increase visibility is to allocate anchor text with no weight to a hyperlink. Probably the most common example remains the *Click here...* phenomenon. See Figure 3.7 for an example.

Instead of the words *Click here*, information about the products and services could have been provided in the anchor text of Figure 3.7. A possible example could be: *DoubleClick offers digital advertising products and services* as anchor text.

When generating the anchor text for a hyperlink, care should be taken not to create what appears to be spamdexing. The same rules apply here as for metatags. Use keywords extensively but not to the point where senseless repetition occurs or where the content does not read well. Also do not use the same anchor text for all hyperlinks. This might appear to some search engines as being auto-generated, which some do not approve of.

It is suggested that the familiar *Click here*, *Homepage* or *More information* not be used as anchor text. If this kind of text is used as anchor text, the webpage rankings will be high only if a user searches for *Click here*, *Homepage* and *More information*.

Google bombing

Ample proof of the value attached to and the power of anchor text lies in the initial *success* of the Google bombing episodes. It is claimed that there are around a hundred known Google bombs (Cutts et al., 2007). A Google bomb is created when enough webpages use similar anchor text as part of hyperlinks pointing to one target webpage. In all known cases the anchor text had no relation to the content of the target site. This bomb then *explodes* when large volumes of unsuspecting Internet traffic is directed to the target website based purely on the strength of this unrelated anchor text. In most of the known cases, the motives were non-commercial (Chellapilla and Chickering 2006), sometimes humorous or political in nature. The term Google bomb has been criticised as being too specific – it should be *link bomb*, since the process is not specific to Google only (Cutts et al., 2007).

The first known Google bomb at the end of 1999 (Sullivan, 2002a) was created when a large number of users linked to the Microsoft homepage using the anchor text *more evil than Satan himself*. As a result, the use of this phrase as a search query led the searcher to *http://www .microsoft.com*. Another one used a derogatory remark to lead traffic to a website selling George Bush merchandise (Sullivan, 2000). A third well publicised Google bomb was aimed at the website of a prankster's friend with the term *talentless hack* – this happened in 2001.

Engineers at Google designed a new algorithm which minimises the effect of Google bombing (Cutts et al., 2007) and the press has been quiet about this phenomenon during the last few years.

Metatags

The prefix *meta* stems from Greek and means *over*. As used in *metadata*, it thus implies *data over data*.

Definitions of metadata abound. In a contracted form it could be described as *data about data*. The National Information Standards Organisation provides another definition: 'Metadata is structured information that describes, explains, locates, or otherwise makes it easier to retrieve, use, or manage an information resource' (Franks and Kunde, 2006). Metadata is crucial in setting up an information retrieval system that allows easy and intuitive access to all the documents stored in the system. However, defining the metadata correctly and designing the retrieval system to consistently produce accurate results are not straightforward tasks.

One solution to the problem is to code every term inside a document as metadata to enable the retrieval of any piece of information from that document. Typical Bible Concordances (such as Strong's Exhaustive Concordance, first published in 1890) do exactly this (Weideman, 2001). However, this method requires extensive human involvement, processing power and storage capacity, it creates duplication and it does not address the retrieval of non-textual data – images, videos, sounds, etc.

In its traditional form, metadata is often mandatory – under certain circumstances it has to be designed and/or coded in some form to make certain information accessible. An Apple iPod play list is a set of metadata which has been extracted from the MP3 songs stored in its memory, enabling the user to choose tracks to listen to. The price tag with specifications on a car front window is a set of metadata about the car it is attached to. Where *metadata* is used to broadly describe a collection of information which defines other information, a *metatag* is one small subset of metadata used specifically in webpage design. The original idea behind introducing metatags for webpages was the same as for having metadata in any information retrieval system – to enable accurate and fast retrieval of relevant information. From this point onwards, metatags will be discussed rather than metadata.

These metatags are chunks of text used to describe various aspects of the webpage within which they are coded. In the free-form style of the WWW, metatags inside webpages are not only optional, but can contain any information the author wishes to put there. This information could be completely different from the actual data it is trying to describe, and in fact has been heavily abused in this way by unscrupulous webpage authors since inception. Enter many court cases, disagreement about the use of metatags and uncertainty in the user community about their use. The reader will hopefully find clarity on the use of metatags in this section.

What do metatags look like?

A webpage consists of two major parts: the HEADER and the BODY, respectively. The contents of the header section are not seen by the human reader (except if they specifically view it via the browser menus), and is used by the browser and other programs (see Figures 1.7 and 1.8). The body section is what is displayed on the computer screen for the human viewer to see. (See Figure 3.8 for a simple program in HTML indicating these two sections.) Figure 3.9 indicates what this program will display in a browser window. The coding between the <HEAD> and the </HEAD> tags is the contents of the header section, and that between the <BODY> and </BODY> tags is the body. Metatags are coded in the <HEAD> section.

A large number of tags and metatags exist. The ones relevant to website visibility, which will be discussed here, are the following: TITLE, DESCRIPTION, KEYWORDS and ROBOTS. In the first three tags, weight-carrying keywords (e.g. brand names, technical terms,

Figure 3.8   Example of HEAD and BODY sections of a webpage

```
<html>
<head>
<title> My New Web Page </title>
</head>

<body>

<h1> Welcome to My Web Page! </h1>

<p>
This page illustrates how you can write proper HTML
using only a text editor, such as Windows Notepad. You can also
download a free text editor, such as Crimson Editor, which is
better than Notepad.
</p>

<p>
There is a small graphic after the period at the end of this sentence.
<img src="images/mouse.gif" alt="Mousie" width="32" height="32"
border="0">
The graphic is in a file. The file is inside a folder named "images."
</p>

<p>
Link: <a href="http://www.yahoo.com/">Yahoo!</a> <br>
Another link: <a href="tableexample.htm">Another Web page</a> <br>
Note the way the BR tag works in the two lines above.
</p>

</body>
</html>
```

Source: *http://www.macloo.com/examples/html/basic.htm#* (1 June 2009).

descriptive words) should outweigh stop words (e.g. the, that, in, a, and even overused words such as webpage, computer, information, home). These metatags should be coded on all the webpages in a website.

TITLE tag

This tag should be written as a single sentence, very descriptive of what the webpage is about, grammatically correct and loaded with meaningful keywords. The TITLE tag can be any length, but most browsers will only display the first 50 to 60 characters. Therefore care should be taken to ensure that the most descriptive keywords of the TITLE tag appear towards the beginning, in case the last part is cut off by the browser (Anonymous, 2006a). The example TITLE metatag in Figure 3.10 adds up to 102 characters, spaces included.

Figure 3.9   Browser display of the program in Figure 3.8

Source: http://www.macloo.com/examples/html/basic.htm# (1 June 2009).

Figure 3.10   Example of a TITLE tag

<TITLE>Book on website visibility and how to improve
website rankings through webpage optimization</TITLE>

Source: http://www.book-visibility.com (1 June 2009).

DESCRIPTION metatag

This tag should be coded as a single English paragraph, very descriptive of what the webpage is about, grammatically correct and loaded with meaningful keywords. It is therefore an extension of the TITLE metatag. The DESCRIPTION metatag should not exceed 250 to 300 characters – most search engines will index all characters but display only the first part. The example DESCRIPTION metatag in Figure 3.11 adds up to 564 characters.

Even though the content of this metatag is seldom used in the actual information retrieval process, parts of it are displayed on SERPs. As such it should be carefully written, with the most important and descriptive keywords towards the beginning.

Figure 3.11 Example of a DESCRIPTION metatag

<META name="DESCRIPTION" content="Uvasys Grape Guards are patented laminated plastic sulphur/sulfur dioxide generating pads/sheets which protect Table Grapes against Postharvest fungal decay, in particular Botrytis, for up to 4 months. Predictable and consistent Sulphur Dioxide emission means that grapes stored with Uvasys have maximum decay control combined with minimum sulphur dioxide damage. The excellent appearance of the stems and berries. combined with prolonged shelf life make Uvasys the choice of many leading European retailers. Both Dual and Slow release Uvasys sheets are available.">

Source: http://www.uvasys.com (1 June 2009).

KEYWORDS metatag

This tag should be written as a series of keywords separated by spaces. Commas could also be used, but they consume an extra character per keyword. Overused and stop words must not be listed (e.g. computer, information, system, the, that, many, etc.). Each keyword must be descriptive of some aspect of that particular webpage and care must be taken to spell them correctly. At the same time, common misspellings of important keywords could be included. The keywords selected should be repeated a number of times in the body text of the webpage. There should be limited repetition of keywords in the metatag itself, but different spellings (e.g. colour, color) as well as common errors (e.g. acommodation, accomodation, acomodation) could be included. The example KEYWORDS metatag in Figure 3.12 adds up to 77 keywords, and 504 characters. The generally accepted limit for this metatag is around 250 to 300 characters.

Due to extensive abuse by designers, very few search engines recognise the KEYWORDS metatag. However, it is recommended that this metatag be used as a *library* to record the important keywords for a webpage – it has to be done somewhere in any case.

Figure 3.12 Example of a KEYWORDS metatag

<META name="KEYWORDS" content=" ">website web site webpage page visibility index indexes indices indexing search engine engines optimisation optimization rank ranking rankings user users internet traffic technology technologies body key word words keyword keywords hypertext anchor text metatag metatags meta tag tags title h1 description link inlink inlinks outlink outlinks domain submission paid inclusion placement html naming convention spam spamdexing server crawler crawlers bot bots robot robots content duplicate flash frames graphics slow cloaking doorway static dynamic javascript banner advertising>"

Source: http://www.book-visibility.com (1 June 2009).

ROBOTS metatag

The ROBOTS metatag instructs search engine crawlers on how to treat the relevant webpage. The general format of the ROBOTS metatag is:

<META NAME='ROBOTS' CONTENT='x, y'>

where x and y can have the values INDEX, NOINDEX, FOLLOW, NOFOLLOW, ALL, NONE.

The meanings of these values are:

INDEX	Please crawl and index this webpage
NOINDEX	Please do not crawl and index this webpage
FOLLOW	Please follow all hyperlinks on this webpage
NOFOLLOW	Please do not follow all hyperlinks on this webpage
ALL	The same as INDEX, FOLLOW
NONE	The same as NOINDEX, NOFOLLOW

If no ROBOTS metatag is included in the HEAD section, it is the same as including this combination:

<META NAME='ROBOTS' CONTENT='INDEX, FOLLOW'> or
<META NAME='ROBOTS' CONTENT='ALL'>

That leaves another three combinations which make sense, namely:

<META NAME='ROBOTS' CONTENT='NOINDEX, FOLLOW'>
<META NAME='ROBOTS' CONTENT='INDEX, NOFOLLOW'>
<META NAME='ROBOTS' CONTENT='NOINDEX, NOFOLLOW'>

Since this book is about increasing visibility, the use of the ROBOTS metatag can be ignored in this context. If a webpage has no ROBOTS metatag, crawlers will visit and index each page they find as if it had one that instructed them to do so.

Why use metatags?

Firstly, the use of metatags could improve the visibility of a website to search engine crawlers. Most search engines attach considerable weight

Figure 3.13 How the TITLE tag is seen by the user during normal browsing

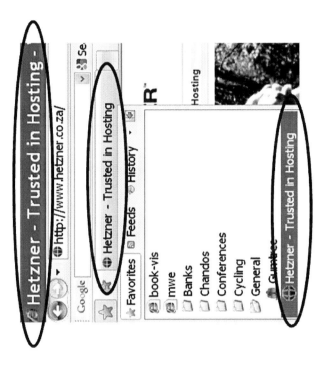

Source: *http://www.hetzner.co.za* (1 June 2009).

Figure 3.14 How the TITLE tag is seen by the user on a search engine result page

hetzner website hosting   Search   Advanced Search
                                                    Preferences

Web

Hetzner - Trusted in **Hosting**
Advanced Web hosting plan. Our Advanced package. Only R279 p/m. Save R199 on setup.
Hetzner's TruServ™ servers are on special in June ...
www.**hetzner**.co.za/ - 13k - Cached - Similar pages - Note this

Customer Login	Web support FAQ
Web Hosting	Managed Dedicated Hosting
Contact Us	TruServ Dedicated Hosting
Support Centre	Resellers

More results from hetzner.co.za »

Hetzner: Advanced **Web hosting** plan
Hetzner was established in 1999 and is South Africa's largest **hosting** company, with well
over 20% market share. **Hetzner** - Trusted in **Hosting**.
www.**hetzner**.co.za/index.php/hosting/specials/advanced-**webhosting**-special/ - 13k -
Cached - Similar pages - Note this

Source: http://www.google.com (1 June 2009).

to the text inside the TITLE tag, and it deserves some time and effort to code properly (Dawson and Hamilton, 2006). As mentioned above, the TITLE tag coding is invisible to the casual browser, since it is embedded in the webpage coding (header section). However, when this webpage is viewed by any user, the wording will be visible in the reverse bar, as well as in tabbing and the Favourites section – see Figure 3.13.

Furthermore, when this webpage is displayed on, for example, a Google result page, the TITLE tag will again be visible as the first line of the result summary – see Figure 3.14.

How to add or edit metatags

To add metatags to any existing webpage, the user needs access to the source code of the webpage, an ASCII editor or word processor, but requires no programming experience. One could use Windows Notepad or any ASCII editor, MS Word or Wordpad. However, to upload the changed webpage will require Internet access, the use of any FTP-type program (can be downloaded freely) and FTP password access to the actual website to which this webpage belongs.

Contradictory evidence on metatags

The need for metadata in webpages was clear-cut after it was released, namely that it should serve as a description of the contents of that webpage. As has become abundantly clear since then, metatags have been abused to draw traffic to webpages and search engines in general do not use them in the way originally intended. Both the TITLE and DESCRIPTION metatags, however, should be used and play a definite role in website visibility. The KEYWORDS metatag has some value, and this situation has led to confusion among users regarding their use in webpage design.

Empirical research on relationships between users and webpage metadata has been carried out previously and 12 links between various elements have been identified. One was inspected in detail, and it was found that website coders made very little use of metatags on webpages, which would have enhanced the user's searching experience (Weideman, 2004b).

Some arguments for the use of metadata include the following:

- The TITLE tag plays an important part in website visibility and is displayed prominently by most browsers.

- Some search engines insist on certain metatags being present before indexing a webpage (including *http://www.ananzi.com*, South Africa's biggest search engine).

- Creating metatags forces the website owner to think about the purpose and content of the website.

- It is considered to be one of the '… easiest legitimate technique(s), often overlooked …' of improving website visibility (Goldsborough, 2005: 40).

- The value of metadata in principle is claimed to be undeniable (Dawson and Hamilton, 2006).

Some quotes from other research confirm the statements above.

> Websites with meta tags have a much better chance of being listed on search engines – and listed higher in the rankings – than websites with no meta tags. (BusinessLink, n.d.)

> Some search engines recognize metadata in webpage coding, and use it to properly categorize the webpage in its index. This should produce high quality answers when a user does a search. (Weideman, 2002a)

> … metadata has been seen as the panacea for the problems of finding information on the internet. (Dawson and Hamilton, 2006)

> There are several meta tags, but the most important for search engine indexing are the description and keywords tags. (BusinessLink, n.d.)

> To accomplish this end, information about the content, context, and structure of records must be recorded and managed. Many experts believe metadata is the key to meeting this challenge. (Franks and Kunde, 2006)

> They might help designer and publisher ensure that their materials are found when appropriate searches are executed. (Alimohammadi, 2004)

The mere fact that metatags have been the focus of a number of court cases underlines their value. In most of these cases, one organisation has used keywords in a metatag which *belongs to* another organisation, and the second has sued the first (Woods, 2007).

On the negative side, arguments against the use of metatags include the following:

- Search engines ignore metadata (Sullivan, 2002b).
- It is too time-consuming and complicated to create.
- Metadata is subjective and can therefore be misinterpreted.
- Creating metadata has no borders – it could carry on forever.
- A webpage can incur spamdexing penalties if metatags are created incorrectly (Mbikiwa, 2005).

Again, there are references to underpin these claims:

> ... unfortunately, only Infoseek and Hotbot currently factor meta-content into their formula ... (Sullivan, 2002b)

> Currently, however, few search engines actually use metatags to determine the relevancy of websites ... (Woods, 2007)

> There are many reasons for the success and public acceptance of the market leader Google, but metadata is not one of them. (Dawson and Hamilton, 2006)

Many studies exist which prove that metatags are often not used to their full potential and that they have positive effects on visibility. Some conclusions from these studies are listed below.

During a study of 33 of the 36 university websites in South Africa in 2002 (three were offline at the time), the following transpired:

- one website (3 per cent) used no metatags at all;
- 19 (58 per cent) used only the basic 'TITLE' metatag;
- four (12 per cent) made basic use of the relevant metatags; and
- the remaining nine (27 per cent) made reasonable use of the relevant metatags (Weideman, 2002a).

The following results were also found from various studies, claiming various facts about the use of metatags.

- One study on the use of metatags in e-commerce websites indicated that they were seldom used (Weideman and Kritzinger, 2003a).
- Another author studied the websites of 33 e-journals and discovered that 19.6 per cent of them made use of metatags (Visser, 2007).
- A study in 1998 proved that the KEYWORD metatag improved access to webpages via search engines (Alimohammadi, 2004).

It is clear where the confusion around metatags originates from – experts openly disagree on their value. This author makes a recommendation on this issue at the end of this section.

Metatag examples

Some examples of *good*, *medium* and *bad* metatags follow. In each case reasons for the rating are supplied. The ratios given for each example refer to the number of keywords (indicated in bold in the text) versus the number of stop words. In the example *7:3 – 70 per cent*, there were seven keywords and three stop words. The percentage is the ratio of keywords against the total, with a higher percentage indicating a better metatag composition. However, reaching 100 per cent would certainly result in gibberish, since a grammatically correct sentence cannot be constructed without using some stop words. Furthermore, a good TITLE tag should have a percentage of around 50–80 per cent, while a good DESCRIPTION metatag would probably reach 40–60 per cent. Ratios are not given for KEYWORD metatags since they should all be 100 per cent – there is no need to build sentences using stop words to make them read well.

Good

http://www.uvasys.com

<TITLE>Uvasys: Uvasys sulphur / sulfur dioxide generators control postharvest fungal decay in table grapes</TITLE>

This TITLE tag manages to pack a high percentage of keywords into a single sentence, without creating gibberish. The brand name appears twice, which should not raise the spamdexing flag. Both the UK and US spelling of an important keyword are used. It could have been a little longer. Ratio: 10:4 – 71 per cent.

http://www.hetzner.co.za

<META name='DESCRIPTION' content='Hetzner is South Africa's largest specialist web hosting company. We provide reliable and robust web hosting solutions coupled with outstanding customer support. Trusted in Hosting'>

This example competes in the overfull technology section, but manages to do a fine job by steering clear of relying only on overused technical terms. Ratio: 14:11 – 56 per cent.

http://www.book-visibility.com

<META name='DESCRIPTION' content='Website visibility: the theory and practice of improving rankings is a book on optimising web site contents for high search engine rankings. Both positive and negative factors influencing the rank of a webpage are prioritised and discussed. Inlink count, body keywords, spamdexing, amongst others, are covered.'>

This DESCRIPTION metatag is complete, although filled with technical detail. Ratio: 39:43 – 48 per cent.

Medium

http://www.bmw.com

<TITLE>BMW automobiles – website of the BMW AG</TITLE>

This tag repeats the most important keyword twice only, and uses two other weight-carrying terms. However, it is too short, includes the totally meaningless term *website* and misses out on the opportunity to load the tag with more keywords (e.g. some model numbers (Z4, 320i, 760Li,), head office or factory locations (München) and other motor-car specific terms). Ratio: 4:3 – 57 per cent.

Another argument could be that a high-profile homepage like *http://www.bmw.com* does not need any special attention to keywords or optimisation, since regular users would simply type the URL in instead of searching for it. However, this example should serve as a general guideline.

http://www.cape-epic.com
<TITLE>**Absa Cape Epic** presented by **Adidas** | The **Magical + Untamed African MTB Race**</TITLE>
The brand name of this event and two of its sponsor names feature prominently, plus the well-known abbreviation *MTB* (mountain-bike). The two punctuation signs add no value, but consume some character positions in the valuable first 60 or so positions. It is also too short, and could have included some more specific terms describing the event and the route (e.g. bike, bicycle, 966km, fynbos, nature reserves, world's toughest, stages). Ratio: 9:5 – 64 per cent.

http://www.ananzi.co.za
<meta name='DESCRIPTION' content='**Ananzi South Africa**, search engine and web portal. Giving you access to the latest **news, property, motoring, shopping, dating** and job **services**.'>
This example suffers from relying on too many overused terms (e.g. search, engine, portal, access), but does manage to survive the tough world of finding unique terms in the technology sector. Ratio: 9:13 – 41 per cent.

http://www.uvasys.com
<META name='KEYWORDS' content='uvasys grapetek tedmark sulphur dioxide table grapes botrytis postharvest laminated pad sheet generator plastic fungal decay litchi lychee grey mould mold fungus uvaspec sulphite laminated grape guard sodium metabisulphite protection preservation red globe south african thompsons residues'>

http://www.bmw.com
<meta name='KEYWORDS' content='BMW international automobile automobiles vehicle vehicles cars car brand service interactive products insights driver driving pleasure 1 Series 3 Series 5 Series 6 Series 7 Series X3 X5 Z4 M3 M5 M6 pre-owned used configure compare models buy search dealer countries country'>

http://www.hetzner.co.za
<META name='KEYWORDS' content=' web hosting hosting in South Africa linux servers data centre co-location shared hosting dedicated

hosting co-located hosting server hosting root server hosting managed hosting php mysql postgres domain registration'>

http://www.sa-cycling.com
<META name='KEYWORDS' content='road bikes roadbikes cycle cycles road cycling roadcycling ride SA cycling SA-Cycling sacycling team cycle club cycling club cycling South Africa cycling cycle touring cycle tour WP cycling best cycling tours fun ride funrides cicling bicycle bicycling rapport giro del capo giro cape argus david cowie bike touring RIP hill cycle news cycling news pedal power PPA WPPA track cycling rules of cycling Tour de France professional cycling pro cycling procycling track fixed-gear ride'>
The repetitive use of the term *cycling* could be problematic in this example.

Bad

http://www.kapstadt.diplo.de/Vertretung/kapstadt/en/Startseite.html
<title> - Homepage</title>
No comment – there is no excuse for having a single-word TITLE tag, where the word choice is useless in any case! When a browser loads a webpage like this, it will display the word *Homepage* at the top – a valuable marketing opportunity wasted!

http://www.welcomebaby.com/
<title>**baby gift**-personalized **baby gift**-buy **baby gift**</title>
This example has only two (debatable) keywords, but repeats each one three times and has the appearance of a spamdexing type heading.

Conclusion and recommendation on the use of metatags

Even while some comments about the use of metatags are contradictory, no evidence was found about their presence having any negative effects on a webpage. Apart from the time taken to create and code them, and the negligible space they are taking up as part of an HTML page, there is no reason to omit them. In fact more than enough reasons exist to include metatags in every webpage of a website.

Every webpage has an *owner* – the person or organisation that stands to benefit from it and who normally provides the content (possibly indirectly). This *owner* should generate the three metatags as described below, and ensure that they are coded into the header section of the relevant webpage(s).

Do not make use of automated online services (e.g. *http://www.web-ignite.com*) to generate metatags, with or without payment (BusinessLink, n.d.). These services mostly use a program, based on an algorithm, to identify keywords on your webpage and then build up metatags based on those. No program can write more accurate metatags than the website owner. This is the person with the strongest motivation to generate traffic to a website, and often the best understanding of the business represented by the website. In conclusion: the use of the TITLE tag is not negotiable – it plays a major positive role in website visibility. For the others, there appear to be two sides to the story – either use them, or do not use them. No evidence could be found that they have any detrimental effect on a webpage, except of course if they contain spamdexing. While they do take time to generate, their presence can only benefit the website owner.

Therefore the following is recommended for any webpage where more human traffic would be beneficial:

■ Discuss with role-players or otherwise determine the purpose, target audience and content of the webpage.

■ Determine the most important keywords for each webpage and ensure they are present in all three metatags.

■ Summarise the most basic message of the webpage in one heavily laden sentence, based on the guidelines for the TITLE tag above – create the TITLE tag with this sentence.

■ Expand the TITLE tag into three or four full sentences, again using a high percentage of keywords as opposed to stop words – create the DESCRIPTION metatag from this.

■ Scan the webpage and the two tags above for at least 100 weight-carrying keywords – create the KEYWORD metatag from them.

■ Double check all tags for spelling mistakes – have them proofed by more than one outsider for comments.

■ Ensure that these metatags are coded into all webpages and uploaded (without duplicates).

■ Manually submit at least the homepage to Google, Yahoo! and MSN.

Duplicate metatags can be avoided by considering what is different or unique about every webpage and rewriting those elements as differing metatags. See Figure 1.8 for an example of a simple but complete set of these three tags.

TITLE tag

As mentioned earlier, the use of keywords plays a major role in increasing the visibility of a website. Arguably keywords used correctly in a webpage's TITLE tag is the most important of these instances (Brown, 2007; Dawson and Hamilton, 2006; Kritzinger, 2007).

Apart from playing a major role in positively influencing the visibility of a webpage, there are other reasons for writing proper TITLE tags for each webpage in a website.

- This text appears in the reverse bar at the top of the user's browser window while viewing this webpage.

- When a user adds this webpage to their favourites, this text is stored with the address.

- When a search engine displays this webpage as part of a SERP, the TITLE tag will appear in the first line of the result section.

The TITLE tag and its implementation are discussed in detail in the previous section.

H1 tag

A webpage coder could specify that the text in the body of a webpage occupy one of a number of levels of importance. These levels are indicated by number in the HTML coding and by font size on the screen. However, it has been proven that crawlers also attach value to especially the H1 heading, which indicates the highest level of importance of text. Figure 3.15 shows the HTML coding of an imaginary webpage in which three levels of headings have been used. Figure 3.16 indicates what this webpage will look like when displayed by a browser.

Most crawlers assume that whatever appears inside the H1 tags on a webpage will be the headings physically on top of the screen. They further assume that this information is important and gives an indication of what the webpage is about. It follows then that designers should incorporate a basic description, similar to the TITLE tag of that webpage, in an H1 tag. The font, colour and size of text can still be controlled by using other technologies (such as cascading style sheets), which makes certain look-and-feel environments possible.

Figure 3.15 HTML code indicating different H-levels

```
<H1>Gary Marescia</H1>

<H2>Cycle Lab</H2>
<H2>Shop C3A Northgate Island</H2>
<H2>1 Section Road</H2>
<H2>Northgate Estate</H2>

<H3>Cape Town</H3>
```

Figure 3.16 Browser display of the webpage in Figure 3.15

Gary Marescia

Cycle Lab
Shop C3A Northgate Island
1 Section Road
Northgate Estate

Cape Town

Outlinks

This element refers to the quality of the hyperlinks from within the website to outside webpages. The correct use of keywords inside these links is important. This could be especially so for newer websites, which suffer an inherited disadvantage of not having a well-aged domain and the associated trust behind them. Being associated with highly trusted and above-board domains rubs off through outlinks to these domains. Some experts consider this element to be 'almost equally important' as inbound links, which occupies the first position on the SEO practitioner's list (Fishkin and Pollard, 2007). It is no coincidence that this factor, number seven on the ranked list of positive factors (see Table 2.16), occupies position number six (in its reversed form) on the list of negative elements (see Table 2.16). In other words, if the external links from a website point to low-quality sites, specifically those branded as containing spamdexing, it will certainly degrade the website to the point of possibly getting it red-flagged by the search engines.

Age of site

This is one element over which a website owner has little control – one cannot increase a website's age except by waiting for time to pass! A domain name which has not been involved in spamdexing and has existed for a long time will probably have been found by most crawlers. This means it has been visited by many users and has built up an element of trust which is difficult to come by in any other way.

However, one can learn from the importance of this element by realising that newly registered domains automatically start with a disadvantage. This implies careful planning when deciding on a corporate domain since, once chosen, this domain should remain as an active website for as long as possible. The path to a successful Internet presence does not lie in the registration of numerous new domains and the creation of as many new websites. Take note that while a domain name will remain constant (e.g. *http://www.abc.com*), the associated URLs might change (e.g. *http://www.abc.com/contact.htm* might change to *http://www.abc.com/aboutus.htm*).

Domain names

Domain names have been chosen to convey a message from the early Internet days. Some examples of existing, descriptive URLs are:

- *http://www.apple.com*
- *http://www.audi.com*
- *http://www.coca-cola.com*
- *http://www.mp3playerbuying.com*
- *http://www.youtube.com*

An instinctive tendency has been, and will probably remain, to choose a URL that is short but descriptive of the business represented by the website living at that URL. Similarly, the use of a brand name (as in some of the examples above) is a highly coveted area of domain name choice. However, every URL can only have one owner, and the number of short, descriptive ones is limited. For example, there are only 26 one-letter .com domains: *http://www.a.com*, *http://www.b.com*, etc. However, both one- and two-letter domain names have been reserved in any case – after some of these domains were already registered (including *http:// www.aa.com* for American Airlines, *http://www.ba.com* for British Airways and some others). An attempt to load *http://www.a.com* and *http://www.b.com* will be unsuccessful, although, for example, *http://www.z.com* was successfully registered by Nissan.

This situation has given rise to the phenomenon of cybersquatting, defined as:

> ... registering, trafficking in, or using a domain name with bad faith or intent to profit from the goodwill of a trademark belonging to someone else. The cybersquatter then offers to sell the domain to the person or company who owns a trademark contained within the name at an inflated price. (Wikipedia, 2008b)

Some of the victims of cybersquatting include Hertz, Avon and Panasonic. It is claimed that 10 per cent of all cybersquatting claims are from pharmaceutical companies, 25 per cent of claims are settled without intervention and 85 per cent of all settlements in the past were awarded to the claimants. In these cases, the original owner of the domains at stake (i.e. the cybersquatter) had to sell it to the claimant for a reasonable fee (Anonymous, 2008a).

The issue at stake here, however, is the role the domain name plays in website visibility. A research methodology was proposed to determine empirically what the effect of domain name choice is on website visibility (Hamdulay and Weideman, 2006). At the same time, the previous element discussed (age of website) also needs to be considered. For example, suppose a website owner decides that their current domain name is not a good choice and wants to register a new, more descriptive one. Subsequently they move the website over to the new domain name. The advantage gained by having a *better* domain name could be offset by the disadvantage of exchanging an old, trusted domain for a new, unknown one.

Experts from the SEO industry make the following claims regarding the value of having a domain name containing (a) descriptive word(s):

- A well aged domain containing a keyword (without hyphens) has achieved 25 per cent of the work to get top rankings.

- Joining two keywords loses its value for search engines (e.g. *http://www.buycars.co.za*) since they cannot see the two keywords, *buy* and *cars*, as separate words.

- Whatever a domain name is, it will be listed in other websites' links and will be shown on SERPs. This leads to more exposure, so the presence of keywords can only have a positive effect on visibility (Fishkin and Pollard, 2007).

The situation of an overfull domain name space has given rise to a relatively new phenomenon: the hyphenated domain name. For example, if *http://www.buycars.co.za* already exists, simply register *http://www.buy-cars.co.za*. This would be perfectly legal, assuming the *buy-cars* domain is still available. Furthermore, one advantage in this example is that crawlers will actually recognise the two words as separate, weight-carrying keywords. The *buycars* domain has less value in this case, since *buycars* as one word is not a recognised English word which describes anything.

Having said that, however, hyphenated domain names should be treated with care. They are often associated with attempts at spamdexing (the typical *http://www.get-rich-quick-from-home-now.com* brigade). The possibility also exists that much wanted traffic can be directed away from your website. If your domain name is *http://www.sell-books.com*, this name can be inadvertently translated (verbally, in writing or typed in e-mails) to *http://www.sellbooks.com*, which is likely to be a competitor.

To summarise:

■ If you have an existing, established domain name containing a single, important keyword, do not register a new one to replace it.

■ Do some research on keywords before registering any new domain name, especially for commercial intent.

■ Consider the competition and what domains they are using.

■ In general, do not combine two keywords into one word.

With the heightened awareness of the branding value of short, descriptive domain names, it is fairly certain that all of these have been taken. This is especially true in the .com domain. If a new domain has to be registered, consider a two-word, hyphenated domain, where the two words are the main keywords describing the website. The supporting website for this book is a good example: *http://www.book-visibility.com*. A quick check on the availability of domains on, for example, *http://www.register.com* will indicate whether a certain domain already used in the .com domain is still available in others (e.g. .net, .biz, .info, etc.).

Search engine submission

If a new website is created and hosted but no links point to this website and no search engine submissions are made, no user will ever be able to find the site. A search engine can only find (and index) a webpage if it finds it via another hyperlink or if somebody submits the URL of the webpage to a search engine. Two methods exist to submit an existing URL to a search engine, simplistically referred to as automatic and manual.

Figure 3.17 Potentially suspect automated submission service

Free Search Engine Submission

✳ ✳ ✳ ✳ ✳

(86 votes)

Add Url - Free automatic search engine registration and url submission service

3
diggs

digg it

Submit your website URL to over 100 search engines, for free. Why submit your site manually to each search engine, when you can submit your URL from one place to all of them just by filling out one simple form that only asks for your web site URL and email address. Add your URL below to submit to altavista, excite, go, google, hotbot, infoseek and lycos. We recommend checking our our hints and tips and trying our free metatag anlalyser, metatag generator and broken links checker before using this service.

1. Link to us:

Please make sure you put this button or a link to us on your page, that's all we ask in exchange for our great service! Just copy and paste the code below into your page!

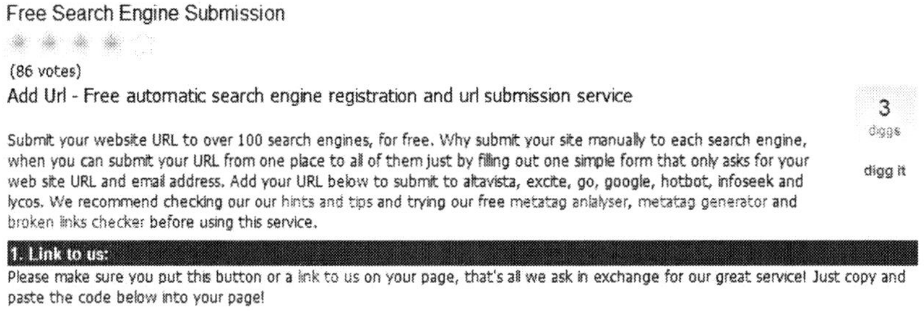

Source: Not shown (1 June 2009).

Automatic

Automatic submission involves the use of an online service to submit your webpage to *hundreds* or even *thousands* of search engines. Sometimes a small fee is charged, sometimes it is free, but almost always the user's e-mail address is requested. In many cases these services are scams, where the main purpose is to obtain a *live* e-mail address which is in turn sold to spammers. The example in Figure 3.17 has not been tested and it could be a trustworthy service, but its appearance is typical of the suspect automated services.

It is suggested that automated submission services not be used. The risk of more e-mail spam and, more seriously, being red-flagged by a search engine is not worth the time saving.

Manual

Manual submission of a webpage involves completing a form on a search engine's website where at least the URL of your webpage is supplied. The search engine crawler or human editors should then visit the webpage and take a decision on whether or not to index it. There is no guarantee that they will actually visit, and if they do it could take from one to a number of weeks, even months. However, the user is guaranteed that the information submitted is in good hands and that the URL is supplied to the source of one possible way to get into the index of a search engine. To submit a URL to Yahoo!, for example, one has to follow the link titled *Suggest a Site* right at the bottom of their homepage – see Figure 3.18. For Google, the URL is *http://www.google.com/addurl/*.

Figure 3.18 Submitting a webpage address for indexing: Yahoo!

Source: *http://www.yahoo.co.uk* (1 June 2009).

Others

Paid inclusion service

Paid results refer to paying a search engine in exchange for a potential or guaranteed increase in ranking for a website. In contrast to SEO, paid results involve an *inorganic* process – simple payment (sometimes regardless of the content of the website) could get the owner top rankings (Köhne, 2006).

Paid inclusion (PI) is a basic paid service which guarantees that a website will be included in the index of the search engine. This is *not* the same as guaranteeing ranking at a certain position. However, it does overcome the first hurdle towards higher rankings by at least knowing that the search engine to whom payment is made will visit the webpage and include it in the index. Google is one notable exception to search engines offering this service.

If PI is not good enough for a given website, the next step is to pay more, but be assured that the website will actually appear on a SERP, in other words that it will actually *rank* somewhere in a predictable fashion.

Paid placement service

PP, also referred to as *pay-per-click* or PPC, involves a website owner allocating marketing funding in a controlled way to ensure high rankings for the website. This is a very obvious form of advertising in an attempt to increase sales and it is surrounded by concerns similar to those with normal advertising. For example, some ethical issues were raised when it was considered that users could be faced with search engine results in top positions earned by payment instead of by virtue (Weideman, 2004a). The website owners put in a bid for a keyword or key phrase considered to be important for a specific website. For example, they might decide to bid an amount of $0.10 per click for the keyword *flowers* (which they consider best to describe their online flower-selling business). This choice is made after determining that the highest existing bid from competitors for the same keyword is currently $0.09 per click. Once an account has been opened with a search engine and a monthly limit set, this advertiser's website will appear in the number one position on that search engine's result page when a user has executed a search with the keyword *flowers*. An amount of $0.10 will be debited to the account every time a user now actually clicks on this top-spot link to the flower business (Weideman, 2007).

It is clear, however, that it is certainly possible to achieve top rankings using PPC when the keyword entered by the user has no relation to the content of the destination website. Furthermore, competitors can inflate the flower-seller's expenses (without the accompanying revenue) by simply clicking on this link repeatedly. This is referred to as click fraud (see below), but search engines have ways of dealing with this situation. This form of website exposure increase is also referred to as cost-per-click (CPC) advertising (Sullivan, 2007a).

A recent study has proven that more users prefer clicking on organic search engine results than those clicking on paid results (Neethling and Weideman, 2007). However, an attempt was not made to determine the difference in sales produced by these different numbers of clicks. It could be that more income was generated by fewer clicks executed on the PPC system.

The three leaders in the PP industry are currently Google AdWords, Yahoo!'s Search Marketing and Microsoft's adCenter. AdWords uses a variety of factors to determine actual ranking, including the webpage quality, the bid price and the click through rate. Initially the Yahoo! system only considered bid price in determining rankings, but its latest Panama development also considers the same elements as AdWords (Sullivan, 2007a).

When using PPC, one should be aware of what competitors are bidding on a particular keyword. It is suggested that readers follow the guidelines given on: *http://www.google.com/adwords/learningcenter/ text/18722.html* and *http://services.google.com/awp/en_us/breeze/5310/ index.html.*

Click fraud

One flaw in the much-used PPC system is the assumption that all Internet users are honest and prepared to do business in an open way. It is quite easy to find a PPC advertisement of a business opponent and continuously click on this link without purchasing any product or service. This action would increase the opponent's advertising expenditure without producing the expected income and it is termed click fraud. As with spamdexing, search engines have ways of identifying these actions and subsequently refunding clients. However, click fraud is complex and this solution is far from ideal.

A relatively new development which bypasses this problem is the PPA or CPA system – Pay Per Action or Cost Per Action. This is a pricing model where a charge is levied for a specified action which is not just a click on a hyperlink as is the case with PPC. This action can be set to whatever the system designer decides, but in this case it is likely to be the payment for a product ordered. Both eBay and Google are incorporating PPA into their online advertising systems (Wikipedia, 2008e).

Age of document

This element is similar to *age of page*, covered earlier in this book. If an HTML file (or MS Word document accessible from within a webpage) has retained the same URL in a trusted domain for a long period of time, it will have a small positive effect on website visibility.

HTML naming conventions

The website designer has full control over what to name HTML pages created for the website. For example, a page containing the contact details of a company could be named: *http://www.abc.com/contact-details.htm*. This element has limited value, although these links will show up in inlinks from other sites. They might also be visible on SERPs, depending on how the search engine displays results. When creating a new website, it is worth the effort to use sensible names, but not in the case of an existing site with thousands of pages.

Age of link

This element is similar to *age of page*, as already covered above.

Other categories

The last two categories (i.e. *Topical relationship of linking site* and *Relevance of site's primary subject matter to query*) are considered of too low importance to be covered here.

4

The bad ones

According to the Weideman model (see Figure 2.6), two kinds of spamdexing occupy the top positions: link and keyword spamdexing. Cumulatively these two elements earned 26.6 per cent of the votes, out of a list of 17 elements with a negative effect on website visibility. It is clear that search engine companies have been very active in identifying and combating these kinds of activities. Similarly, any website owner interested in high rankings without resorting to unethical methods or incurring search engine penalties should be very aware of how these two kinds of spamdexing are defined by the search engines.

Link spamdexing

Many search engines rely on link analysis for ranking determination and put a premium on the quantity and quality of the links pointing to a given webpage (Sullivan, 2002c). The more and/or higher the quality of the links pointing to this page, the higher its ranking will be. As a result, yet another form of abuse has become evident: link farms or *free for alls* (FFAs). A link farm is a webpage/site with the primary purpose of listing thousands upon thousands of links to other pages (Thelwall, 2001: 118). There could also be some automatically generated but seldom useful content in an attempt to fool search engine crawlers. Often one can simply add one's own URL to this list (hence the name FFA) or buy your way in to have your URL added to the list. The argument is that if you add your URL to many different link farms, your total *inlink* count will be higher, yielding better rankings for your page. See Figure 4.1 for an example of a FFA website.

One variation on this theme is swapping links – a banner (with an embedded hyperlink) is put on webpage A, pointing to webpage B, with the reverse happening on webpage B (Thelwall, 2001: 120).

Many authors claim that link farms are considered to be spamdexing, and guilty websites could be blacklisted by search engines (Thurow, 2003a: 224; Rowlett, 2003; Goldsborough, 2005).

Figure 4.1 A free-for-all links site

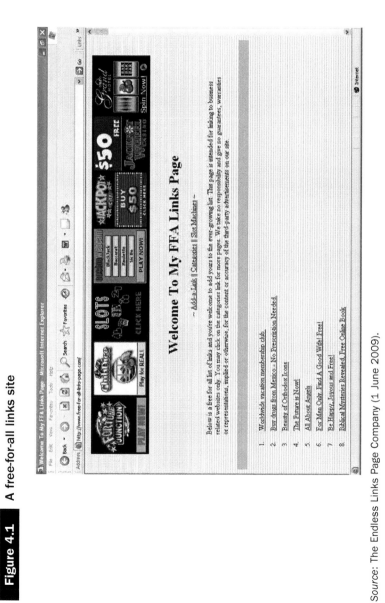

Source: The Endless Links Page Company (1 June 2009).

However, as the most important positive and negative factor, one should be aware of how to create inlinks without resorting to spamdexing. A website owner must identify the website neighbourhood where a website belongs – is it the real estate world? Book and CD sales? Academic publishing? Games programming? Once this has been established, an effort must be made to establish hyperlinks to and from other (especially reputable) websites in the same neighbourhood. Links to a website should occur naturally, and linking to and from unrelated neighbourhoods will raise suspicions. Such an effort was made to establish exactly this set of valuable links on the book website – see *http://www.book-visibility.com*. This could be done by simply contacting the website owners of these neighbourhood sites in a professional way, and establishing communication with the intent of gaining reciprocal links.

Keyword spamdexing

Invisible text

When a computer user views a webpage on a computer screen, he or she will see what the browser finds in that webpage to display. If this user views the HTML code of the webpage the same text will be visible on the screen, but this time embedded inside HTML code. However, there are ways to code text inside a webpage to make it visible to the crawler and the human viewer (via the source code), but invisible when the browser displays it. This means that the human viewing that webpage through a browser will not see the invisible text, while the crawler reading this same webpage will.

One way to achieve this is by simply specifying the background and the text font colours to be the same (e.g. blue text on a blue background). This text will be quite visible if viewed as source code, and crawlers will be able to read it, but the browser will not show it on the screen. See Figure 4.2 for an example of source code which lists some text to be

Figure 4.2   HTML code to generate hidden text

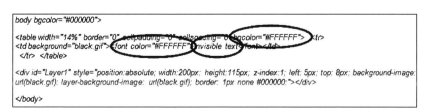

```
body bgcolor="#000000">

<table width="14%" border="0" cellpadding="0" cellspacing="0" bgcolor="#FFFFFF"> <tr>
<td background="black.gif"><font color="#FFFFFF">invisible text</font></td>
   </tr> </table>

<div id="Layer1" style="position:absolute; width:200px; height:115px; z-index:1; left: 5px; top: 8px; background-image:
url(black.gif); layer-background-image: url(black.gif); border: 1px none #000000; "></div>

</body>
```

displayed (the words 'invisible text'), but specifying a white background with a white font colour ('FFFFFF').

The screen dump in Figure 4.3 indicates what should have appeared on the screen had the text been displayed in black text. However, since it is in white text, the user will see Figure 4.4 on the screen.

However, search engine algorithms can easily pick up via the HTML code that the text and background are in fact the same colour. Since this situation strongly implies spamdexing, most crawlers will flag this webpage and either just not index it or blacklist the webpage to ensure that is not indexed in future. Many authors describe this and similar phenomena in detail (Kay, 2007; Mbikiwa and Weideman, 2006; Anonymous, 2006a; Goldsborough, 2005; Thurow, 2003a: 222; Anonymous, 2002). Other known tactics are to hide text behind layers, to place text at the bottom of oversized pages or even to hide text inside metatags (Chambers, 2005: 57; Dunn, 2004; Weideman, 2004a; Introna and Nissenbaum, 2000: 57).

Figure 4.3 Hidden text as it would have appeared on the screen

Figure 4.4 Hidden text as it does appear on the screen

| Figure 4.5 | Example of JavaScript being used to hide text |

```
<script type="text/javascript">
document. write ('<'+'script
type="text/javascript"
src="'+document.location.protocol+'//stats1
.clicktracks.com/cgi-bin/ctasp-server.cgi?
i=CODE"></'+'script>');
</script><noscript><a
href="http://www.clicktracks.com/"><im
g src="https://stats1.clicktracks.com/cgi-
bin/ ctasp-server.cgi?i=CODE&g=1"
alt="Web Analytics"
border=0></a></noscript>
```

In a similar vein, text can be coded to be so small that a browser will not display it, or possibly display what appears to be a thin line across the screen (Goldsborough, 2005). Again some algorithms have been programmed to detect and flag this type of coding. Finally, JavaScripting could also be used to create invisible text (Anonymous, 2006a) – see Figure 4.5. The <NOSCRIPT> tag could be used to hide text on a webpage, while that webpage might not even contain any JavaScript (Thurow, 2003b). Once again, many search engines either ignore this tag or decrease its weight when determining relevance.

Keyword stuffing

Search engines use keywords in various ways to determine the ranking of webpage content – see Table 2.7. Weight-carrying words are termed keywords – see Figure 1.6 and surrounding text for an example of weight-carrying versus less important words (often referred to as *stop words*). Keywords are descriptive terms which, on their own, add value to and describe the content of a webpage. Stop words are non-descriptive but are needed to write complete sentences.

Since keywords are so important in search engine rankings, it follows that their implementation also offers many opportunities for abuse by unscrupulous website authors. In its simplest form, keyword stuffing refers to mindless repetition of the same word or phrase inside a webpage, with the hope of resultant high rankings when a searcher types in those keywords/phrases. This practice is also called keyword stacking (Kay, 2007; Thurow, 2003a: 221).

To hide the presence of this kind of spamdexing, authors could list these repetitive keywords right at the bottom of a very long web page. It could even be at the bottom of a splash page which few users are likely to scroll down to (Wilkinson, 2004). Fortunately, search engine algorithms are continually updated to detect this situation, and they are likely to exclude or even blacklist websites guilty of this practice (Wilkinson, 2004).

A variation on this theme is the use of excessive keywords not in the webpage body, but in the metatag(s) of a webpage – specifically the KEYWORDS metatag. A large number of authors describe this practice in detail (Wikipedia, 2008f; Weideman, 2004a; Wallace, 2003; Alimohammadi, 2004: 240; Sherman, 2002). A further variation is to use more than one TITLE tag (Anonymous, 2006a).

The value of the KEYWORDS metatag to crawlers has been reduced to just about zero owing to the abuse by spammers shortly after its introduction. However, it is suggested that this metatag still be used as a storage area of important keywords required during webpage design. Experience has shown that if the three basic metatags have been properly written, their contents can be used over and over again elsewhere in the body. For example, the TITLE tag can be copied and used after minimal changes in the main H1 body tag. The DESCRIPTION metatag could be used in parts of the body text and the KEYWORDS metatag could be used as a continuous reminder of the website's important keywords. These keywords could be reused in Alt tags, body keywords, hyperlink anchor text and H1 header tags.

Server accessibility to bots

This element is fairly simple, although the user might not realise this to be a problem before it is too late. If a website server is down, all the websites hosted on that server will be inaccessible to all Internet users. This includes access by search engine robots, which would normally crawl these webpages and index them.

Users probably do not check whether or not their sites are live all day and will therefore not be alarmed immediately if a server goes down.

One SEO expert claims that a webpage will drop from a search engine index quickly if a server is down for 48 hours or longer. Another states that if a website is hosted with a hosting company whose servers are down regularly, its content is probably not worth being ranked in any case (Fishkin and Pollard, 2007).

It is also possible that a webpage will exclude crawlers by specifically asking them not to crawl the page. Privacy can be one of the reasons for wanting to keep crawlers out of a certain page, as well as the belief that the contents of this webpage could be misleading for indexing purposes. Some webpages might contain large amounts of information which is of no use to any user and will only slow down servers if they are indexed. These include usage logs and programs.

This exclusion of a crawler (from the complete website or only parts of it) can be done by using the *robots.txt* file. This file must be in the top-level directory of the website. If it exists, a robots.txt file can easily be viewed – try *http://www.book-visibility.com/robots.txt*. Whereas the ROBOTS metatag (discussed in Chapter 3) has an effect only on the webpage where it is coded, the robots.txt file affects the whole website. If this file exists with certain content without the owner wanting to exclude crawlers, it would explain why crawlers did not index the contents of a given webpage in the first place.

All crawlers will be excluded if, for example, the robots.txt file contains the following:

User-agent: *
Disallow: /

It is also possible to exclude one specific crawler from one subdirectory:

User-agent: CrawlBot
Disallow: /MyDirectory/

Many other combinations are possible. More detail can be found on the webmaster pages of three large search engines:

- *http://www.google.com/support/webmasters/bin/answer.py?answer =40364*

- *http://help.yahoo.com/l/us/yahoo/search/webcrawler/slurp-03.html*

- *http://help.live.com/help.aspx?mkt=en-za&project=wl_webmasters*

However, if a webpage does exist where absolute privacy is required, it would be best not to use the robots.txt file. If a search engine crawler stumbles across this private webpage via an inlink and not via the homepage, the robots.txt file will not protect it from being indexed. In this case the use of the ROBOTS metatag will protect the specific webpage from being crawled.

Google webmaster tools strongly suggest adding the location of the sitemap in the robots.txt file. This sitemap is primarily for the search engines and neither applicable nor relevant to the user. The sitemap ensures that the crawlers are able to find all the web pages on that particular website. For an example, view *http://www.mpginvestments .co.uk/sitemap.xml*.

Another useful reference for more detail on the robots.txt file and the ROBOTS metatag is *http://www.searchtools.com/robots/*. Finally, an important announcement regarding the way the big three search engines sees this issue was made in June 2008. For more detail, see *http://www .searchtools.com/robots/robots-exclusion-protocol.html#rep-june-08*.

Similar/duplicate content

It is possible to implement a method to potentially increase website traffic: make many copies of a webpage, give each copy a unique filename (leave the contents identical) and submit them all to search engines (Anonymous, 2006a). Some website authors actually go one step further by modifying the content of each one slightly, so as to lead crawlers to believe that each page is actually unique. For example, at least the TITLE metatag is changed, to mislead a search engine to list each page as if it is a new one (Anonymous, 2002; Thurow, 2003a: 226). Once again this practice will fill up the indices of search engines with (not necessarily useless but certainly duplicate) content (Dunn, 2004).

In the case of an unscrupulous website owner employing this strategy, both the search engine and the user will lose out. The search engine index will contain duplicate webpages, consuming space and processor time to index, store and display these duplicate pages. The user will waste time by making choices from SERPs to view *different* webpages while hunting for answers, just to find that the content is identical. The overall effect of duplicate content is one of dilution of value.

However, it is possible that duplicate content is generated unknowingly or without malicious intent. Assume that a certain portion of text with a large weight in terms of value to the user is published on a given webpage (for example, an important speech, a late breaking news item, etc.). Various website owners might have access to this text and decide to host it on their existing webpage. The result will be two webpages in totally different domains with duplicate content.

Flash

Flash is software product, initially marketed as *Shockwave Flash* and then *Macromedia Flash*, currently distributed by Adobe Systems. It enables the designer to create various types of animations, integrate video into webpages and in general develop rich Internet applications. It is often used to create an introductory video on a homepage, in which case the user is initially faced with a blank screen requesting them to wait while the Flash video loads – see Figure 4.6.

After loading, the video often starts playing automatically, sometimes with sound. It also often displays an option to skip over the Flash introduction and move straight to the content (see Figure 4.6, at the bottom).

Industry researchers claim that Flash has a negative effect on website visibility. One specific claim is that 50 per cent of a subset of websites (athletic clubs) had their visibility reduced by the use of Flash (Gault, 2005).

On the one hand, Adobe Systems claimed that over 98 per cent of users in the USA at one stage had the Flash Player application installed (Wikipedia, 2008d). On the other, industry research has proven that many users prefer not to view Flash pages (Yahoo! Answers, 2008; Nielsen, 2000). Some authors also claim that Flash breaks with the traditional web interface, leading to user frustration. The mere fact that Flash users code an escape button, typically *Skip Intro*, is an indication that they realise and accept that users might want to bypass the Flash introduction. Even though all these sources are not peer-reviewed academic by nature, they do indicate that there is concern over the use of Flash.

Whether or not to use Flash is clearly one of many debatable issues. It did receive the fifth highest score (out of 17 competitors) on the scale of unwanted elements. This is an indication that it deserves to be treated with caution if website visibility is of importance.

A webpage which only plays a Flash animation has no content for search engine crawlers to index. There is no text, no keywords and no

Figure 4.6   A typical Flash image busy loading

Source: *http://www.irvan.com/* (1 June 2009).

hyperlinks, and when crawlers visit this kind of webpage, they mostly leave empty handed. If the designer does not implement very specific measures to compensate for this lack of a textual harvest, webpages containing Flash would not be indexed by crawlers. There are methods which enables designers to include text on a Flash page, bypassing this problem to an extent. These include the creation of descriptive TITLE and metatags, the use of regular text hyperlinks and textual descriptions of what the Flash image is representing (Wall, 2006).

It has been claimed that some search engine crawlers can index Flash content to a limited extent. This is a development which holds promise for those webmasters insisting on using Flash (Anonymous, 2006b). Furthermore, the <NOSCRIPT> tag can be used for non-Flash content, which will improve visibility.

External links to low-quality/spamdexing sites

The Google bombing phenomenon discussed earlier has proven the high weight of anchor text in hyperlinks in enhancing website visibility. Anchor text is a word or phrase embedded inside a hyperlink, and this text is displayed on the screen as being the visible part of the hyperlink. The user would click on the anchor text to follow the hyperlink. In a similar way, the webpages linked to from a given webpage have an influence on the ranking of the originating page. If some of these hyperlinks link to spamdexing webpages, it will decrease the ranking of the originating webpage.

PageRank, Google's ranking algorithm, is partially based on the strength of links to a given site. Any link to any webpage is taken to be a vote of confidence in that webpage, very much like a statement of trust. The Internet is loosely structured around communities of like-minded human beings, often remote from each other by thousands of kilometres. These communities manifest in blogs, DSNs (digital social networks such as Facebook and MySpace) and the use of hyperlinks. If one webpage hyperlinks to another, it can be implicitly assumed that these two pages are part of the same community.

Any web designer should be careful when linking to a webpage. The target webpage should at least be viewed first to establish its identity and purpose. Most importantly – does it present the content it promises by virtue of its title and/or author and/or the community it belongs to? Does this website belong to the same community that it links to? A website owner should consider these issues for every external link on the website.

Frames

Introduction

Frames are used to make a webpage easier to use and more attractive to the human user. A framed website is divided (sometimes by invisible lines) into separate areas or rectangles, each one reserved for a different type of information. Typically, a rectangle across the top is used for titles, logos or other pertinent information; another one down the left-hand side of the page is used for navigation while the rightmost, largest rectangle contains body content. Every frame is stored as if it is a separate html page. See Figure 4.7 for a simplified layout of a framed webpage.

The real advantage of frames become evident when one starts scrolling around inside this web page which occupies more than one screen. When the user reads and scrolls down the body text, the navigation frame would remain stationary, allowing the user to view and use the navigation controls without scrolling back to the top. Figure 4.8 (a)–(c) shows a series of screenshots, taken successively while a user does exactly this. Note how the centre block of text moves upward as the menus in the left box remain where they are.

However, the use of the latest technology in website design without carefully considering the roles of all the players is not advisable. The user has arguably the most important role (see Figure 1.2), while the designer, the website owner and search engine crawlers are others. Frames, dynamic pages, scripts and image maps are some technologies which

Figure 4.7 Simplified example of a framed webpage

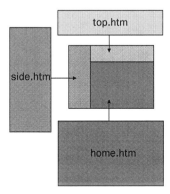

Source: Anonymous (2007) (1 June 2009).

Figure 4.8 Screenshots of a framed website while scrolling

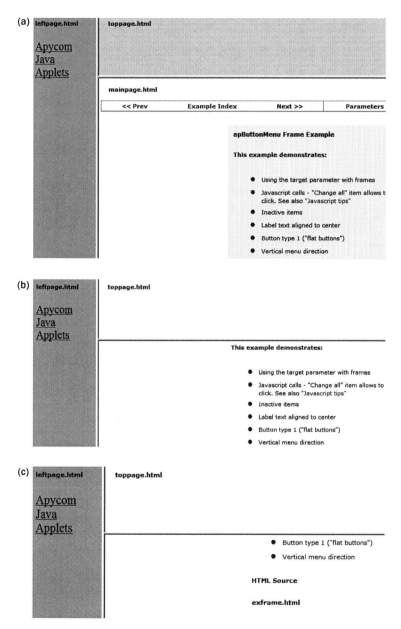

Source: http://www.apycom.com/website-buttons/exframe.html (1 June 2009).

could confuse the search engines (Dahm, 2000). There appears to be two schools of thought – those who believe that high rankings are possible while using frames, and those who do not (Roy, 2001). Clarification will be sought in this matter below.

The case for the use of frames

As mentioned above, retaining the view of pertinent information while moving around on a webpage is one reason for wanting to use frames. Furthermore, a table of contents for a whole website could be displayed consistently, as the user moves from one webpage to another across a website (Zeeger, 2008). From the coder's point of view, frames make for easy updating of especially large websites (Whalen, 2000). This could of course also benefit another role-player – the owner, who has to pay for the time spent on maintaining his/her website. Therefore it appears as if frames could please the user, the coder and the owner, while upsetting only the search engine crawler. Cascading style sheets (instead of frames) are also used to create an architecture that requires only a single update which is instantly applied to all webpages.

One example of the use of frames to deliver a functional webpage is given in Figure 4.9. The horizontal menu bar in the top one third remains in position while the body text is being scrolled up or down.

Figure 4.9 A framed website

Source: *http://www.flysaa.com* (23 April 2009).

The case against *the use of frames*

However, contradictory arguments about the use of frames in webpage design are as old as frames themselves. The most important of these are discussed below.

Some experts argue that a typical webpage should not exceed the height of one user screen in any case, since some users have an aversion to scrolling down to see more content. They argue that this obviates the need for frames and that the information to be displayed should instead be broken up and spread over a number of pages (Zeeger, 2008). This larger number of webpages will again find favour with the crawlers.

Ideally a website wanting to draw many visitors via search engine clicks should consist of many pages with useful, well laid out and truthful information. If frames are used, the number of webpages to which a search engine can link in your website is reduced to one.

The typical coding of a framed webpage contains very little text for search engine crawlers to harvest, and no links for the crawlers to follow to the really useful text (Whalen, 2000). Figure 4.10 lists the HTML code of a typical imaginary framed website, indicating that the really useful body content is stored elsewhere. Crawlers cannot follow the links to this useful content as it is coded below.

Search engine crawlers might ignore webpages beyond the homepage of a framed website, thereby omitting them from the indices and making them effectively invisible to human visitors (Weideman and Haig-Smith, 2002). While the crawler can index the homepage, it used to ignore linkages to other framed pages referred to on the homepage (Dahm, 2000). This is no longer a serious issue, as some crawlers can bypass this problem. Some older browsers cannot interpret frames at all, and the user will be faced with a blank page or a partial display when visiting a framed web page. It is claimed that this figure was as low as 2 per cent (Dahm, 2000), but others believe it is still a factor to consider.

Figure 4.10 HTML code of a typical framed webpage

```
<HTML>
<HEAD>
<TITLE>The best secondhand bicycles in the world - ABC Bicycle Workx</TITLE>
</HEAD>
<frameset cols="30%,70%">
<frame src="navi-bar.htm" frame="left">
<frame src="homepage.htm" frame="right">
</frameset>
</HTML>
```

It is also claimed that coding framed websites adds yet another complexity to the design process – the coder has to consider browser compatibility with frames to ensure a high percentage of satisfied clients.

During everyday use, many users print the content of useful webpages and some bookmark those they would like to return to or share with friends. Both these actions become problematic with framed webpages. Printing a framed webpage might produce only a section of the required content on paper – normally the frame which contained the cursor – without any explanation to the confused user. Bookmarking saves a link to one frame of a webpage without any comment, and when a user later follows this bookmark, he or she might find themselves back at the homepage, which is not the page originally bookmarked (Zeeger, 2008).

Possibly one of the most serious arguments against frames is that they '... disrupt the entire fundamental concept for the web ...' (Zeeger, 2008). A detailed discussion of this statement is outside the scope of this book.

Other authors claim that website visitors cannot link to framed webpages, with the result that potential customers can be lost. A framed online CD store with the normal homepage and many sub-pages for different artists, for example, will prevent visitors from linking to the sub-pages and from finding these sub-pages via a search engine. Meanwhile it is exactly these pages which will be content-rich and laden with keywords, the ideal target for crawlers.

Does an existing website use frames?

As described above, when a (typically) left-hand navigation bar or a banner at the top of a webpage remains in place while you scroll downwards through the body of a web page, it is frames-based (Whalen, 2000). You can double check by clicking on an option in the navigation block. If the body contents change according to what you have clicked on but the navigation area remains the same, you are likely to be viewing a frames-based site. Since other technologies can also be used to create a frames-like view, it would be safer to check the source code for the presence of frames coding.

Try the following:

- Load the webpage in the browser window.

- View the source code (*View* menu, *Source* option), or right click on an unused screen area and select the *View Source* option.

- Place the cursor at the start of the coding, and do a search (Ctrl + F) for the word *frameset*.

- If you find this word, the webpage does make use of frames.

How to include frames with minimal damage

It is possible to use frames and bypass some of the problems associated with crawlers and frames. The NOFRAMES HTML tag can be included in a framed webpage, plus all the content of the actual webpage, to expose crawlers to the important keywords (Roy, 2001). In effect a complete webpage is to be added inside this tag, which was designed by Netscape (an earlier, popular browser) for backward compatibility (Dahm, 2000). A typical imaginary webpage coded this way looks like the code in Figure 4.11.

Furthermore, webpage visitors can be disgruntled since they might arrive at a sub-page of a website and not see any navigation links at all, since the frame containing the navigation is not being displayed. Some authors refer to these pages as orphaned webpages, since they contain no indication of their origin. A simple solution to this situation would be to put at least a link back to the homepage on each 'inside' webpage, but preferably a simple structure with links to all the subcategories of the website (Whalen, 2000).

Final confirmation that the use of frames is controversial is the existence of a number of hate sites against their use. In one example, the use of frames is discouraged in a number of languages – see Figure 4.12.

Figure 4.11   HTML code of inclusion of valuable text-rich code

```
<HTML>

<HEAD>
<TITLE>Your keyword-rich descriptive title goes here.</TITLE>
<META NAME="Description" CONTENT="Your one- to two-sentence keyword-rich
marketing description goes here.">
<META NAME="Keywords" CONTENT="Your important relevant keywords and
keyword phrases go here.">
</HEAD>
<FRAMESET>
<FRAME SRC="navigation.html" NAME="nav">
<FRAME SRC="main.html" NAME="main">
<NOFRAMES>
<p>
Here is where you should copy all the HTML code for what I have named main.html. Be
sure that you have all your navigational links to the rest
of the site also in here for the search engines to follow.
</p>
</NOFRAMES>
</FRAMESET>
</HTML>
```

Figure 4.12 Contents of part of a frames hate site

Source: http://members.tripod.com/~daGecko/hatefrm.html (1 June 2009).

Recommendation on the use of frames

- If a website has to be designed from scratch, avoid using frames at all (Roy, 2001).

- In an existing, simple but framed website, rewrite it and omit the frames.

- If an existing framed site is complex, rewrite only the homepage without the use of frames. Secondly, depending on the number of webpages on the next level down (i.e. *below* the homepage), rewrite that level if resources allow it. Carry on moving down in this way until either all the webpages have been redone or you run out of resources to sustain the process.

Duplicate title/metatags

This method of increasing exposure differs from plain duplicate content (discussed earlier), as will be seen further on in this discussion.

One way to ensure higher visibility to search engines is to have more webpages hosted on the Internet with content about your product/company. The hard way to get this done is to create more websites or increase the number of webpages in one website, making them all visible to crawlers. These extra webpages should all have different, new and unique content. This will certainly earn higher visibility in an ethical way.

A much shorter but unethical and risky way to achieve this same goal is to simply copy existing webpages, give them new filenames, host them on the Internet and submit to search engines. This way (theoretically at least) search engines will find the content, hopefully index it and increase the chances of attracting visitors. If the entire webpage is duplicated this way, everything about the webpage will be a duplicate (except the URL). This includes certainly the visible content, but also the (invisible to the user) metatags, TITLE tag, etc.

However, if more exposure is sought this way, a number of problems could crop up, which might or might not be of concern to the *perpetrator*:

- The content created this way is a copy of existing content and does not add any value to the Internet as a source of information.

- This extra but duplicate content will clog up search engine indices with *useless* information, since it already exists elsewhere in the index.

- SERP content will decrease in value – repeat listings will occur on user screens.

- Search engine processing power and storage space is wasted on duplicate content.

- Search engine algorithms can and are programmed to identify cases of duplication, with resultant penalties in ranking or even exclusion from indices altogether.

As a result, this method for increasing exposure is not to be advised. Duplicate content can sometimes be excusable as a result of purely copying important or relevant information from a single source and publishing it on different webpages. However, for these webpages to coincidentally have the same TITLE tag and metatag information is highly unlikely.

As an example of how webpages on the same website can be allocated different metatags, view some of the metatags on different webpages of *http://www.book-visibility.com*.

Graphics

The (correct) use of graphics on webpages has many positive results and should be encouraged for many reasons. Much Internet traffic generated by searches originates from image searches. Some of these reasons are as follows:

- A picture is worth a thousand words – one small image in the correct spot explains to a user what a few words (in a language that user might not be able to read) could not do – think of the overused but still popular house picture indicating a link to the homepage.

- Webpages with only text, especially in large quantities, often do not increase stickiness (the tendency for a user to spend more time on a webpage, indicating useful content). Users do not like to read passage after passage of text – if a few images can convey part of the message, the user experience is much more pleasant.

- Using images as navigation aids is well established and understood by the user community (Ngindana and Weideman, 2004).

- Graphics in various forms support the passive user syndrome – the tendency of users to *want to be entertained*, to want to do less work while the computer displays information in a way that is easy to assimilate.

However, there is a fine line between the correct use of graphics and irritating the user with overuse. Probably the most important culprit here is the use of animated graphics. Images with continuous movement, which initially attracts and entertains, can quickly start to frustrate. Figure 4.13 claims to be *The World's Worst Website*. Whether or not this is true, it does provide a good example of how *not* to design a website. What will not be visible to the reader of Figure 4.13 but which a website visitor will experience includes:

- the title (first line of text) moves left and right, in a ping-pong way, continuously;

- the *Welcome To My Website!* (not visible here due to colour restrictions) moves across the screen continuously;

- the grainy spots in the background flicker continuously.

Figure 4.13 The World's Worst Website

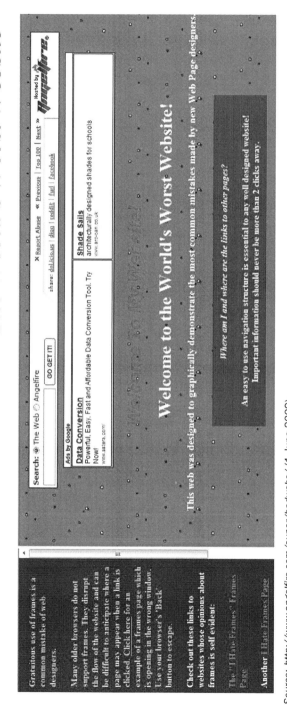

The World's Worst Website

Source: http://www.angelfire.com/super/badwebs/ (1 June 2009).

Numerous other animated graphics become visible as you scroll down, as further examples. An irritating, repetitive music clip starts playing when this webpage is loaded, and the choice of colours is not kind to readers' eyes.

A visit to a NASA webpage at *http://spaceflight.nasa.gov/shuttle/archives/sts-108/flash/sts108.swf* provides another good example of the overuse of movement in an attempt to draw users. Readers susceptible to sea-sickness should not view this page! The focus of this section, however, is on graphics and website visibility. The problem is very easy to describe: a graphic image or video on a webpage normally offers the user something: a quick way to make menu choices, a funny moment, a sharp way of conveying a message – basically a good user experience. However, it offers the search engine crawler nothing! The crawler cannot read the contents of the image; it can harvest nothing from the image itself, even if the image is a keyword or a text string. Figure 4.14 contains a screen dump from a very popular website, showing an image in the top left-hand corner. This image contains some descriptive text which is not only part of the URL, but also the website's name, and it contains two crucial keywords for this website. It occupies the prime spot on the webpage (top left), which is a good choice of location (Enquiro, 2008; Nielsen, 2006). However, it is still an image – although the human visitor can read it, the search engine crawler will not be able to harvest any value from it.

This does not mean that graphic images on a webpage should be reduced to an absolute minimum to enhance website visibility. There is an easy way to provide the crawlers with useful, keyword-rich text associated with each image used. It is called the ALT tag (short for *Alternate*) and simply has to be coded with each image. What the very important TITLE tag does for a webpage, the ALT tag does for an image – it provides a keyword-rich summary of what it is associated with. Secondly, it will be displayed on the screen while a user waits for an image to download. An added benefit of well-written ALT tags is the information they provide to blind and partially sighted users who depend on text readers to read webpage contents to them aloud. With no ALT tag associated with an image, these users would not even be aware that a certain image is on a webpage. Text readers will read out the text of an ALT tag, however, giving them an idea of what image on the screen they are not seeing. For example, a descriptive ALT tag to go with the photo in Figure 4.15 could be:

<img src='mountainbike.gif' width='240' height='180' alt='silver Merida Mission 3000 dual suspension mountain bike with Shimano XT Deore components'>

Figure 4.14 Webpage with an image containing text

CNN.com INTERNATIONAL

HOME | ASIA | EUROPE | U.S. | WORLD | WORLD BUSINESS | TECHNOLOGY | ENTERTAINMENT | WORLD SPORT | TRAVEL

Hot Topics » America votes • Eye on France • China quake • Euro 2008 • French Open • more topics »

Make CNN Your Home Page

June 3, 2008 — Updated 1404 GMT (2204 HKT)

Top Stories

- Admiral: Bush doesn't want war with Iran
- Ahmadinejad: West fueling food crisis
- Sex scandal F1 boss wins vote 51 min
- Bush condemns tactics in Zimbabwe
- Mugabe could be stripped of knighthood 52 min
- CNNMoney: GM to close 4 truck plants
- Iraqi leader goes to Iran for security talks
- Al Qaeda linked to embassy attack
- Israel under fire over settlement plans
- Blog: Should children get cash for behaving?
- Taxi drivers lead fuel protests in Paris
- Teachers, architects among child porn arrests
- Somalis warn of worsening crisis

Source: http://www.cnn.com (3 June 2008).

Figure 4.15   An image to go with the Alt tag as described

Photo taken by M. Weideman at the Cape Epic event, Knysna, 28 March 2008.

An ALT tag should describe the image and the text around the image. As a result, the ALT tag should also be in line with the TITLE tag and header tags of the webpage. Finally, making use of images in the primary navigation on an important webpage should be avoided. Search engines value keywords used in the navigation highly for the same reason as using headings on a webpage.

Others

Very slow server response times

An Internet user expects that when a URL is typed into a browser, or when a hyperlink is clicked, that a (different) webpage will appear on the screen. Many factors play a role in making this seemingly simple event occur. The response of the server on which the website is hosted is one of the more important ones, as is the size of a webpage. Larger webpages (for example, those with many graphic images, especially if they are of a high resolution) will obviously take longer to load, if all other factors remain constant. Consistency in the *serving* of this website is of high importance here.

A website which has been well designed in terms of visibility but is inaccessible at any one time has no value to the user. Neither can a search engine crawler read and index it while it is not accessible. To the average user and the search engine crawler, there is often no difference between a server that is down and one which takes a long time to respond. Both browsers (i.e. as seen from the user's side) and crawlers (as seen from the search engine side) have built-in time-outs. If a website does not load within a certain time period, the request is terminated. A user will either navigate to another website or possibly attempt to load the webpage again. A crawler will simply move on to the next webpage to index.

Previous research has indicated that Internet users have little patience in waiting for their screen contents to update after having initiated a change of some sort. Some of the findings of both academic and practitioner research are listed below.

- A website usability expert states that three times are important in human–computer interaction: 0.1 second for the user to receive feedback that the system is responding to an action, 1 second for the user's flow of thoughts to remain uninterrupted and 10 seconds to keep the user's attention focused on the dialogue (Nielsen, 2007).

- Nah (2004) claims that users can only wait for two seconds: 'Web users' tolerable waiting time and the tolerable waiting time for information retrieval is approximately 2 s.'

- Ceaparu and others claimed that web browsing, e-mail and word processing were the applications causing the most user frustration (Ceaparu et al., 2004). Long download times are listed as one of the reasons for these frustrations.

- As long ago as 1968, decades before the birth of the Internet, it was claimed that '... thinking continuity essential to sustained problem solving ...' is not possible if a user has to wait as long as 10 seconds for a system response (Miller, 1968: 268).

Although no one single figure can summarise this acceptable delay, it is clear that a computer interface must provide quick responses to user interactions. Any time longer than approximately 10 seconds is simply too long to keep the user's concentration fixed on the task at hand. There are many factors influencing the delay, and some of them are outside the website owner's control. However, choice of service provider is not one of them.

Before any website is hosted for the first time, the website owner has to make a choice as to which service provider is to be used for hosting.

It does not make economic sense for a website owner to go to the expense and technical complexity of setting up an Internet server with all the software and procedures required just to host one website. Fortunately, there is no shortage of companies who provide this service for a reasonable fee. Furthermore, hosting a website has no relation to the physical address of the owner or business (although it is possible, for example, to restrict searches to geographical location using IP addresses). If better hosting is available in a city or country different from where the owner is situated, it presents few problems to *move* the website elsewhere. Figure 4.16 lists some of these hosting companies available in South Africa.

However, running a reliable hosting company is technically and financially demanding. The most basic requirement is to provide servers which are *up* as close to 100 per cent of the time as possible. Hetzner is the leading South African hosting company, with one in five websites in the country being hosted by them and an uptime of 99.9 per cent (see Figure 4.17).

Unfortunately, these kinds of claims are sometimes difficult to verify – experience with the hosting company over a period of time is the only reliable method. In the Hetzner example, claims of reliability and service excellence have actually been confirmed, based on the following kind of interactions:

- The company's own website is well designed, always accessible and easy to interact with.
- Basic interactions like registering a new domain and querying an account can be done online.
- More than one line of support is available (human telephonic and e-mail support, physical location is known, etc.).
- Response time on queries is short (human-based answers to e-mail queries are quick and relevant).
- Answers to technical queries are simple and to the point, without overwhelming the user with technical details.
- Websites hosted with the company are consistently available and uptime appears to be 100 per cent.
- Many other related services are offered – e-mail accounts, a free website design program, domain searching, administrative software tools, etc.

Potential website owners are urged to do some research before taking a decision on a hosting partner. It is a relationship which is not known to the

Figure 4.16   Website hosting companies

Storm Web Hosting and Website Design Services - Website Design, Web Hosting, Graphic Design ...
Relevance: ||||||||||||||||||||| (83%)
Storm **Web Hosting** has basically taken the internet, well... by STORM, Starting off as a small business venture, to accomplish a need that was really not covered by other Website Design and **Web Hosting Companies**. SERVICE ...
http://www.stormwebhosting.co.za/

Web Hosting Directory of South Africa | Web Hosting South Africa
Relevance: ||||||||||||||||||| (80%)
Web Hosting South Africa. **Web Hosting** Directory of South Africa. **Web Hosting Companies**, **Web Hosting** Articles, **Web Host** Submission, **Web Host** Rankings, **Web Host** Uptime Monitoring and **Web Host** Advertising.
http://www.web-hosting-directory.co.za/

Web design | Website Hosting | SEO - Home
Relevance: ||||||||||||||||||| (80%)
graphics, logos, graphic design, webdesign, **web hosting**, domain name registration, graphics, logos, graphic design, , **web hosting, web** design south africa, website, **hosting** service, **hosting companies**, **web** development, **web** design, **web** ...
http://www.hosting-webdesign.co.za/

Web Hosting - Affordable Web Hosting Company - Ubuntuhosting : Home
Relevance: ||||||||||||||||||| (79%)
Ubuntuhosting offers affordable **web hosting** for all types of **hosting** needs. Ubuntuhosting provides reliable and affordable **web hosting** packages for individual and business **web** site **hosting** solutions
http://www.ubuntuhosting.co.za/

WebNow – Hosting, Broadband and more
Relevance: |||||||||||||||| (77%)
WebNow is a Cape Town based **hosting company** offer windows **hosting** on shared or dedicated servers. We also provide domain name registration, internet and **web** design.
http://www.webnow.co.za/

Source: *http://www.ananzi.com* (1 June 2009).

user and normally does not feature anywhere on a hosted webpage, but is one which plays a large role in the Internet experience of the website owner. Competition in this field is strong, which results in a large field of players for users to choose from. Website owners should investigate the result of the kind of interactions listed above before making a decision.

Figure 4.17   Hetzner services

About us

Hetzner - Leaders in South African Web Hosting

At Hetzner South Africa we are passionate about web hosting – it is our core business. We don't offer web design, marketing or consultancy, leaving us free to do what we do best: to provide reliable and robust web hosting solutions coupled with outstanding customer support to the SMME and mid-corporate markets.

Established in 1999, our share of the South African web hosting market exceeds 20%. Hetzner is a financially stable company, and with profits continually reinvested into infrastructure and operations, we currently service over 70,000 active domains – making Hetzner South Africa's largest, specialist Web Hosting Company. Our affiliation with Hetzner Online AG in Germany enables us to share even more skills and expertise.

Source: *http://www.hetzner.co.za/index.php/hosting/about/about-us/* (1 June 2009).

The bottom line remains: if a website is not live, or appears to be so because the server is slow, no human or crawler can access it!

Inbound links from spamdexing sites

This is another feature which is very much outside of the website owner's control. However, it is unlikely that a number of inlinks from spamdexing websites to a non-spamdexing website will simply be created out of nowhere. If a website has been involved with spamdexing in some or other from, these kinds of links can be expected. One extreme solution to the problem is to simply register a new URL, ensure that the website has no internal references to the old one, and move the whole website over to the new URL, making sure that the old one is cancelled at the same time.

Dynamic webpages

Every webpage on the Internet can be classified as either dynamic or static. This difference has a bearing on the visibility of these pages and this difference is highlighted here.

Static webpages are actual HTML pages which have been designed, coded, stored and uploaded to a server manually. If a user types in a static URL, that exact page will be displayed on his/her browser. The page contents will not change until a human coder physically makes these changes and uploads the new file to the server again. Therefore, static pages actually exist somewhere on the server, and their contents can only change by human intervention. Static webpages mostly have simple URLs, without characters such as *?* and *&*. Examples of static webpages are:

- *http://www.book-visibility.com*
- *http://www.uvasys.com/htm/contact_us.htm*
- *http://www.cs.hm.edu/~peters/SoSe2008/MW_CiE_SoSe_2008.pdf*

In contrast, dynamic webpages do not exist on a server in the format the user views them on the screen. They are *created* from the contents of a database the moment a user does a query, for example. If this happens, they are displayed on the screen, and disappear again the moment the window is closed. If the same query is done 10 seconds later, the new dynamic page could have different contents. For example, suppose a user goes to his or her online banking website (the homepage is static and does not change often), typically:

- *https://www20.encrypt.standardbank.co.za/ibsa/InternetBanking*

This user now logs on with username and (sometimes more than one) password, selects one of ten accounts, and asks for a statement. The banking system will retrieve, from that one account, all transactions of the past 30 days plus the latest balance. It will then create a dynamic page and display this *virtual* page on the screen. This dynamic URL could be:

- *https://www20.encrypt.standardbank.co.za/ibsa/InternetBanking/balance.php?page_id=c45g&title=/Account Cheque*

The page does not exist in this format on the server, and if the user repeats the process 10 seconds later, the system might have registered a payment which has gone through and the new dynamic page will show a different balance. This all happened without a human coder having changed and uploaded a webpage manually.

The problem with all of this is that crawlers can index static pages, but can often interpret dynamic URLs only up to the first *?* or *&* character. Therefore dynamic webpages often cannot easily be indexed by crawlers. This makes sense, since the dynamic page does not exist for the crawler to index, so where would the crawler go to find the content? A dynamic page only exists on the human visitor's screen, and theoretically a crawler cannot query a browser.

As a result, the whole database of a large online book store, for example, cannot be indexed by search engines. This is crucial, since this database contains thousands of important keywords, like book titles, author surnames, keywords from the book contents, etc. This is exactly what searchers and potential buyers will use as a search engine query when trying to find and buy a book.

It is thus clear that dynamic pages decrease the website visibility to crawlers. However, many large websites cannot exist without these pages, since manual maintenance of thousands of webpages with rapidly changing content is simply impossible. Online banking systems, large volume stores (i.e. books, other small items), airline booking systems and other similar websites have to use dynamic pages to manage these pages. On the positive side, however, the situation with dynamic pages having low visibility seems to be improving. Google, for example, does consider the '=' indicator by reading up to three of these parameters in a URL. Some advanced programming can categorise product detail from a catalogue database and populate a landing page with this detail. This means that a webpage can now be optimised for certain keywords which would normally have been hidden in the database.

In addition, so-called content management systems (CMS) are often used to create complete websites. This allows the website owner flexibility since it is now possible to change website contents without any technical knowledge. One example of a source for such a system is a German company called Conmasys – see *http://www.conmasys.de* for details.

It is suggested that static pages be used whenever possible. As mentioned before, this would be impossible for large, complex websites. Where dynamic pages are present, some static pages should be created with most of the important keywords which would otherwise be visible to humans only on the dynamic pages. In this way crawlers will find the important keywords for indexing.

However, the search engines are working hard at minimising the negative effect of dynamic pages on website visibility. For example, Google claims that its crawler can now actually fill in forms (Sullivan, 2008b). The negative effect of dynamic pages is bound to decrease as search engines concentrate on minimising this negative aspect of visibility.

Cloaking

This term was derived from the concept of a human wearing a piece of clothing which will hide his or her true identity. Cloaking refers to one website with a set of two webpages being coded – one to please the search engine crawler (loaded with keywords but unpleasant to read) and another to please the human viewer (easy to read but not much content to be harvested by a crawler). When a crawler visits the website, the crawler-designed page is offered to the program, which is likely to rank it highly for certain keywords. However, human viewers are unlikely to read much of this type of webpage, so when a non-crawler visitor (assumed to be a human) arrives, the human-designed version is offered to the browser. This is also referred to as bait switching, or bait-and-switch technique – implying that one web page is used as bait to draw a visitor (the crawler designed one), but the bait is replaced by the human-designed page just before the user *bites*. Many authors describe this process in detail (Kay, 2007; Rowlett, 2003; Thurow, 2003a: 227).

Figure 4.18 shows an example of a typical cloaking page, designed for the crawler. Note the repetitive use of the phrase *women's clothing* and the terms *women, fabric, fibers, cotton* and *rayon*. This page seems to be

Figure 4.18   Example of a cloaking page – the crawler version

Source: *http://www.snkkattle.com/fezz/main.html* (1 June 2009).

normal after just skimming over it. However, if read in detail, the reader might feel uneasy due to the excessive repetition. The human viewer will never see this page – he or she will be served with the webpage in Figure 4.19 which is attractive, well designed and easy on the human eye.

Controversially, some authors dispute whether or not this technique qualifies as spamdexing. Some actually imply that search engines use this technique themselves (Sullivan, 2003). Others argue that cloaking is not spamdexing, since it does not do anything to illegally satisfy a search engine's algorithm – instead, it guarantees that targeted content is delivered. It is also claimed that some authors use cloaking since Flash content and dynamic pages are unreadable by some search engines. As a result, website designers quite innocently code an extra static webpage for crawlers to index (Sullivan, 2003).

In contrast, Thurow states that all the major search engines consider cloaking to be a form of spamdexing (Thurow, 2003a: 227). This same author claims that crawlers will accept cloaking if it is delivered via a trusted feed program.

Figure 4.19   Example of a cloaking page – the human version

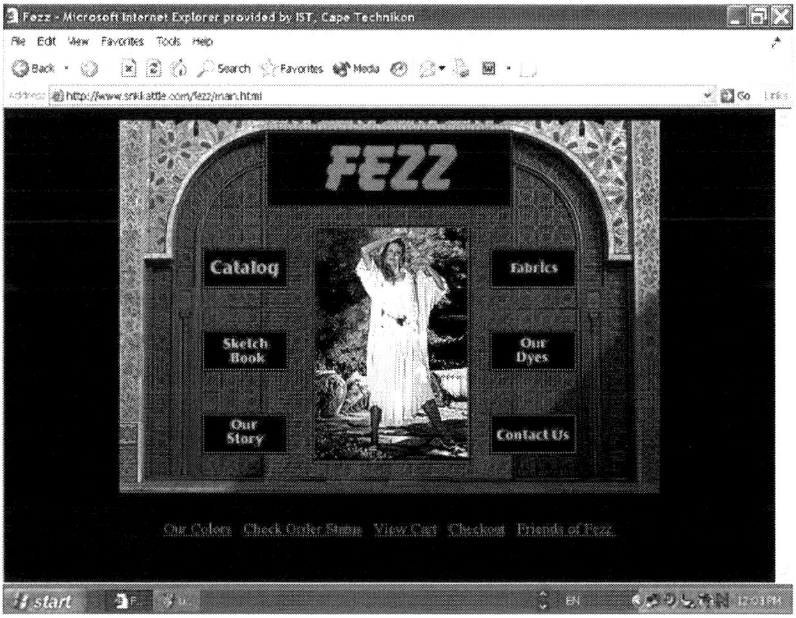

Source: http://www.snkkattle.com/fezz/main.html (1 June 2009).

Doorway pages

As the name suggests, doorway pages are webpages which (similar to cloaking) serve as a conduit to lead users via a *false* webpage to the real one with useful content. This second webpage might even be hosted on a different URL (Sullivan, 2003). Once again, the main reason behind going to the trouble of generating doorway pages is to attract more potential clients to the main website (Thurow, 2003a: 227).

For example, a company selling motorcar tyres might register and host its useful and important information at *http://www.tyres.com*. At the same time, however, they might also register (and host some web pages at each of) the following URLs:

- *http://www.tyres.co.uk*
- *http://www.tyres.co.au*
- *http://www.tyres.jp*

These other *tyres* websites are optimised for search engines, have little valuable content, but they all point straight to the .com website. The last three websites are termed doorway pages (Sullivan, 2003). One parallel that does exist between cloaking and doorway pages is that both are questionable, while at the same time some authors advocate them as being beneficial, useful and legal. Many companies exist that specialise in creating even thousands of doorway pages for one website based on a number of keywords or key phrases (Thurow, 2003a). The same author claims that doorway pages should be avoided, since they tend to clog search engine indices with *junk pages*, full of keywords which sometimes include gibberish, but do not add any value for the user (Thurow, 2003a: 227). Sullivan (2003) claims that cloaking and doorway pages often go hand in hand.

In contrast, other authors simply warn against having too many doorway pages, since it could be viewed as spamdexing. This implies that it is acceptable to have some doorway pages – just not too many (Nobles and O'Neil, 2000: 166). Yet another author claims that the doorway page practice was only popular until 2000, when it was labelled as one of the most obvious forms of spamdexing (Dunn, 2004). Figure 4.20 shows a typical commercial doorway page generator service.

At the same time it should be noted that there are legitimate uses for doorway pages. Collins (2006) provides an example of a network messaging tool application, with other webpages explaining the security risks and another the benefits of internal messaging. These extra pages will in effect direct more traffic to the main page (Collins, 2006).

Figure 4.20 Example of a doorway generator service

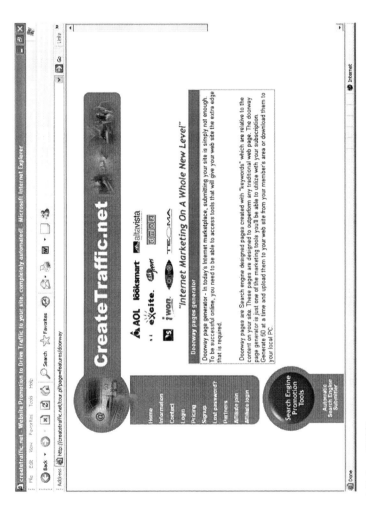

Source: CreateTraffic.net (1 June 2009).

JavaScript

JavaScript is a scripting language used for developing user-friendly website elements and was based on a number of other programming languages. Probably one of the most common uses is to create drop-down menus on webpages – see Figure 4.21 for an example.

In one empirical research project, an attempt was made to determine the relationship between website visibility and the use of JavaScript (Weideman and Schwenke, 2006). A literature study has proven that there is some contradiction with regard to claims for and against JavaScript and its effect on website visibility. A test website was designed, containing many data files and a menu structure, and it was hosted. JavaScript-based hyperlinks to these files were used to check whether or not crawlers would follow the links to the data files on other webpages. Both methods of including JavaScript in the HTML code and calling it an external file were used. Different ways of specifying links inside JavaScript were also considered.

After hosting the website and submitting it to a list of 13 search engines, a time period (463 days) was allowed to enable crawlers to visit the homepage, index it and follow hyperlinks to other webpages. The actual visits of search engine crawlers were recorded, as listed in Table 4.1.

Figure 4.21 Example of JavaScript usage

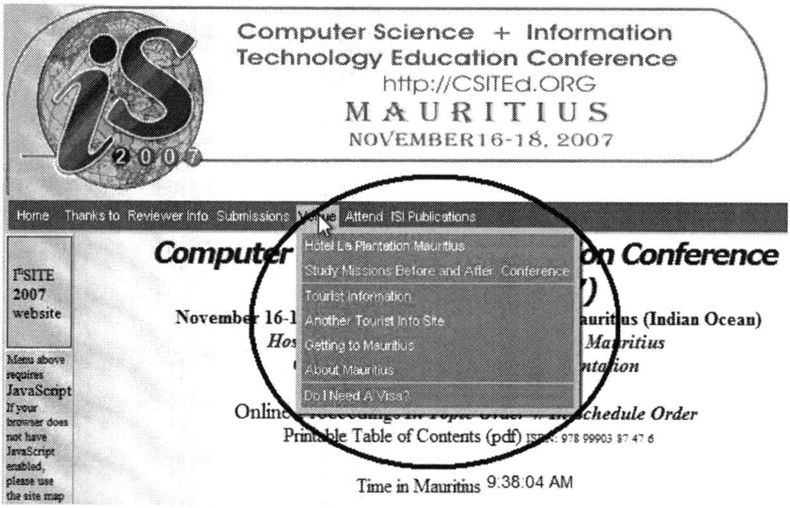

Source: http://csited.org/ (1 November 2007).

Table 4.1 Crawler visits via JavaScript hyperlinks

Types of links used (an X indicates that the crawler did in fact follow the link)

Crawler name	Completely dynamic JavaScript™ links (JavaScript™ menu)												JavaScript™ includes the links in the HTML (document.write())												JavaScript™ links accessed via <A HREF> tags (JavaScript: open Window())												Text
	Absolute URLs						Relative URLs						Absolute URLs						Relative URLs						Absolute URLs						Relative URLs						
	External script			Internal script			External script			Internal script			External script			Internal script			External script			Internal script			External script			Internal script			External script			Internal script			
	1	2	3	1	2	3	1	2	3	1	2	3	1	2	3	1	2	3	1	2	3	1	2	3	1	2	3	1	2	3	1	2	3	1	2	3	
aipbot/1.0							O																														O
Ask Jeeves/Teoma																O																					O
ConveraCrawler/0.9c																																					O
ejupiter.com																																					O
Googlebot/2.1							O									O												O									O
ia_archiver				X						X	X					X	X					X	X					X	X					X	X		O
jongaim pj/1.02				X	X		X						X						X						X						X						O
jongaim pj/1.03				X	X		X						X						X						X						X						O
LinkWalker																																					O
MJ12bot/v 1.0.5																																					O
msnbot/0.3																																					O
msnbot/1.0																																					O
NutchCVS/0.7																																					O
psbot/0.1																																					O
SietsCrawler/0.1																																					O
UbiCrawler/v0.4beta																						O															O
Yahoo! Slurp													O																								O
ZyBorg/1.0													O																								O

Source: Weideman and Schwenke (2006) (1 June 2009).

An *X* in a cell indicates that the specific crawler attempted to follow the specific type of link but was unsuccessful. An *O* indicates that a crawler did follow this link. The rightmost column of Table 4.1 shows that 17 out of 18 crawlers did follow the text-based hyperlinks. However, out of these 17 crawlers, only seven attempted the JavaScript links, with only four of these seven being successful at doing so.

These results prove that crawlers prefer text-based hyperlinks to index webpages and tend to ignore JavaScript-based hyperlinks. Certain types of JavaScript links were not followed at all.

If a reason exists to have JavaScript-based navigation links on a website, it is suggested that these be complemented by standard text-based links.

Banner advertising

As the second last element on the list, banner advertisements are not regarded as a serious threat to website visibility. In fact, much research has proven that banner ads were doomed to failure due to user reactions to them and terms such as *banner blindness* became common (Burke et al., 2005; Yoo and Kim, 2005; Cho, 2004; Weideman and Haig-Smith, 2002).

However, website designers should still take care to not produce areas on a webpage which appear similar to banner ads, since users are unlikely to view or respond to these areas.

Low levels of visitors

As the last on the list, this element does not carry much weight. A website owner has many reasons to want to have a high number of visitors to the website and will probably do everything possible to achieve this. A low number of visitors is likely to be the result of many contributing factors, and cannot be addressed by implementing or avoiding one specific element of website visibility.

A word from the search engines

Search engines are in effect one of the two targets of the efforts of website designers (the user being the other). Therefore it might be useful to turn to what the specifications are from search engines regarding the negative elements discussed in this chapter (Anonymous, 2008b). An asterisk below (*) is an indication, added by the author, that this negative element has been discussed in this book.

Google:

> Basically, Google's position is that we prefer no hidden links,* no hidden text,* no automatic tools used for positioning, and no cloaking.* We prefer that Googlebots get the exact same page that users see.* In general, you can assume that we're as conservative as possible. We don't like hidden links/text* in divs/layers/iframes/css, or links that are inconspicuous or punctuation, for example. Similarly, we don't like cloaking* or sneaky redirects in any form, whether it be user agent/ip-based, or redirects through JavaScript, meta refreshes, 302s, or 100 per cent frames.* ... However, certain actions such as cloaking,* writing text that can be seen by search engines but not by users* or setting up pages/links with the sole purpose of fooling search engines may result in permanent removal from our index.

Yahoo!:

> The following list includes some of the qualities with which Yahoo! does not wish to be associated:

- pages that harm the accuracy, diversity or relevance of search results;
- pages that direct the user to another page, such as doorway pages;*
- pages that change the user's browser preferences, reset default home pages, resize browser windows, or otherwise interfere with a user's ability to navigate, without permission;
- pages with automatic software downloads including viruses, adware, spyware, or other self-installing programs;
- pages offering or promoting bulk marketing products or services if the stated or implied use of the product is unsolicited spam;
- pages with text that is hard to read,* such as text that is too small,* is obscured by the background of the page, or is located in an area of the page not visible to users;*
- pages designed to artificially inflate search engine ranking;*

- pages built primarily for search engines or pages with excessive or off-topic keywords;[*]
- pages that seem deceptive or fraudulent;[*]
- pages that are outdated or result in 'product not available' messages.

MSN Live:

Techniques that may prevent your site from appearing in Live Search results. The following techniques aren't appropriate uses of the Live Search index. Use of these techniques may affect how your site is ranked within Live Search, and may cause your site to be removed from the index.

- attempting to increase a page's keyword density[*] by adding lots of irrelevant words. This includes stuffing ALT tags that users are unlikely to view;
- using hidden text[*] or links[*] – only use text and links that are visible to users;
- using techniques, such as link farms,[*] to artificially increase the number of links to your page.

The message from these three policy statements is clear: stay away from those negative elements discussed here. Some authors claim that the same time spent on creating spamdexing in various forms could be spent on creating good content and/or optimising websites without the resulting penalties (Cutts, 2005; Thurow, 2003a: 218).

5

The ugly ones

A fight – or a partnership?

Some authors consider the ever-changing and rather sensitive relationship among the search engines, the SEO specialists and competitor websites to be a fight. Others agree that there is a fight, but are not clear who the participants are: spamdexers, return on investment (ROI), the search engines, website owners, SEO specialists – the list could go on (Hill, 2008; Murray, 2008; George, 2005: 7; Ramos and Cota, 2004). One author actually lists seven techniques used to harm competitor sites: Google bowling, tattling, Google insulation, copyright takedown notices, copied content, denial of service and click fraud (Schwartz, 2007). In a sense, it certainly appears as if there is a fight taking place in the SEO world – see Figure 5.1.

What is clear, however, is the following:

- There are conflicting motives for spending time on websites apart from just coding the basic information.
- There is a strong element of competition present.
- Many of these role-players are interdependent.

Search engines spend time and other resources crawling, indexing and critically evaluating website contents. They are motivated to index only high-quality websites, resulting in high quality SERP content and returning users (clients). There is also the obvious motive of surviving financially in the highly competitive market.

The SEO specialist spends much time on websites to ensure that they are finely tuned for content and layout to satisfy visiting crawlers and ultimately to make it into the top rankings. These participants in *the fight* are motivated to gain top rankings, fuelled by financial motives and an element of pride.

| Figure 5.1 | One view of the relationship between SEO and the search engines |

Search engine optimization is all about technique. Just like martial arts, styles make the fight. Every day is a battle in the SERPs (search engine result pages) as multiple SEO techniques duke it out **behind the scenes** to see who dominates the top 10.

Source: *http://www.seodesignsolutions.com/blog/search-engine-optimization/seo-styles-make-the-fight-10-deadly-seo-techniques-to-avoid/* (1 June 2009).

The definition of what *competitor websites* are depends on the angle of the viewer. Any website with content similar to your own, or with a motive to draw the same paying customers as your website, can be viewed as a competitor. If this is true, owners of competitor websites are motivated to draw more traffic with higher conversion rates than your website. A competitor website can also be viewed as one trying to rank well for the same keywords as another, irrespective of the industry it is in. Essentially, therefore, a financial motive seems to be overriding here.

Spamdexers have one straightforward motive – to achieve top rankings regardless of the methods used or ethical arguments against them. However, they are walking on the edge of a narrow ridge with intolerant users on the one side and distrusting search engines on the other. Falling down either side of the ridge would make them unpopular and their websites lose rankings. Why are they doing this? The answer is, yet again, for financial gain.

So it appears that the only common factor in the fight is financial. At the same time, however, many of the role-players depend on each other for survival. If the search engines did not exist, SEO specialists and spamdexers would have no job. If these last two groups did not exist, SERP contents would be predictable and remain stable (and uninteresting).

In summary it appears as if this fight is really a partnership, with many role-players, motives and complex relationships. Both SEO specialists and spamdexers are attempting to please search engine algorithms to achieve high rankings for the websites they are working on. If they break the rules, search engines will penalise them. In the end the user seems to gain much from these partnerships. After all, it is the user's preference for clicking only on the top positions and not bothering to look further down SERPs that is driving this rush for top rankings (Neethling, 2008; Waganer, 2008; iProspect, 2006). In exchange, the users receive better products at lower prices and higher quality information from the choices they make on SERPs.

So in the end what appears to be ugly – a fight between highly paid professionals and multi-billion dollar companies – can actually be viewed as a potentially benign partnership with the user reaping many of the benefits.

The hats

The SEO industry refers to the two main groups of professionals as the white hat and the black hat practitioners respectively. Depending on their emphases, these two groups make use of a variety of techniques to improve the rankings of their customers' websites. White hatter methods include judicious keyword use and placement, correct use of metatags, manual submissions and sitemap implementation. Black hat techniques include keyword spamdexing, cloaking and the use of link farms.

There is no clear dividing line, however, between these two types of techniques. What one search engine or SEO practitioner considers white hat another will call black hat. Furthermore, black hat practitioners often do not see themselves as black hat and will normally not advertise their services as such. Fortunately, some techniques are clearly in the one camp or the other, as discussed in Chapters 3 and 4. Other techniques are on the dividing line – also termed grey hat techniques – and are the subject of heated debates in the industry. Some experts actually accuse search engines themselves as being guilty of implementing black hat techniques!

White hat

In general, the techniques listed and discussed in Chapter 3 can be classified as white hat. They do not attempt to pretend that a website is different to what it appears to be in terms of the content and value that it offers to the reader. This is in essence the difference between white and black hat techniques. Some examples of simple websites where white hat techniques have been implemented and black hat techniques avoided are *http://www.uvasys.com*, *http://www.louwcoet.co.za* and *http://www .book-visibility.com*.

Black hat

Similarly, the elements of website visibility discussed in Chapter 4 can be classified as black hat techniques. These are to be avoided and can in many cases result in complete banishment from the search engine index.

Probably the most well known example of banning is that of the homepage of BMW Germany (*http://www.bmw.de*), which was banned from Google in February 2006. Surprisingly they used an old and well-known black hat cloaking technique which presented different content to users and search engine spiders. This event was reported in many of the top platforms in the SEO world (Sullivan, 2007b; BBC News, 2006; Baker, 2006). Once the banning order became known, BMW apologised, removed the offending pages and the site was restored. A Google search for 'gebrauchtwagen bmw' (used car bmw) listed *http://www.bmw.de* in the first position (July 2008).

Some of the black hat operators claim that the end justifies the means. Some would not classify themselves as black hat SEO implementers. All of them are specialists – it is easier to achieve high rankings using white hat techniques than black hat. In some cases they blatantly advertise their services (see Figure 5.2). Others practise their art but refuse to be called black hat operators.

Some authors unashamedly promote black hat techniques, without always identifying them as such. In one example, a practitioner (Sekhar, 2000) advocates the use of cloaking (p. 41), doorway pages (p. 52) and multiple domain registrations (p. 53).

Grey hat

A third rather vague category lies somewhere between white and black hats. One author labels them as '... black hat wannabes ...' (Jackson, 2007). Figures 5.3, 5.4 and 5.5 present some definitions from SEO experts and bloggers. What is important to notice, however, is that the focus is not on illegal behaviours, but rather on ethically questionable techniques.

Figure 5.2 Black hat SEO advertising

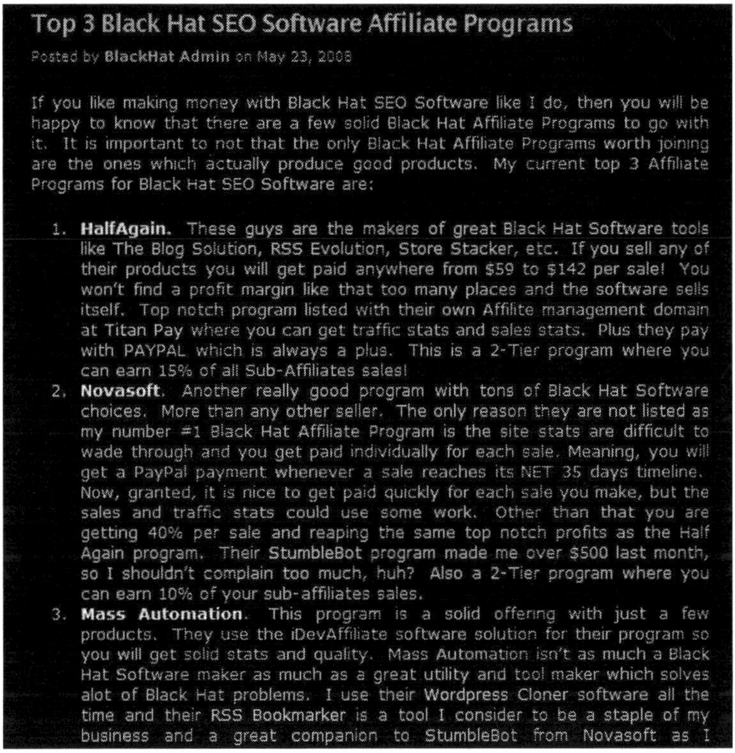

Top 3 Black Hat SEO Software Affiliate Programs

Posted by **BlackHat Admin** on May 23, 2008

If you like making money with Black Hat SEO Software like I do, then you will be happy to know that there are a few solid Black Hat Affiliate Programs to go with it. It is important to not that the only Black Hat Affiliate Programs worth joining are the ones which actually produce good products. My current top 3 Affiliate Programs for Black Hat SEO Software are:

1. **HalfAgain.** These guys are the makers of great Black Hat Software tools like The Blog Solution, RSS Evolution, Store Stacker, etc. If you sell any of their products you will get paid anywhere from $59 to $142 per sale! You won't find a profit margin like that too many places and the software sells itself. Top notch program listed with their own Affilite management domain at Titan Pay where you can get traffic stats and sales stats. Plus they pay with PAYPAL which is always a plus. This is a 2-Tier program where you can earn 15% of all Sub-Affiliates sales!
2. **Novasoft.** Another really good program with tons of Black Hat Software choices. More than any other seller. The only reason they are not listed as my number #1 Black Hat Affiliate Program is the site stats are difficult to wade through and you get paid individually for each sale. Meaning, you will get a PayPal payment whenever a sale reaches its NET 35 days timeline. Now, granted, it is nice to get paid quickly for each sale you make, but the sales and traffic stats could use some work. Other than that you are getting 40% per sale and reaping the same top notch profits as the Half Again program. Their StumbleBot program made me over $500 last month, so I shouldn't complain too much, huh? Also a 2-Tier program where you can earn 10% of your sub-affiliates sales.
3. **Mass Automation.** This program is a solid offering with just a few products. They use the iDevAffiliate software solution for their program so you will get solid stats and quality. Mass Automation isn't as much a Black Hat Software maker as much a great utility and tool maker which solves alot of Black Hat problems. I use their Wordpress Cloner software all the time and their RSS Bookmarker is a tool I consider to be a staple of my business and a great companion to StumbleBot from Novasoft as I

Source: *http://www.blackhatsoftware.net/* (1 June 2009).

Figure 5.3 Grey hat definition number 1

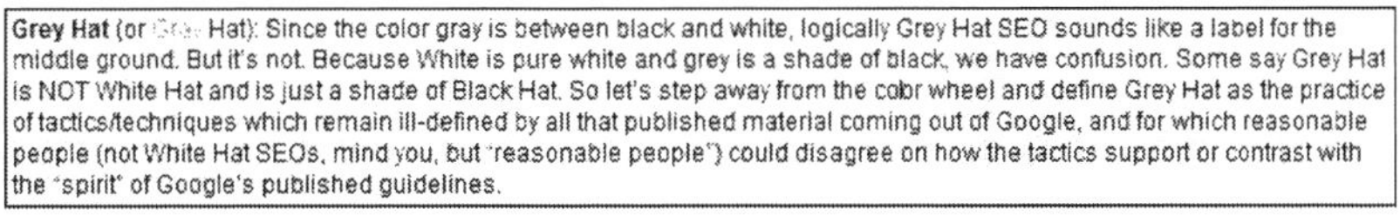

Grey Hat (or Grey Hat): Since the color gray is between black and white, logically Grey Hat SEO sounds like a label for the middle ground. But it's not. Because White is pure white and grey is a shade of black, we have confusion. Some say Grey Hat is NOT White Hat and is just a shade of Black Hat. So let's step away from the color wheel and define Grey Hat as the practice of tactics/techniques which remain ill-defined by all that published material coming out of Google, and for which reasonable people (not White Hat SEOs, mind you, but 'reasonable people') could disagree on how the tactics support or contrast with the 'spirit' of Google's published guidelines.

Source: *http://www.johnon.com/220/white-hat-sissies.html* (1 June 2009).

Search engine policies and penalties

Being penalised by a search engine is one of the ugliest events in a website's life, especially if this involves banishment from the index. Neither Google nor Yahoo! publishes a clear policy which states on what basis they would exclude a website from their index. Both list some black

Figure 5.4 Grey hat definition number 2

Gray Hat SEOs

Gray Hats are often, but not always, black hat wannabes. They may stuff some keywords into the alt text. They will probably have a link at the bottom of every page of a site that has "keyword A" linking to the home page. They may create a bunch of "information pages" that are strictly built to try to rank for a particular keyword but have little use to the end user/visitor of the Web site. Another method that some would consider "gray" are the buying of text links on various Web sites. There are certainly a number of other tactics that most would consider "gray," but I'm just highlighting a few. Some competitive situations may make a white hat go a little gray on occasion, but most of the things gray hats get involved in are what white hats would consider ethically questionable, such as keyword stuffing, etc.

Source: http://searchenginewatch.com/showPage.html?page=3626787 (1 June 2009).

Figure 5.5 Grey hat definition number 3

Gray Hat

Gray hat SEO is changing in that some things that were once white, are now gray. Gray hat SEO includes things like publishing duplicate content. Multiple, otherwise white hat, sites that have the same content. Gray hat SEO also includes mild artificial linking schemes.

So if you were doing gray hat SEO you would perhaps use a tool like the Digital Point Coop Ad Network. You would probably more aggressively include keywords within your site's content. You would certainly also do all the optimizations a white hat SEO would do, but you might take them a little further. For instance you might overly use image ALT tags to put in more keywords, even when it is unrelated to the specific image. With gray hat SEO you aren't afraid of link exchanges and may even do an off-topic link exchange (dark gray to be sure) if you think it'll raise your PageRank.

Mostly, gray hat SEO includes things that may be frowned upon, or could even result in a penalty, but they are very commonly done and they aren't forbidden as strongly as black hat acts. For instance gray hat linking schemes may get your links devalued, whereas black hat linking schemes could get your site banned.

Source: http://www.websitepublisher.net/article/white-gray-black/ (1 June 2009).

hat SEOs which would earn a website disfavour from the search engine, but neither has a central policy that clearly spells out this detail.

South Africa's largest search engine, Ananzi, does, however, have a clear policy on this issue. This is set out below (Ananzi, n.d.). Some interesting points, on which they specifically exclude a website from being indexed, are given as:

- website content which is not related to South Africa;
- webpages without metatags;
- webpages with repetitive content;
- submission forms completed only in capital letters;
- websites which are link farms.

Ananzi takes pride in providing the best possible search engine experience for our users. By submitting a site to Ananzi, users agree to the following terms and conditions governing the use of Ananzi's services. Please verify the following before you proceed:

Ananzi consists of two sections: the Search Engine (SA Web) and the SA Directory. After your site has been reviewed and accepted by Ananzi's administrators, it will become searchable via the Ananzi search bar and will be located in the SA Directory under the category to which you have submitted it (although Ananzi's search adminstrators might change this should a more appropriate category be available).

Please note that sites must either be based in Southern Africa or cover a topic that is relevant to Southern Africa. Please do not submit sites which have no bearing on Southern Africa.

Ananzi reserves the right to reject directory submissions, as well as to remove entries or move them to other categories at any time and for any reason.

Ananzi only allows one entry per site in our SA Site Directory. Only in exceptional cases will we consider allowing a duplicate entry.

Meta tags play a definitive role in determining the searchability and ranking of a site and we recommend to site owners to add meta tags to their web sites. (Click here for guidelines on adding meta tags to your site.)

Keywords and meta tags used to describe sites must accurately represent their content. Any attempts at spamming may result in exclusion from Ananzi.

Ananzi can reject sites the contents of which are essentially repetitive in nature, whilst just containing different contact details (e.g. sites advertising the same product or network marketing programs).

No submissions will be accepted if the submissions form has been filled in only in capital letters.

The excessive use of punctuation marks and symbols in titles (to boost site listings) will not be allowed.

Ananzi does not accept any affiliate sites as these sites make it nearly impossible for owners of brands to get a good listing on search engines.

Ananzi does not accept any link farm sites due to the fact that Ananzi is a search engine in its own right and should not be used as merely a stepping stone to get a good ranking in international search engines.

Ananzi cannot guarantee that any sites submitted via automated submissions programs will be received and accepted.

If your site has been accepted and, in future, you want to make any changes to your site's listing, please complete the form at http://www.ananzi.co.za/comments/change.html.

Ananzi cannot be held responsible for the content of pages hosted under our free service. We do try to review all pages for content before they are posted. However, we reserve the right to remove any page from our servers which we determine to be in violation of our rules and ethics.

Ananzi reserves the right to discontinue free of charge listing in our SA Directory and search engine. You will be notified of any change of policy concerning this amendment.

If you have not found an appropriate category to submit your site to, please view our category list or e-mail the Directory Administrator.

It is certainly worth the effort to make a detailed study of this policy for all the target search engines to which a website is to be submitted. This might imply studying a number of webpages of the search engine where these exclusions might be spelled out.

Banning

If a website has been banned from a search engine index, it is one of the worst fates it could experience. The example of the BMW homepage discussed earlier gives an indication of how this can affect a company negatively. Any website owner should consider banishment from a search engine index to be downright ugly.

Google lists a number of reasons why they would ban a website:

- if they believe law obligates them to do so;
- if a website does not meet the guidelines for quality set by Google;
- if a website hinders a user in finding relevant information;
- the use of cloaking or invisible text;
- participation in a link farm scheme. (Google, n.d.)

A number of other publicised banning examples exist. During 2005, Webmasterworld was banned for apparent transgressions of Google spamdexing rules. In June 2006, the *New York Times* optimised certain pages for search engines and it was claimed that they also used a form of cloaking, resulting in banning (Sullivan, 2007b).

Banning a website from a search engine means that it is not listed in the index, although it possibly has been listed before. Simply searching for the domain in a search engine, both with and without the *www* part at the front of the query, will determine if it has been banned or not. If neither of these two actions produces a listing containing this website, it is not in the index (Jackson, 2008). Alternatively, using the *site* operator in Google will also indicate whether or not a site is in an index: *site:www.book-visibility.com* for example (Bobnar, 2005).

The most obvious reason for banishment to have taken place is of course the implementation of black hat techniques on the website. These could include any number of the elements listed in Chapter 4.

Another reason for a website to be banned could be that the domain has a suspect past. The previous owner of the domain may have been involved in spamdexing practices, so search engines have blacklisted it and are not aware of its new owners' approach. One such case and its solution is described in a blog (Webb, 2007).

From bad to ugly: the top two

In summary, it seems appropriate to upgrade the two worst offenders in terms of degrading website visibility (see Figure 2.6) from *bad* to *ugly* status. Either one of them could easily cause a website to be banned. Number one is *link spamdexing*; number two is *keyword spamdexing*. Both involve some form of excess, both involve the use of crucial keywords and both attempt to promote a website as having content other than what really is the case. Most search engines would ban or at least drop the ranking of a website if either one of these two is present. Some academic authors have done research in an attempt to find counter-measures to combat these kinds of spamdexing (Wang et al., 2007).

Even Google itself is taking a serious stand on fighting keyword spamdexing by providing guidance on detecting spamdexing on a website (Matthews, 2008).

6

Case studies

Introduction

A number of unrelated case studies are presented here to indicate the success achieved by the application of website visibility research in practice. Note that these case studies were executed at various stages before this book had been written. In some cases it involved the early models mentioned in the book, and in no case are the guidelines of the Weideman model implemented. One example where this has been done is the book's website (*http://www.book-visibility.com*).

The SA-Cycling study was selected to prove that it is possible to redesign a homepage with website visibility as the main focus, without changing the look and feel. The *old* and *new* looks of the two homepages are virtually indistinguishable, while a large number of changes have been made to the design of this webpage. However, the *new* website was never hosted, so it serves merely as an example of how visual appearance can remain constant with dramatic changes of coding.

The second case study, based on a small law firm (Louw & Coetzee), is actually spread over a number of studies. Initially it was proven that the implementation of one of the models discussed earlier in this book can improve visibility substantially. A number of competitor websites were then tested in parallel with the test website, comparing their visibility. Finally it was proven that the initial optimisation done on the test website withstood the test of time well, by retaining its high rankings virtually unchanged over a period of one year.

A third study is discussed to prove that only ethical (white hat) techniques need be implemented to again dramatically improve website rankings. No use was made of black hat techniques. The ranking of the website of Grapetek (Pty) Ltd (*http://www.uvasys.com*) jumped from being non-existent to top spot on all three large search engines.

Finally a basic investigation was done on a dual-language website, as an indication of how to test the current visibility of a website. Again this is only a basic example and does not include a *before* and *after* testing situation.

SA-Cycling

A pilot study was conducted to provide evidence that it is possible to change an existing webpage to be visible to search engine crawlers without altering the user view of the page (Weideman and Chambers, 2005). An active website was chosen (*http://www.sa-cycling.com* – see Figure 6.1), which has been hosted for a number of years.

Initially an evaluation program was used to determine the *before* status, including current ranking, use of keywords, etc. The recommendations of this program were dissected, and reasons for low rankings or any other situation that could be improved were sought – see Table 6.1. Trends on the *before* website were monitored on a daily basis and as a comparative measure *after* comparison.

A series of changes to the website, which would be virtually invisible to the user, were discussed with the website owner. These changes were based on the Chambers model (Chambers, 2005). They include changes to the TITLE, KEYWORDS and DESCRIPTION tags. It was proposed that the logo should be changed from an image (which provided no content for crawlers) to plain text. Frames had to be removed, and coding was to be done on a single, static HTML webpage. All images had to provided with descriptive ALT tags and a text-based site map was also to be added.

Based on these changes, a *new* webpage was designed while attempting to keep the visual look and feel identical to the *old* one. Noticeable differences were slight, and included the following (see Figure 6.2):

- The menu bar at the left was changed from a JavaScript coded structure to pure text. A visual comparison only would not reveal any differences, but the absence of mouse-overs and pull-down menus would indicate the difference in actual use.

- The heading was changed from an image with text to a small image with the flag, but the title in pure text. Visually the two are very close to being perceived as identical.

Figure 6.1 Initial layout of test website

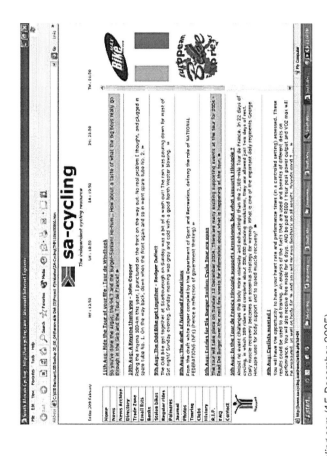

Source: http://www.sa-cycling.com (15 December 2005).

Table 6.1   *Before* feedback report

Area description	Current count for SA-Cycling	WebPosition Gold's Suggestion	Proposed action
TITLE area keyword frequency	2	1	Decrease key word frequency
TITLE area word count	4	5–10	IncreaseTITLE word count
TITLE area key word prominence	44.40%	53%	Increase key word prominence in TITLE
Meta keywords word count	10	15–37	Add more key words describing the site
Meta description area keyword prominence	42.90%	62%	Increase key words prominence in meta description
ALT area keyword frequency	0	1–20	Increase key words in ALT area
ALT area word count	0	52–100	Increase key words in ALT area
ALT area keyword prominence	0%	59%	Increase key word prominence in ALT area
Body text word frequency	0	1–10	The key word frequency should be increased if the frames are removed
Body text word count	10	257–385	The suggested word count should be implemented if the frames are removed
Body text keyword prominence	0%	55%	The key word prominence should increase if the frames are removed
Whole page word count	6	293–555	The overall page word count would increase if the frames are removed

Source: Weideman and Chambers (2005) (1 June 2009).

- The webpage title was changed from just the site name and address to a keyword-dense, accurate description of the content of the webpage.
- The final major change is the removal of the frames. Once again this would not be noticed by just viewing the two pages. Interaction would

Figure 6.2 Final layout of test website

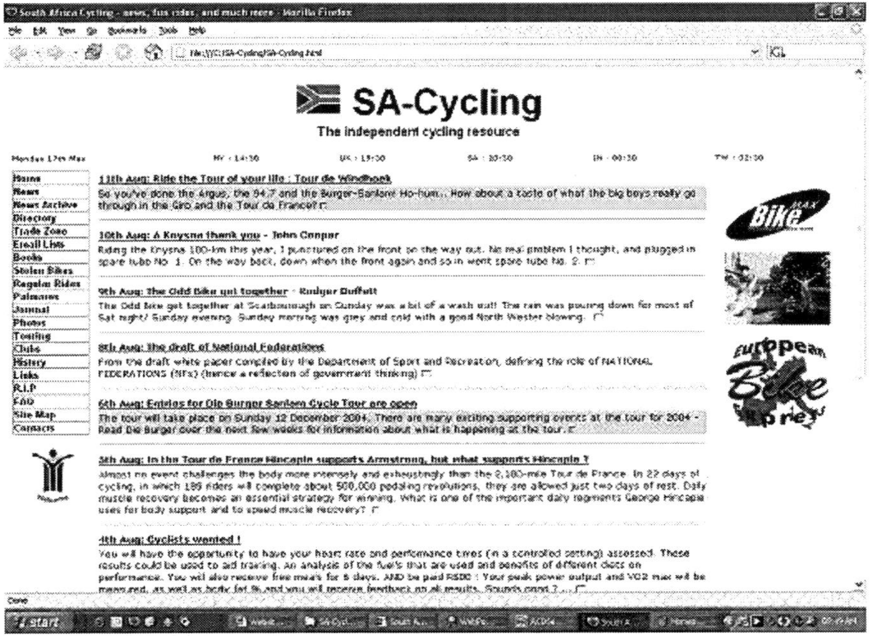

Source: *http://www.sa-cycling.com* (15 December 2005).

be required, which would reveal that scrolling down would have only moved the main body of the webpage, not the title and menus.

The new website was not hosted, so actual before/after comparisons could not be carried out. However, it did prove that a website does not have to lose its original look and feel when altered to become visible.

Louw & Coetzee

An empirical experiment has proven that organic optimisation can establish top rankings for a website (Visser et al., 2006). Paid inclusion or PPC was specifically excluded in this study. Furthermore, as a follow-up, a comparative study was carried out to determine how well competitor sites in the same industry (small law firms in South Africa) were ranked. At the same time, an evaluation was done to see how well the original site maintained its ranking over a period of one year, without any further optimisation having been done (Kritzinger et al., 2007). It was not known how the test website would stand up during one year of no improvements or further optimisation while search engine algorithms and competitor sites were updated. As will be seen, this second study proved that the high rankings of the first phase remained virtually unchanged.

First study

The client was a small law firm, Louw & Coetzee, situated in Durbanville, Cape Town (*http://www.louwcoet.co.za*). Their website had been hosted for a number of years under the same domain and has remained fairly static over this period. The owners were concerned that their website was not used as an entry point to their business by new customers and required that something be done to improve the situation.

Phase 1

Identical testing under the same circumstances was carried out during the three phases. The same keywords and testing software were used on the test website. The client produced a list of 105 keywords and phrases which are relevant to their business, while the test software listed 430 accessible search engines worldwide. Some of these keywords/phrases were: *louw & coetzee attorneys, administration of estates, legal advice, agent, analysis, attorney, attorneys, mortgage bond* and *building contracts*.

The 430 search engines included both organic and paid systems, for example: Google, Google (Paid), Google Directory, Google Directory (Paid), Google Groups and Google Groups (Paid). Since this study focused on organic systems only, all paid systems were excluded, leaving a subset of 34 search engines to be used. These are listed in Table 6.2.

Had the 105 keywords been tested across all of them simultaneously, it would impose a tremendous processing load on the search engine servers. As a result, the keywords were divided into three equal-sized blocks, named A, B and C. Similarly, the search engines were divided into four blocks, named 1, 2, 3 and 4. The tests were run on the cells formed in this way – A1, B1, C1, A2, etc. – one group of four cells at a time (see Table 6.3).

Table 6.2 Search engines used

Search engines			
A9.com	Galaxy	Mamma	Ananzi.co.za
About.com	Go	MSN	Google.co.za
AllTheWeb	Google	Netscape	za.msn.com
AltaVista	HotBot	Open Directory	Mweb.co.za
AOL Web Sites	ICQSearch	Search.com	
Ask	ISleuth	Tygo	
Earthlink	Ixquick	Webcrawler	
Entireweb	Jayde	WiseNut	
ExactSeek	LookSmart	Yahoo Directory	
Excite	Lycos	Yahoo Web Results	

Source: Visser et al. (2006) (23 June 2008).

Table 6.3 Keyword and search engine subdivisions

	Keywords		
Search engines	A: 1–35	B: 36–70	C: 71–105
1: 1–10	A1	B1	C1
2: 11–20	A2	B2	C2
3: 21–30	A3	B3	C3
4: 31–34	A4	B4	C4

Source: Visser et al. (2006) (23 June 2008).

However, it was considered important to run the various instances as close together timewise as possible. All tests were done on the same day by running the same keywords on different search engines using four parallel computers. Had a single one been used, the test would have been spread over four days, decreasing the reliability of the results in the process. Therefore A1 to A4 were run simultaneously, for example. After this block of tests was done, the Internet connection was broken and re-established using different usernames and passwords. This caused the IP addresses to be different as seen by each search engine and prevented the search engines from blocking the tests based on the continuous bombarding from the same IP address.

The test environment described above was used for phase 1 and all results were recorded. Thus the test website was checked in its original state, without any attempt to implement or remove any of the elements identified in this book as having an effect on website visibility.

Phase 2

After completion of phase 1, the test website address was submitted for indexing (on the same day) to those search engines that allowed free submission. Only seven of the 34 did, so the pool was reduced again, as expected, to: Ananzi, DMOZ, Entireweb, Exactseek, Google, Jayde and Yahoo!. A waiting period was allowed for the crawlers to visit and index the website, and during this time the website was redesigned completely (offline). The differences in visual appearance were minimal, but technically the prescriptions of the Chambers model were implemented (see Figure 2.2). At this stage the (less dated) Visser model did not exist and the Chambers model provided the best guidance. The emphasis was on simplistic design, using only static pages with no JavaScript, Flash or frames.

Phase 2 involved a repeat of the previous test battery, after allowing a short waiting period. Constraints of the research project specified the length of time. The website was still in its original state while the new design was being tested and checked offline. Customer feedback and testing on the new website was carried out regularly to ensure that the usability aspect was not neglected. The results of phase 2 were also recorded in exactly the same fashion as before.

Phase 3

Phase 3 involved hosting the new website and resubmitting to the search engines again. Visibility was tested yet again and results recorded. Figures 6.3, 6.4 and 6.5 list the three sets of results for the most

Figure 6.3 Results: Phase 1 of the Louw & Coetzee case study

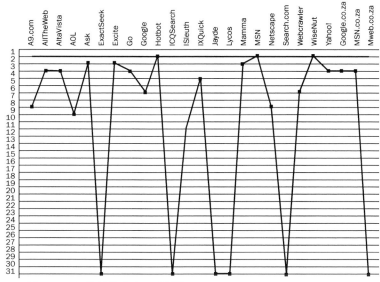

Source: Visser et al. (2006) (1 June 2009).

Figure 6.4 Results: Phase 2 of the Louw & Coetzee case study

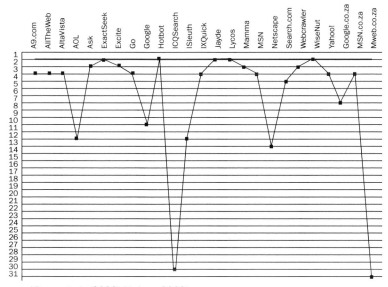

Source: Visser et al. (2006) (1 June 2009).

Figure 6.5 Results: Phase 3 of the Louw & Coetzee case study

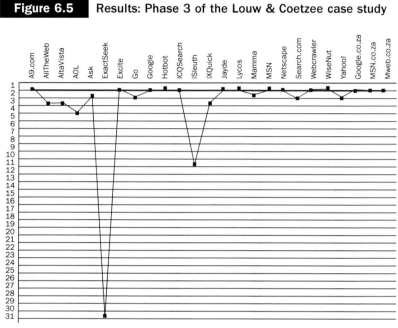

Source: Visser et al. (2006) (1 June 2009).

important keyphrase specified by the client: *attorneys conveyancers western cape*. In each case only the top 30 results of each SERP were inspected. Furthermore, 25 out of the 34 search engines listed results in the top 30, hence only those 25 were included in the results.

An interpretation and comparison of these three graphs will highlight the improvement in ranking experienced over a period of time. The *x*-axis represents the 25 search engines with their names listed along the top. The *y*-axis lists the ranking of the test website for the corresponding keyphrase. The best ranking for any website, i.e. position number one, corresponds to a *1* on the *y*-axis. The horizontal line at rank one for all search engines represents the perfect situation – the test website achieving first position on all 25 websites. In an attempt to represent *not indexed* on the same graph, a value of 31 was chosen – just outside the limit of the first 30 results. Therefore the negative visual effect of those *not indexed* cases is not as strong as it should be. A website that is not indexed at all constitutes a serious situation and does not deserve a place on the graph. However, to represent this in some way, a value had to be chosen.

The closer any point on any one of the three graphs approaches the line at the top (ranking one), the better its ranking. Therefore the more *peaks* toward the top, the better the ranking. At the same time, the more *troughs* evident on the graph (graph shapes pointing towards the bottom), the lower the ranking is.

From a simple visual scan of the three graphs, it is clear that the graph *moved upward* in general through the three stages. Compare Figures 6.3 to 6.5 to see this upward movement. Figure 6.6 provides a summary and a visual indication of the trend in these three graphs.

The black bar (first column) decreases from 6 to 2 to 1, indicating how the *Out of Index* listings have shrunk over time. This implies that at each stage, more of the search engines indexed the test website.

The grey bar (second column) changed from 15 and 15 to 9. This implies that the number of rankings between position two and ten decreased over time. The reason is simple – those that disappeared moved up to ranking position one (see below).

Probably the best success indicator is the lightly shaded column growing steadily from 3 to 5 to 14 top ranking positions. Two of the last stage's 14 top positions were for top search engines – Google and MSN. Yahoo! boasts second ranking position after the third phase.

Seen overall, this study has proven that it is possible to improve the ranking of a website by applying basic guidelines for good design practice.

Figure 6.6   Results summary of three phases

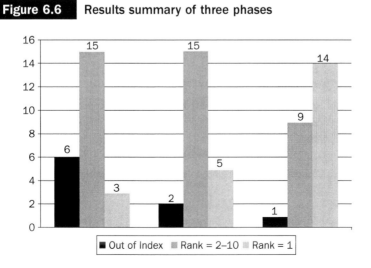

Second study

It was not known how a website's ranking would change over a period of a year in which with no changes to the website were carried out. During phase 1 of this second study the exact same testing was carried out as in the previous study, using the same 25 search engines and the same 105 keywords. Furthermore, another test was carried out in phase 2 (of the second study) to determine how well competitor websites ranked. A questionnaire was sent to potential participants (small law firms in South Africa which had an existing website). The recipients were asked to identify four-, three-, two- and one-word phrases which were highly descriptive of their businesses. Only 7 of the 96 questionnaires were sent back. It was assumed that a perception of mistrust was the cause for the low response rate as the participants were all law firms dealing with a stranger (the researcher). These keywords/phrases were then used to test their website's visibility in the same way as the test website.

Phase 1

It is clear from the three sets of results from this phase that 9 of the 25 search engines indicated improvement in the results, compared to the same sets of results from the previous year. Eleven showed no change at all, but 10 of these 11 were (and still are) in position one, so although deterioration was possible, no improvement could occur. Five of the results showed a decrease in ranking over the year period, but only one of them is affiliated to (receive their search results from) one of the top five search engine companies, namely Ask.

Therefore it can be stated that the test website held up very well over time, with some improvements evident in this period. These were probably as a result of the fact that the website now had a longer time to lie and wait for crawlers to visit. This is in contrast to the short time (11 and 13 days respectively) during the first study. It suggests that one has to allow enough time for crawlers to visit after having submitted a website to search engines.

The 10 rankings which retained their first positions was another encouraging result, proving that basic SEO using good practice guidelines can sustain or improve rankings. Only one out of 25 search engines indicated a drop in rankings over one year. This could be attributed to the fact that no further optimisation or resubmissions were done to the test website.

However, it is not advisable to leave a website untouched in terms of optimisation for any extended period. Search engine algorithms often change and, probably more importantly, competitor websites are changed and added constantly. SEO elements need to be constantly updated and improved, rankings checked and compared, and competitor websites analysed.

Phase 2

In this second phase, seven results were received, where others were incomplete or not returned. One of the seven was from the owners of the test website of Louw & Coetzee (LC).

The test results of four-keyword searches indicated that the test website (LC) scored a total of 15 first positions out of a possible 25 search engines (see Figure 6.7). The second best result set was from Firm 3, which scored 8 out of 25, followed by Firm 7 with 2 out of 25. The remaining participants were omitted (Firms 2, 4, 5 and 6) since they produced no results in the top 30 for any of the 25 search engines. Firm 1 is listed as the only other with some rankings, although none are in the first position.

The test result for three-keyword phrases proved that LC scored 17 first positions out of 25 search engines. Figure 6.8 summarises these results. Firm 7 was second with six firsts, while Firms 4 and 6 were omitted since they produced no results in the top 30.

A summary of the test results for two-keyword testing showed that Firm 7 was the leader here with 17 out of 25 first positions. It is followed by LC with one first position and several scores between positions

Figure 6.7   **Results summary of phase 2 – four-keyword series**

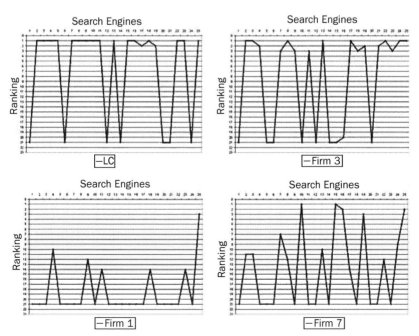

Source: Kritzinger et al. (2007).

Figure 6.8 — Results summary of phase 2 – three-keyword series

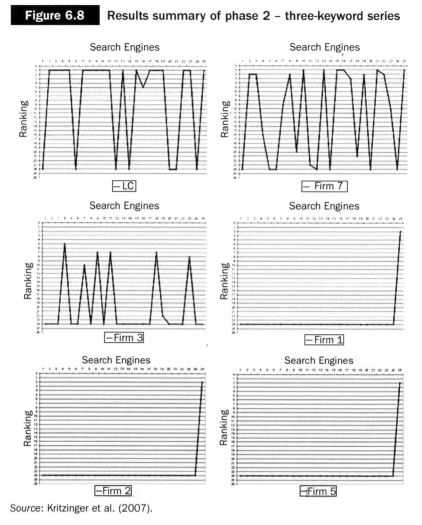

Source: Kritzinger et al. (2007).

2 and 11 – see Figure 6.9. Again firms without any results in the top 30 were omitted: 1, 2, 4, 5 and 6.

It is notable how firms start dropping out of the rankings as the number of keywords decreases. It appears to be easier to achieve higher rankings with more keywords.

One-keyword results showed that achieving high rankings with single keywords is difficult. This implies that optimisation for a single keyword is also difficult. LC achieved the highest ranking, namely tenth, for one search engine. Again those firms without any sub-31 rankings were omitted: firms 2, 4, 5 and 6. Figure 6.10 shows this summary. In general, the number of peaks in the graphs can be seen to drop (i.e. the rankings drop) if the reader scans through Figures 6.7 to 6.10.

Figure 6.9 Results summary of phase 2 – two-keyword series

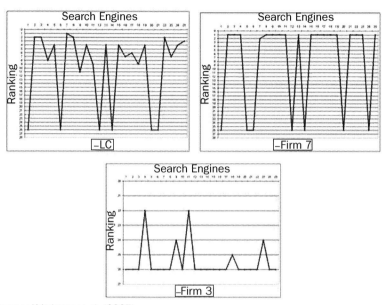

Source: Kritzinger et al. (2007).

Figure 6.10 Results summary of phase 2 – one-keyword series

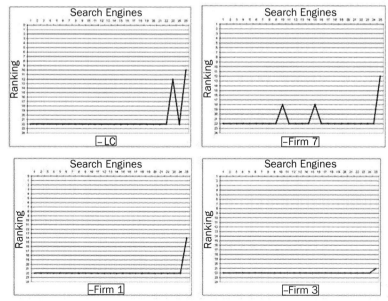

Source: Kritzinger et al. (2007).

In summary, LC proved to have, almost without exception, the highest ranking of the seven companies. Further calculations were done to determine an *average* ranking over all the tests carried out in this study, and LC was in first position with 51 per cent, followed by Firm 7 with 42 per cent and Firm 3 with 18 per cent. Closer inspection of Firm 7's website revealed that a web design and marketing company was responsible for their website, which probably explains their relatively high ranking compared to LC. No evidence could be found that a company with marketing expertise was involved in any of the other five website designs.

Conclusion

Overall, it was again proven that guidelines such as the Chambers model could improve rankings dramatically and sustain them over time. This happened without spending large amounts of money on paid placement or similar schemes to ensure top rankings. It is also important to note the interesting relationship between number of keywords and ease of achieving first position. The more keywords optimised for, the easier it is to achieve top rankings. Top rankings for single keywords are rather difficult to achieve. When comparing the graphs used in the four-, three-, two- and one-keyword results above, a *downward slide* is evident. This relationship bears interesting similarities to another study which proved that better Internet searching results were achieved when more keywords were used (Weideman and Ngindana, 2004).

Grapetek – Uvasys

An empirical study was carried out in an attempt to prove that it is possible to achieve top rankings in the world's top three search engines by applying only white hat techniques (Weideman, 2007). No paid placement systems or black hat techniques were used. A literature study has indicated that many techniques are available to improve rankings – classified as either white or black hat. However, no evidence could be found that a study has been done to prove that the application of basic website visibility techniques could dramatically increase the visibility of an international company for single-word searching.

A real-world industry website was chosen as the test site (*http://www.uvasys.com*). A Cape Town-based company, Grapetek (Pty) Ltd, manufactures a chemical product used to protect fruit against rot during export. The product name is Uvasys, also termed generator sheets or sulphur dioxide generator sheets. Their existing website has been hosted for a number of years, was fairly passive and had no indication of number of hits, page views or visitors.

A *before* study proved that, even though the website had been live for a number of years, it had no visibility with the top three search engines (Figure 6.11). The website owners provided a series of important keywords and keyphrases, and these were used during both before and after testing. An industry standard program was used for testing (WebPosition Gold, as suggested by Sullivan (2000)), linked with the keywords supplied by the owners. The top three search engines were specified (Google, Yahoo! and MSN), based on research on their and others' market share (Sullivan, 2006, 2008a).

The adapted Visser model for website visibility (see Figure 2.3) was used. Emphasis was on the *Essentials* components and, as the model proposes, the *Cautions* or *Dangers* were specifically excluded. Of the *Extras*, the HTML filenames were given descriptive names, but the domain name was not changed. Care was taken to place the important keywords correctly on especially the homepage, as seen in Figure 6.12. The basic rules of concentration towards the top, frequency and density were applied.

Figure 6.11   Before testing on *http://www.uvasys.com*

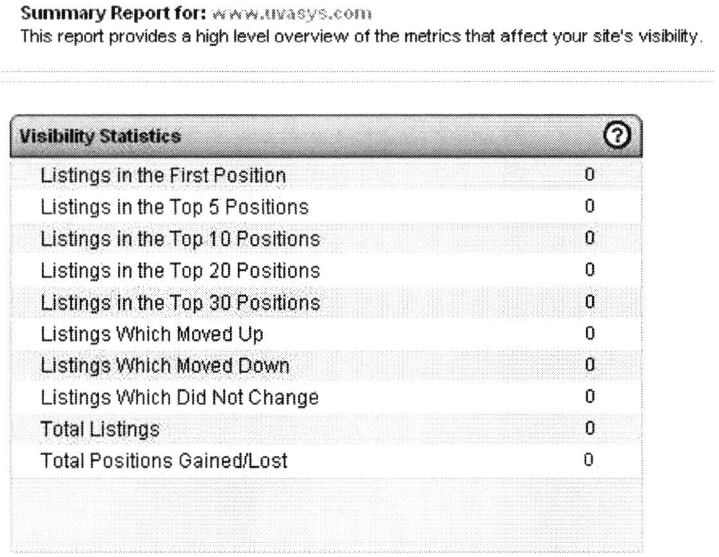

Summary Report for: www.uvasys.com
This report provides a high level overview of the metrics that affect your site's visibility.

Visibility Statistics	?
Listings in the First Position	0
Listings in the Top 5 Positions	0
Listings in the Top 10 Positions	0
Listings in the Top 20 Positions	0
Listings in the Top 30 Positions	0
Listings Which Moved Up	0
Listings Which Moved Down	0
Listings Which Did Not Change	0
Total Listings	0
Total Positions Gained/Lost	0

Source: Weideman (2007) (1 June 2009).

Figure 6.12 Keyword location on homepage

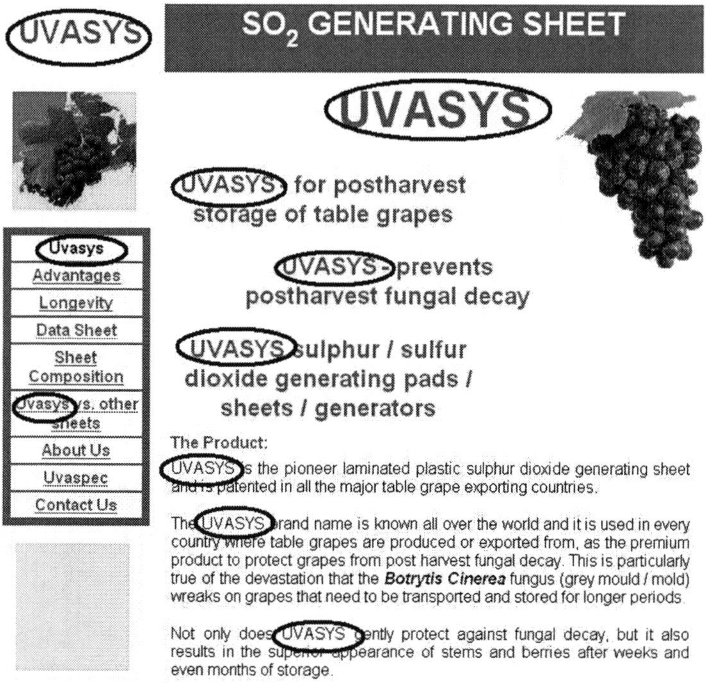

Source: http://www.uvasys.com (1 June 2009).

Using the guidelines of the Visser model, proper metatags were written – see Figures 6.13 and 6.14. The original TITLE tag contained only two words, of which one was non-descriptive. The new one is descriptive, repeats the main keyword and concentrates the most important words towards the beginning of the sentence.

The original DESCRIPTION metatag was non-existent, thereby losing an opportunity to increase the keyword content and improve the

Figure 6.13 Original and improved TITLE tags

ORIGINAL	IMPROVED
<TITLE>Uvasys > Home</TITLE>	<TITLE>Uvasys: Uvasys sulphur / sulfur dioxide generators control postharvest fungal decay in table grapes</TITLE>

Source: http://www.uvasys.com (1 June 2009).

Figure 6.14   Original and improved DESCRIPTION metatags

ORIGINAL	IMPROVED
	<META name="DESCRIPTION" content="Uvasys Grape Guards are patented laminated plastic sulphur/sulfur dioxide generating pads /sheets which protect Table Grapes against Postharvest fungal decay, in particular Botrytis, for up to 4 months. Predictable and consistent Sulphur Dioxide emission means that grapes stored with Uvasys have maximum decay control combined with minimum sulphur dioxide damage. The excellent appearance of the stems and berries, combined with prolonged shelf life make Uvasys the choice of many leading European retailers. Both Dual and Slow release Uvasys sheets are available.">

Source: *http://www.uvasys.com* (1 June 2009).

visibility. A new DESCRIPTION metatag was compiled, being keyword-rich and repeating the main keyword (Uvasys). Both the English and American spellings of one keyword were included.

The original KEYWORDS metatag contained an ASCII Carriage Return and Linefeed, denoted by &#13 and &#10 respectively. These were removed and replaced by spaces. The keywords were also expanded to contain the most descriptive words (see Figure 6.15).

The results were very satisfactory, especially for the main keyword. Where the website had zero visibility initially, it now produced, for a single keyword search, top position on all three major search engines – see Figure 6.16.

Other keywords and phrases specifically optimised for did well too. Those listed in the top 10 of the three search engines are given in Table 6.4.

Figure 6.15   Original and improved KEYWORDS metatags

ORIGINAL	IMPROVED
name="KEYWORDS" content="Uvasys
 Postharvest ;
 Table Grapes ;
 Grapetek ;
 Tedmark ;
 Litchis ;
 Sulphur Dioxide ;
 Sulfur Dioxide ;
 " >	<META name="KEYWOR DS" content="Uvasys Grapetek Tedmark Sulphur Dioxide Table Grapes Botrytis Postharvest Laminated Pad sheet generator Plastic Fungal decay Litchi lychee Grey mould mold Fungus Uvaspec Sulphite Laminated Grape Guard Sodium Metabisulphite Protection Preservat Residues">

Source: *http://www.uvasys.com* (1 June 2009).

Figure 6.16 Top positions in top three search engines

Google   **Web** Images Video News Maps **more »**
uvasys   Search Advanced Search
                                                    Preferences

Web

Did you mean: *evosys*

Uvasys: Uvasys sulphur / sulfur dioxide generators control ...
Uvasys Grape Guards are patented laminated plastic sulphur/sulfur dioxide generating
pads /sheets which protect Table Grapes against Postharvest fungal ...
www.**uvasys**.com/ - 31k - Cached - Similar pages

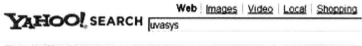

YAHOO! SEARCH   **Web** Images Video Local Shopping
                 uvasys

Search Results

1. **Uvasys: Uvasys sulphur / sulfur dioxide generators control**
   postharvest fungal decay in table grapes
   Uvasys Grape Guards are patented laminated plastic sulphur/sulfur dioxide ...
   The **UVASYS** sulphur dioxide generating sheet produces a predictable and ...
   www.**uvasys**.com - 31k - Cached - More from this site

Live Search   uvasys
                                         ☐ Only from South Africa
   Web   Images   News   More ▾

uvasys Page 1 of 7 results · Options · Safe Search Moderate

Uvasys > Home
The **UVASYS** brand is synonymous with unparalleled quality and
performance. Simple to use . Cost effective . Reliable . These
three features of the **UVASYS** SO 2 gas-generating sheet have
found favour ...
www.**uvasys**.com/Default.aspx?tabid=1

Source: http://www.google.com, http://www.yahoo.com, http://www.msn.com (1 June 2009).

| Table 6.4 | Top 10 positions for other keywords |

Search phrase	Google	Yahoo!	MSN
decay in table grapes	7	2	0
grapetek	5, 6	7	1
postharvest fungal decay	1	3	0
sulfur dioxide generators	6	4	0
sulphur dioxide generators	4	1	0
tedmark	0	6	0
uvasys	1	1	1

Source: Weideman (2007) (1 June 2009).

Conclusion

In conclusion, it has been proven that a website owner does not have to spend inordinate amounts of money on PPC or make use of black hat techniques to achieve high rankings. Top rankings cannot be guaranteed for any website under all conditions, but an improvement in rankings is almost always possible.

The kind of results listed in Table 6.4 is one of a number of tests for the successful website visibility of a given webpage. To simplify this kind of test, the following steps are suggested:

- Identify at least one keyword, preferably a few plus some key phrases, which are crucial in describing the content of the webpage.

- Repeat multiple searches on at least the three major search engines.

- Decide on how many results are to be inspected – first 10? first 30? The higher this figure, the more results will be found, but the lower down they will be in the ranking on the average.

- List the occurrences of the webpage under inspection as in Table 6.4.

The lower (numerically) the ranking figure, of course, the better. If any keyword or phrase does not appear in the table, it should either be discarded or the optimisation process must be repeated with this keyword in mind.

In closing, an example taken from the tourism industry can be given to put these results into perspective. The tourism industry is well represented on the Internet. A search for *hotel accommodation London* on Google produced 323,000 answers, including the top 11 being PPC ads. A quick scan through the first three SERPs indicated that *all* results were relevant – they all advertised hotel accommodation in London and surrounds. This level of relevance on a SERP is rare in the search engine world and is good news for the user.

On the other hand, for a new tourism website it cannot be expected to guarantee that all these results in terms of rankings can be bypassed by simply adding a few relevant keywords to this new webpage. The tourism industry is highly competitive, and achieving guaranteed high rankings in this environment should be done through paid ranking systems. Thus the results of this case study must be seen in the light of *density* of competition.

XiCrypt

Another example of a website with every reason to be crawler friendly and widely listed is the case study on XiCrypt Technologies (Weideman, 2008). XiCrypt is an Austrian company providing secure online transactions to public administration bodies, private users and other companies. The long-term storage of digitally signed documents is part of this service. Although XiCrypt is in a German country and has many German-speaking customers, they claim also to serve the English-speaking community. They host both a German and English version of their homepage.

However, this short investigation of their website visibility produced alarming results. Empirical testing was carried out, which proved that the English version of the homepage (*http://www.xicrypt.com/index_en.php*) had no visibility at all. The world's top three search engines were used, and six keyword queries supplied by the company as being important to their vision. The first 30 results of each SERP were considered, which yielded $3 \times 6 \times 30 = 540$ webpages which were inspected. The homepage did not appear anywhere in this set.

The investigation was repeated, this time using the same six keywords translated into German on the German homepage. Using a group of 35 German students as a check, the eight most-often used German search engines were identified and the test above was repeated. This time the German version of the homepage was used (*http://www .xicrypt.com/index.php*), but the results were only marginally better. Again the homepage was not listed anywhere on any one of the 1,440 resultant webpages (8 search engines × 6 keywords × 30 results = 1,440 webpages). Three search engines (*http://www.msn.de*, *http://www.web.de*

and *http://www.yahoo.de*) listed one of the sub-pages once each within the first 30 results. In each case it was for the same keyphrase.

Again the XiCrypt homepage was not indexed by any of the eight German search engines for any of the six keywords. The reason for this virtually total lack of visibility was impossible to determine and could be ascribed to a number of factors. This short study suggested that even commercial websites do not achieve a high degree of website visibility automatically. Visibility has to be *earned*, either through SEO or paid systems.

Conclusion

It is clear that website visibility has to be reached through careful planning and does not just happen. Furthermore, it is better to design a website with visibility as one of the objectives rather than to panel beat an existing site to achieve visibility. In none of the case studies above was this done, and the price to be paid included extensive changes and, in some cases, the complete redesign of the entire website.

7

Recommendations and the future

Recommendations

Recommendations for the implementation of website visibility elements are spread throughout the text. A website owner has one of four choices, as explained at the end of Chapter 1: either do not implement any SEO, which will probably cause the website to retain its current level of visibility, or invest in either organic SEO or paid systems, or fourthly use both.

Investing in both is certainly the most effective, but the most expensive and labour intensive. If quick ranking improvements are needed, paid systems are the answer. If a website already has keyword-rich and descriptive content (or it could be added easily) and financial constraints are present, organic SEO will be the best.

In summary, a checklist for SEO is supplied below. Consider the fact that the application of technical SEO alone will not lead to top rankings. It will create a website that appears to be *safe* in terms of pleasing the crawlers. If there is no content of value, no human touch, it will not rank well and visitors will not be pleased.

Ensure that each point has been addressed before starting to submit the website to search engines. The sequence of the headings below is an approximation of the Weideman model – the first are the most important (see Figure 2.5). All the points of the checklist below should be implemented before an increase in rankings can be expected.

Content

- Does the website as a whole contain content of value to the human visitor, with many related inlinks and keyword-rich text?

Neighbourhood and links

- You can choose where your website lives – who are your neighbours and who are your competitors?

- Attempt to gather high-quality inlinks to your site – contact similar trusted websites.

- Have you included outlinks to all the well-known leader sites in your topic area?

- Check each outlink – are they all pointing to trustworthy sites?

- Are you aware of any inlinks from suspect neighbourhoods?

- Does the website have a text-based site map linking to every internal page?

- Do you have a plain text link from the homepage to the site map page?

- Is there a clear menu structure on the homepage, leading to every other webpage?

- Is every hyperlink in the text surrounded by descriptive keywords?

Keywords

- Identify all important keywords – record them in the KEYWORDS metatag.

- Write hyperlink anchor text for every hyperlink as descriptive keyword-rich semi-sentences.

- Create a high-density DESCRIPTION metatag based on the most important keywords.

- Use the most important keywords in the TITLE tag of all webpages.

- Use these keywords in grammatically correct, full sentences in the body text.

- Employ a professional writer if needed to write the body text.

- Ensure that a descriptive page title, using a choice of keywords, is written inside an H1 tag.

- Consider keyword location – concentrate keywords closer to the top of the webpage, use them less towards the bottom.

- Consider keyword frequency – use the most important keywords often, without creating nonsensical, spamdexing word sequences.

- Consider keyword proximity – keep the words of a keyword phrase close together.

- Ensure that every image on every webpage has an ALT tag where the same keywords are used correctly.

Finalisation

- Once this checklist has been completed, manually submit the site to all the big search engines. This will increase exposure and subsequent inlinks.

As an example of the implementation of this checklist, view the book's website at *http://www.book-visibility.com.*

Management vs the technical guys

The conceptualisation, design, implementation and maintenance of a corporate website are complex tasks. If the website is mission-critical, it is crucial that these steps be executed in a planned and methodical way. There often exists a *distance* between management and technical personnel in terms of their perception of how this should be done. For example, management might have a clear idea of what the business is aiming to achieve, what products or services are important and how to market these. The website coder, however, focuses on technology, how best to design the website according to a different set of perceptions of what is right. These perceptions might include ease of coding and maintenance, the use of new software technologies or the implementation of good programming practice.

These two sets of perceptions, those of management and those of technical staff, often do not coincide. If matters are left to themselves, the chances are that either one or both groups will be dissatisfied with the website or with the actions of the other group.

In this author's experience, there needs to be a *middleman* who can act as a buffer between these two groups. This middleman's task is to ensure that a visible and usable website is produced using the best and most relevant software technologies while meeting the requirements of management. He or she has to focus on getting a highly ranking website hosted while incorporating management's wishes and considering technical staff limitations, perceptions and resources. This is not an easy task and contains more elements of project management than of technical excellence in SEO.

This middleman would need to have the following:

- a basic understanding of website visibility, as outlined in this book;
- a clear understanding of the company's vision, operations and products/services;
- above average communication skills;
- the motivation to improve a website's ranking;
- project management skills.

Search engine developments

Standard Internet searching is and has always been free for the user. However, search engine companies need to survive to maintain this much needed service of *free information*. One way to survive is through advertising, whether through online advertisements or paid listing services such as PPC.

The highly successful models implemented by some search engine companies have proven that this goal of providing a free information service and creating revenue can be achieved. In a personal interview between a search engine company employee and this author, it was admitted that they are not interested in searching. Their service is purely there to attract users, while their main driving force is marketing and financial gain. The provision of a free searching service is used to expand the free e-mail user base, to sell more advertisements and to reach new markets.

It is expected that this trend will continue. The chances of search engines starting to charge users for what used to be free are slim.

Many academic information services require registration and payment for access. There is a strong drive towards open access – that is, removing these payment borders. This cannot be achieved without compensation in some form for the loss of revenue. New financial models will need to be found for this process to continue.

Future trends

It is unlikely that the established pattern of the Internet offering ever increasing volumes of information will change in the near future. New websites appear by the second, traffic volumes increase causing networks to groan under the load and users expect shorter response times and immediate fulfilment of their information needs. An interesting development is making available more and more of the masses of information trapped in the invisible Web. The availability of rich media and other non-traditional content is also increasing at disproportional rates. In parallel with this increase is of course the need to find these kinds of content. Traditional crawler harvesting of text does not work for images, video and sound searching. Most search engines are expanding research in these areas to satisfy user demands.

The game being played out in the search engine field is bound to have an interesting finish. At the time of writing, Yahoo! has spurned Microsoft's (rather high) bid for their company. This leaves Google as the leader, by far, in the search field. Apparently Microsoft has now experienced failure in their attempt to offer serious competition to Google as the frontrunner of search. In fact, many are wondering if it really is the search technology that Microsoft is after, or is it the 500 million Yahoo! Mail clients they want ...

Personalisation seems to be one of the latest catch words – personalise your presence on the Web via Facebook and other social media sites, personalise your desktop with one of a plethora of toolbars/schemes and other customisable environments, personalise the news you receive with RSS feeds, and of course personalise your search, again with one of many technological tools available for this purpose. This trend is likely to continue, as users are *empowered* more and more by these options. One might even hypothesise that personalisation allows the user to establish a personality on their technological devices. Or is it a matter of *feel-good* technologies that satisfy some selfish drive in users to enable them to establish a bit of their own personality?

Currently English is by far the dominant language of the Web. Other languages have lagged behind, for a variety of reasons. Extended character sets and low connectivity in certain countries and areas are some of the reasons behind this trend. However, the world's largest group who speak the same language (Mandarin) represents about 999 million out of 6,704 million humans believed to inhabit the planet as of 21 June 2008 (Wikipedia, 2008g). English and Spanish, respectively, weigh in at a distant second and third position. This large group of potential users have virtually no slice of the Internet pie in their own language. This situation offers a vast opportunity for service providers, educationalists and marketers.

In summary, the Internet offers both beginner and expert an unlimited field of learning. The author's advice is to always keep an open mind, look for answers elsewhere if not found the first time, and NEVER GIVE UP!

Glossary

Academic – a teacher/researcher who works at a university or other higher education institute. Academics normally specialise in one topic inside a field and teach and/or publish research inside that one field. Most are advanced degree holders (masters and/or doctoral degrees). The author of this book is an academic specialising in website visibility. See also *Practitioner*.

Age of document – refers to how long a document has been part of a webpage on the Internet. The document could be text only, graphic elements or any other non-HTML form of document. In terms of website visibility, documents on a webpage could influence the way crawlers read that webpage. If a document contains text which is highly relevant to and supportive of the topic of the webpage for example, and is readable by the crawler, it could add to the visibility of that webpage.

Age of link – the amount of time the link (hyperlink) has existed in the same format on a given webpage. Older links will add more value than younger ones to the visibility of the webpage they appear on.

Age of website – refers to the length of time that website has existed under the same URL (e.g. *http://www.mwe.co.za*) and with the same content. The older a website is the better in terms of visibility of that website.

Algorithm – refers to an interrelated set of mathematical equations on which a search engine bases its decisions for ranking search results in response to a query from a user. The detailed operation of these programs is a trade secret, although the basic operation is generally known. The most well-known algorithm in the search engine world is Google's PageRank, which uses the number of inlinks to a webpage as one of the factors to determine the ranking of a webpage. The eventual visibility of a website depends to an extent on the way the algorithm evaluates it.

ALT tag – the text on a webpage, chosen by the coder, to describe an image on that webpage. This text is displayed if the image itself cannot be displayed (e.g. while downloading or when the image link is broken). It is useful to search engines for indexing purposes and screen readers will read it out for visually impaired Internet users. The ALT tag is optional, but images without one do not increase the search engine ranking of the webpage they appear on.

Altavista – one of the oldest search engines, and at one stage the leader in terms of index size.

American Standard Code for Information Interchange (ASCII) – a set of standard characters used to transfer information, based on the sequence of these characters in the English alphabet. Every character is allocated a unique code (e.g. A is 65, B is 66, a is 97, b 98, etc.). Generally the characters on a standard keyboard are all ASCII characters, while other methods have to be used to generate non-ASCII characters (like Ω, 2/3, €, ±, ë, etc.). An often used reference to ASCII is the phrase 'an ASCII editor', which refers to a simple program used to code programs or webpages, where this editor is only capable of generating standard ASCII codes.

Anchor text – refers to descriptive text coded as part of a hyperlink on a webpage. This text will be displayed on the screen as the area where the user should click on when wanting to be taken to a different part of the website. These words are also used by search engines as part of the ranking algorithm, and should be as descriptive and unique as possible. The very common 'Click here', 'Next' and other similar non-descriptive word choices for anchor text should be avoided.

Animated graphic – a graphic image which contains some movement, used to catch the user's eye on a webpage. Excessive use of animated graphics has been proven to irritate users and even drive them away to other webpages. Descriptive text should be associated with the graphic to enhance the website visibility of that webpage. Crawlers cannot index the content of the graphic, however descriptive it might be as an image.

Ask – a search service, previously called Ask Jeeves, after the well known butler. It is also referred to as Ask.com, based on its Internet address.

Bandwidth – the amount of data which an electronic communications channel can transmit per time unit, expressed in bits per second or multiples of it (e.g. kb/s or Mb/s). Originally the term was used exclusively in a computer science and networking environment but lately has become common when referring to fast (or slow) Internet downloads.

Banner advertising – an Internet marketing mechanism which displays advertisements in the form of (mostly) horizontal strips appearing at the top of webpages. A different banner may be displayed on every subsequent visit to the webpage, and it could have a static or changing layout. On low-bandwidth Internet connections these ads can slow down operation, and since they have been proven to frustrate users, their popularity has decreased dramatically.

Banner blindness – refers to the tendency among users to block out and simply not see areas on the screen containing banner ads and advertisements in general. It has contributed to the demise of banner ads. Being mostly graphical by nature, a banner ad will also be invisible to a search engine crawler and thus not contribute to the webpage's visibility.

Banning – the action of a search engine removing a website from its index, making it in effect invisible to the user. This could be catastrophic if the website is commercial in nature. Search engines impose this penalty if spamdexing has been detected on a webpage, or if other search engine policies have been violated. Banning reduces a webpage's visibility to zero.

Black hat – refers to a set of techniques whereby webpages are presented differently to Internet users than to search engine crawlers in an attempt to raise their ranking artificially. Some black hat techniques include keyword spamdexing, cloaking and link farms. These techniques cannot be delimited exactly, and a number of differences of opinion exist as to which ones qualify for this dubious honour. White hat techniques are considered to be above board and ethical and should be used to improve rankings. These include correct keyword usage, manual search engine submissions and the use of proper metatags. Grey hat techniques are those which are in the middle between black and white hat techniques.

Body – the main section of a webpage, which will be interpreted by the user's browser and displayed on the screen for the user to see. The body section normally contains text, images and other elements designed to be of interest to the reader – in short, what is perceived to be the content of a webpage. This is in contrast to the header section, which is not displayed. See also *Header*.

Body keyword – the text component inside the body of a webpage, and specifically the occurrence of weight-carrying keywords in this section. The body text section could be the only part of the webpage but is often supplemented by images. Body text is most important for search engine crawlers since they use this text to index and rank the webpage. Incorrect use of keywords inside body text (i.e. mindless repetition of the same word(s)) could be perceived as spamdexing by search engine crawlers.

This could result in the webpage being banned from the index. Sentences inside the body section of a webpage should be descriptive and contain a high percentage of keywords. However, this percentage should not be increased to the point where a sentence appears to be spamdexing. From the crawler's perspective, the body contents are what matters in terms of website visibility, and the focus of using the correct keywords in the body text should be on this area. Below is an example of a sentence using a high percentage of body keywords without raising the spamdexing flag to a search engine (weight-carrying words are indicated in bold):

> **Website visibility:** the **theory** and **practice** of **improving rankings** is a **book** on **optimising website contents** for **high search engine rankings**.

An example of a sentence which will probably raise the spamdexing flag is:

> Buy books from **ABC bookshop** since **ABC bookshop** provides the best value for money – **ABC bookshop** is the world's best online store.

See also *Keyword*.

BODY tag – the HTML coding element, part of the structure of a standard HTML page, which indicates the start and the end of the body section of a webpage. The start tag is coded as <BODY>, and the end tag as </BODY>.

Bomb – see *Google Bomb*.

Boolean operator – a set of keywords which can be used to focus a search by (mostly) excluding unwanted answers – also called a logical operator. Examples include AND, NOT, OR and NEAR. Most search engines add an 'AND' Boolean operator between keywords by default. Google, for example, will treat the following two queries as if they are the same:

- soccer world cup cape town
- soccer AND world AND cup AND cape AND town

Adding AND operators between keywords tends to decrease the number of answers (i.e. narrow the focus) of a search. The OR operator has the opposite effect. See also *Logical search*.

Bot – see *Crawler*.

Breadcrumbs – a set of words, often linked by '>' symbols at the top of a webpage, which informs the user about his/her location on a website. It also indicates the trail followed to get to the current webpage. Breadcrumbs grow in length as one drills deeper into a website and shrink when moving upwards. This term was coined after the Hansel and Gretel fairytale of leaving breadcrumbs to allow return by the same path. The use of breadcrumbs coded as text could increase website visibility, since it provides more weight-carrying text keywords for crawlers to index.

Browser program – a set of programs which users run to display and interact with webpages from the Internet. Early browser examples include Mosaic and Netscape Navigator, while currently Microsoft Internet Explorer and Mozilla Firefox are common. Due to the familiarity of an open browser window on a user's screen, this browser window is often labelled 'the Internet'. Different browsers have different ways of formatting HTML code for display, and the same webpage might appear differently on different browsers.

Cache memory – traditionally refers to high-speed, high-cost and therefore low-capacity random access memory normally used to store often used information in a computer. Lately used in a generic sense by browsers to store the last few visited webpages. This reduces the amount of information which has to be downloaded while browsing the Internet. When navigating the Internet, however, the user might be viewing an old copy of a given webpage from the browser's cache memory. To prevent this from happening, the Refresh function in the browser should be used to download the current version.

Cascading style sheet (CSS) – a programming aid for website developers which makes it possible to code multiple webpages in a consistent way. A CSS describes the presentation of a document coded in, for example, HTML. When a CSS is used in a certain way, it could decrease the visibility of a webpage – crawlers generally would not be able to read external CSS files.

Citation – when one author refers to the work of another. On the Internet, it is used to describe one website linking to another via a hyperlink – generally taken to be a vote of confidence in the content. Google's PageRank algorithm is, among other things, based on citations. In general, having many hyperlinks pointing to one webpage should increase the ranking of the webpage. See also *External link*, *Hyperlink* and *Link farm*.

Click fraud – refers to a type of Internet crime involving the continuous clicking on a paid link leading to a given website without the intention of spending money at the target website. It can be used by commercial operators to increase the advertising expenditure of a competitor without the expected offsetting income. The clicking can be done by a human, an automated script or other computer program. It is the subject of some controversy, since click fraud can be difficult to prove. However, most large search engines claim to have ways of identifying and combating click fraud.

Click through – the action of clicking on a hyperlink on a search engine's result page, leading to another website. It is also used in a more general sense as a click on any hyperlink on a webpage which will lead to another webpage.

Clipboard – a common memory area, used by the Windows operating system to allow the transfer of data from one area in an application to another or between applications. The cut, copy and paste operations are used to transfer and save data using the clipboard.

Cloaking – a technique used to achieve high webpage rankings in search engines in an artificial way, generally considered to be spamdexing. One webpage is designed to be search engine friendly (optimised), i.e. it contains large amounts of keyword-rich text, and this page is offered to crawlers when they visit. It will thus earn high search engine rankings. However, when a human user tries to visit this page, a different page designed to be human friendly is served to them. Cloaking is considered to be a black hat technique and could lead to a webpage being banned from search engine indices.

Coder – refers to a person with the skills and training to generate computer programs, which include Internet webpages and systems. The process of coding webpages often includes the use of many different but supporting Internet languages and technologies, such as JavaScript, cascading style sheets, frames, graphics and others. Also called *Programmer*.

Community – a loosely related grouping of webpages with similar content. Just as like-minded humans tend to spend time with each other, communities of webpages tend to link to each other rather than to link to those with content differing dramatically from their own. In terms of website visibility, it is important to find, link to and obtain links from other reputable websites in the same community.

Concept map – a diagram used to list objects or concepts and the relationships between them. Often blocks or circles contain the objects, and annotated arrows between these blocks indicate the relationships.

Content – a generic term referring to information of value on a webpage. This content could be text, visual elements, audio elements and others.

Useful and relevant content is an important component in the drive towards user satisfaction in webpage usage. A common method of increasing webpage ranking using suspect methods is to host many webpages with similar or even identical content. This is aimed at increasing the occurrence of relevant keywords and hyperlinks, but most search engines have ways of identifying and flagging these duplicate pages.

Content management system – an authoring system that enables companies to manage the content of their website by allowing departments to provide and control the content of their own subsection of the website.

Crawler – a computer program which traverses the Internet continuously, gathering information about websites in the process. Website coders have to understand how crawlers view webpages and code accordingly to achieve high webpage rankings. Also called a *bot*, *robot*, *scutter* or *spider*.

Cybersquatting – the process of buying a domain with the intent of waiting until a company or person will realise the need they have for this domain, and then sell it for an exorbitant price. It often involves a brand or company name, or part thereof, being included in the domain name. Most of the known court cases resulting from cybersquatting have been ruled in favour of the applicant, forcing the squatter to sell the domain for a reasonable price. See also *Domain name*.

Database – a collection of textual, graphic and other records or data, structured in a specific way, which enables users to extract useful information via an interface. This way of organising is done according to a database model, with the relational model being the most common. Other models are the hierarchical model and the network model.

Deep web – see *Invisible web*.

DESCRIPTION metatag – an HTML tag used by webpage authors to provide a description of the content of the webpage for use in search engine listings. This tag plays an important part in website visibility. Part of it is also displayed on search engine result pages, implying that its contents should be written with care. If it is too long, the search engine will only display the first part. This implies that important keywords and keyphrases should be concentrated towards the beginning of the description tag. See also *KEYWORDS* and *TITLE metatags* and *Metatag*.

Digital social network (DSN) – a collection of users all over the world who share messages, ideas, emotions, photos, etc. through a complex set of programs on the Internet. Common examples include Facebook and

MySpace. A participant in any DSN actually becomes part of a virtual or online community, who communicate for educational, emotional, social, professional, business and other reasons. It is expected that some social change will result from the growth of DSNs.

Directory – a search tool which uses human editors to review and categorise websites in a hierarchical directory according to topics. Yahoo! and Looksmart are some examples. As such directories are not search engines, although the two tools are sometimes combined. Often the topic of a website earns it a position in a given directory category rather than the contents of one specific page. See also *Search engine*.

Domain name – a unique text name that companies and private users register to indicate their Internet website address, e.g. *http://www.book-visibility.com*. A user would type this domain name into the URL bar to visit a website. Legal disputes can arise when two persons or companies disagree about which one has the right to use a given domain already registered by one of them. See also *Cybersquatting*.

Doorway page – a webpage designed to rank highly with crawlers but which actually only serves to lead humans to another webpage with human-friendly content. Designers sometimes use doorway pages in an attempt to satisfy both search engine crawlers and human visitors, thus achieving high rankings with search engines while also providing quality content to users. Doorway pages are considered to be spamdexing, which might result in a website being banned from a search engine index. Also known as bridge pages, entry pages, gateway pages, jump pages, portal pages or zebra pages.

Download – the action of transferring a webpage and/or other objects (images, forms, etc.) from a server to a local computer. When a user types a new URL into a browser and presses Enter, a download will start. Excessive downloading (e.g. many users copying movies simultaneously) can reduce service delivery on a network with resultant user frustration.

Dublin Core – a set of metadata conventions designed originally to describe webpage contents, including TITLE, CREATOR and SUBJECT. Dublin Core is now used to describe physical collections in archives, museums and libraries. It is also used to describe video, sound, text, images and other digital materials.

Duplicate – could refer to a variety of elements in terms of webpage content. Website authors could create duplicate content with the intent of improving website rankings. Duplicate metatags could also be used for the same purpose. Generally search engines frown on this practice, since it dilutes the content of their indices, clogs them with repeated information and slows down their servers.

Dynamic page – a webpage which is not stored on a server but is generated by a query before being displayed on a user's screen. As such it is a virtual page since it does not exist in the traditional webpage format but is generated on demand and stops existing when the user moves to the next webpage. Examples include online banking statement webpages and airline booking pages. In general search engine crawlers do not index dynamic pages as easily as they do static webpages. See also *Dynamic URL* and *Static page*.

Dynamic URL – refers to a URL that contains $, %, =, & in its name, which is generated dynamically during a request by a user. These characters are referred to as 'stop characters', because they force crawlers to stop interpretation of the URL at that point. Often copying a dynamic URL and pasting it into a browser will not take the user to the desired webpage, since that specific URL does not exist any more at that time. In general dynamic URLs are not followed by search engine crawlers, meaning that information on those pages cannot be indexed and found by users. See also *Dynamic page* and *Static page*.

e-Commerce – refers to the marketing, distributing, buying, selling and servicing of products or services over the Internet. It could also include electronic data interchange, where one company's computers query and transmit purchase orders to other companies' computers.

Editor – a term which has two meanings. The older one refers to a program which coders use to write other programs with. A very simple editor which could be used for creating webpages is Windows's Notepad. In the second sense an editor is a human who is tasked with scanning websites manually with the purpose of harvesting useful information.

Empirical – normally used to refer to research which involves experiments, observation or measurements and tangible results to describe a given situation. Empirical research can be viewed as opposite to theoretical research.

Exclusion policy – a set of criteria set up by search engines to describe when a webpage would be excluded from their index since it breaks one or more of their basic optimisation rules. It could also list criteria for the submission of websites. However, search engines often do not supply an exhaustive list of exclusion criteria. This could provide guidelines as to which spamdexing techniques website designers could implement without being detected for that specific search engine.

Explorer – refers to a Microsoft program, supplied free with the operating system, used to browse the Internet. It is often abbreviated MSIE, and is represented by a blue lowercase letter 'e' icon surrounded by a yellow ellipse. Since MSIE has become a strong standard in industry, the term 'Explorer' is sometimes used as a generic term to refer to any browser program.

External link – refers to a hyperlink on webpage B, linking to webpage A, where webpage A is the one currently under consideration. A large number of external links from other websites in the same community makes a positive contribution to website visibility. A webpage coder has very little control over the quantity and quality of external links, but the website owner could canvass for external links from other high-quality websites. See also *Citation*, *Hyperlink* and *Link farm*.

Facebook – a social utility on a website which allows registered users to share information, photos, text messages, etc. in a way which creates a virtual community of users with loosely grouped subgroups of 'friends'. Facebook is one of many digital social networks – others include MySpace, Linkedin, Orkut and Flickr.

File – a collection of information stored on a computer under a name and an extension. Common files include word processing documents (e.g. MinutesFeb09.doc), spreadsheets (e.g. BudgetProduction2010.xls), webpages (e.g. index.html) and photographs (e.g. facejohn.jpg). Files can be copied to another location, deleted, renamed and e-mailed as attachments to other Internet users. Search engine crawlers scan through all the readable files they can find on a website, harvesting all the content they can, and store it in the index.

File server – a high-performance computer used to store, manage and 'serve' files and services to many other 'client' computers. Some companies own and manage many servers to allow users to store their websites, for a monthly fee, on them. The reliability and uptime of a file server has an effect on website visibility, since a file server that is down regularly will cause all websites stored on it to be unavailable to users and crawlers.

File transfer protocol (FTP) – file transfer protocol is a network protocol commonly used by website designers to upload website files from their local computer to a file server. The moment the upload has been completed, these files will be available to users on the Internet.

Finder of Information on the Internet (FOIOTI) – a simple interface which forces the user to think carefully about a query before specifying it, with the purpose of improving searching success. See *http://www.mwe.co.za*.

Firewall – a generic term indicating either a security program or specialised hardware, both with the same purpose of protecting a computer against a variety of threats. These threats include computer viruses, auto-install programs, popups and advertisements.

Flash – a multimedia platform for adding visual flair to webpages in the form of interactivity, animation, advertisements and video integration. One of the motivations for using Flash is to improve the navigation of and add to the user experience of a webpage. Some users, however, do not like Flash-based webpages, and not all search engines can index Flash. A webpage containing only a Flash image (so-called Splash pages) has nothing for a crawler to index and will have virtually no visibility.

Focusing – refers to a process whereby an Internet searcher modifies (often lengthens) his/her search query in an attempt to receive fewer but more relevant answers to a query. Any unsuccessful searching attempt should be subject to a process of focusing to increase the chances of success.

Font – (also spelled fount) refers to a complete set of characters of a given typeface, normally in a set style and size. However, the term is often used as a synonym for font size or font type. Most books state the name of the font used to print the contents.

Frame – a technique used in website coding which divides the webpage into separate areas, used mostly to centralise and enhance navigation. The dividing lines between these areas are sometimes not visible, and each frame is stored as a separate HTML file, with one master file to identify each section. The use of frames in webpage design is considered to decrease website visibility.

Front end – refers to the part of a computer program which interfaces with the user. The front end is where the user clicks, makes selections and in general communicates his/her requests to the rest of the program.

Google – currently by far the most popular search engine available, which services several hundred million search queries per day. The company has a very successful financial history and a large body of regular users. The name Google is derived from the term 'googol', which is a very large number (1 followed by 100 zeroes).

Google bomb – a scheme whereby website coders with ulterior motives create large numbers of links to a given webpage, but associate each link with irrelevant text. This could cause innocent searchers to arrive at this webpage while having typed this irrelevant text as a search query. The term is actually a misnomer, and should actually be 'search engine bomb', since the technique will work equally well with any search engine. However, this process has only been done using Google as a vehicle, again proving its popularity. See also *Bomb*.

Graphics – a picture, photograph or other non-textual image used on a website to enhance its usability. A graphic image often presents some other concept or textual phrase. Overuse of graphics on a webpage can lead to user frustration. Graphic images (if not supported by descriptive text) can lead to a decrease in website visibility. They were initially not indexable in general, but lately many search engines offer image searches, proving that they can be indexed.

Grey hat – see *Black hat*.

H1 tag – a piece of code (called the Header tag) used on a webpage to indicate the level of importance of text. It is most often used to identify headings of text. H1 is the highest level, followed by H2 up to H6. Search engine crawlers attach value to the H-levels, and coders should carefully choose what they put inside the H1 tag on every webpage of a website.

Harvesting – the process of scanning through many webpages per day in an attempt to increase the capacity and value of a search engine index. Both human editors and automatic search engine programs called crawlers harvest webpages.

Header – the first section of webpage HTML coding, which is not displayed to the user but is used to store information about the webpage. The body section contains the information to be displayed by the browser. The header section could (and should, for the purpose of achieving higher website visibility) contain various HTML metatags. See also *Body*.

Header tag – see *H1 tag*.

Hidden link – a hyperlink which is hidden from view so as not to irritate or alarm human users but which will be read by crawlers with a resultant increase in visibility for the target webpage. Adding hidden links to a webpage is considered spamdexing, since their inclusion is often aimed at artificially increasing the ranking of a webpage.

Hidden text – text which is hidden from being read by human users but which search engine crawlers will read and interpret. Normally the hidden text is keyword rich or even mindless repetition of the same set of keywords. Text can be hidden in a number of ways: text and background colour can be the same, text can be miniscule so as to appear as a thin line or text can be hidden behind images. Hidden text is considered to be spamdexing and its use could lead to a website being banned.

Hit – the number of requests a web file server receives to download a file. One webpage containing 20 images being downloaded will register 21 hits. As a result, hit counters are often used as a (false) indication of human traffic visiting a webpage since they provide an inflated view of activity. See also *Page impression*, *Page view*, *Visitor*.

Hosting – refers to the action of storing a complete website under a fixed name on a fast computer to allow users from all over the world to access it. Normally a company would offer this specialised service as being the only business they run, since it involves high uptime, fast connections to the Internet and a high level of expertise. Hosting companies whose servers are often down can negatively affect a website's visibility.

HTML naming convention – refers to the way a website designer allocates names and extensions to the files which make up the website as a whole. A sensible name for a webpage containing company detail could be *contact-detail-abcshoes.html*. The descriptiveness of these filenames plays a small part in website visibility.

Human/computer interaction (HCI) – refers to the study of the synergy and interaction between a human user and a computer program, normally via the program's interface. HCI is located on the intersection of a number of other fields of study, including design, behavioural science and computer science. Since the birth of the Internet, HCI has been expanded to include the study of humans interfacing with webpages.

Hyperlink – a word or set of words linked to a different location on the same webpage, a different webpage on the same website or a webpage hosted elsewhere. If the user clicks on a hyperlink, he/she is transported to the destination location. See also *Citation*, *External Link* and *Link farm*.

Hypertext Markup Language (HTML) – a formal document language generally used to create hypertext documents, called webpages, to be hosted in such a way that users can read them from anywhere in the world via their browsers. The user needs this browser program (like MS Internet Explorer) to display the HTML document properly.

Hyphenated domain name – a domain name which consists of two or more keywords, connected by hyphens. If the domain *www.buycars.com* has already been registered, one can instead register *www.buy-cars.com*, which is a hyphenated domain name. Although the single-word version is more popular, the hyphenated version can be interpreted by a search engine crawler. However, an association between hyphenated domain names and spamdexing has been established through the popularity of the get-rich-from-home-quickly brigade. A hyphenated domain name with a large number of keywords designed to draw the reader is typical of these schemes.

Impact factor – the number of times authors have referred to one specific academic journal. This figure (often abbreviated IF) is an indication of the importance of this journal, since many other authors base their own research on articles published in this journal. See also *Web impact factor*.

Index – a large set of files which contain all the data collected by the human editors and/or the crawler(s) of a search engine. When a user submits a search query, the contents of the index is searched, not the live Internet. The index should be updated regularly, and if done, this 'freshness' of the index tends to improve the quality of answers.

Indexing – the process of reading a webpage, then selecting and compiling the weight-carrying words in a searchable format into the index file(s). This process of updating the index file is done on a regular basis and the so-called 'freshness' of the index depends on the frequency of updates. The more regularly an index is updated, the higher the quality of the contents and the fewer 'dead links' it will contain.

Information literacy – the ability of an Internet user to access information from different sources, evaluate it critically and apply it in order to enhance learning.

Inlinks – hyperlinks pointing from other websites to the one under consideration. As such they can be viewed as votes of confidence in the quality of the information on the website and a higher number of 'votes' are taken to indicate higher value. Many search engines use the quantity and quality of inlinks in the ranking algorithm. More inlinks and inlinks from high-quality websites are worth more to the target website. Website owners should attempt to canvass inlinks from highly valued websites in the same community and in doing so use white hat methods to increase website ranking.

Interface – the coupling between two separate entities. A webpage must allow the user to interact with it – or at the least offer some navigation controls to lead the user to some other part of the website. This interaction between user and webpage takes place through the interface.

Internet – a collection of worldwide government, commercial and private computer systems that can interact and share information. These computer systems share data using a packet switching system and connect millions of users simultaneously.

Internet Protocol (IP) address – refers to a packet-based protocol expressed as four numbers that specifies a computer's network location.

Intranet – refers to a network in a company which could contain parts of the Internet and limits access by outside users. It often contains information relevant only to employees or too sensitive to share with the world.

Invisible text – refers to text on a webpage which cannot be seen by the user. The purpose of coding invisible text on a webpage is to create harvestable keywords for search engine crawlers in an attempt to raise the ranking of the webpage. This text will not be read by or even deter human users. Methods to make text invisible include using a very small font size, setting text colour and background colour the same and hiding text behind images. Most search engine crawlers will consider invisible text to be spamdexing and they can normally detect this easily. Also called *Tiny text*.

Invisible web – refers to an area of the Internet containing information which cannot be located through the use of search engines. This information is invisible to search engine crawlers for various reasons, including search engine policy decisions (opting not to index certain formats) and information that is located behind a firewall. Content of the invisible web will normally not be included in search engine indices and will therefore not be found by users. See also *Deep web*.

JavaScript – one of the most popular programming languages that enables website designers to add flair and interactivity to their websites. Netscape developed JavaScript, which is commonly used to enhance webpage navigation through the use of rollovers/mouseovers, pop-up windows and navigation menus. However, some search engine crawlers cannot interpret JavaScript coding and its use could block crawlers from following some links. This could lead to a decrease in website visibility.

Keyword – as in this book, the term *keyword* may be used in one of three contexts.

- It could refer to a single word or phrase typed into a search engine query box. In this sense, the user should try to type in (a) keyword(s) which closely match(es) the topic on which information is required.

- Secondly, it could refer to a single word that accurately describes the contents of a single webpage or website.

- Finally it could refer to the KEYWORDS metatag – an area in the webpage header reserved for listing all the important words which accurately describe the contents of that webpage.

See also *Body keyword*.

Keyword density – refers to the number of keywords used as a proportion of the total number of words in a sentence or paragraph. Keyword-rich text should contain as many descriptive words as possible, without creating text which does not read well. This kind of text could be seen as an attempt at spamdexing. Search engine algorithms could ban these webpages. See also *Keyword frequency*.

Keyword frequency – refers to the number of times a keyword is used on a webpage. See also *Keyword density*.

Keyword placement – refers to the location of keywords on a webpage. Research has proven that important keywords should be concentrated towards the top but diluted towards the bottom of a webpage.

Keyword proximity – refers to the 'distance' between two related keywords. These related keywords should be used close together to improve website visibility for that specific phrase.

Keyword search – an action done on a search engine to find documents containing one or more words that are specified by a user.

Keyword spamdexing – refers to the practice of repeating keywords inside the text or metatag part of a webpage to the extent that a human reader will not consider it to be normal text. This could vary from repeating the same word many times consecutively, to cleverly written text which verges on irritating the human reader due to repetition of the same word(s). Search engines use algorithms to determine when a webpage uses keyword spamdexing but the details of their operation is not known. Keyword spamdexing has been identified as the second most serious spamdexing issue, after link spamdexing. When writing body and metatag text, care should be taken not to exceed the limits of what is considered to be readable, standard text. Also known as *Keyword stuffing*.

Keyword stuffing – see *Keyword spamdexing*.

KEYWORDS metatag – a metatag listing the relevant keywords a user may enter when trying to find a specific category on a search engine. This metatag is not used by search engines anymore as a result of abuse by unscrupulous website authors. However, it is suggested that it is used as a central storage point for the important keywords for every webpage. These keywords need to be stored in a central page, since they are often needed when writing body copy and when creating some of the other metatags. See also *DESCRIPTION* and *TITLE metatags* and *Metatag*.

Link farm – a collection of webpages that contain large numbers of hyperlinks to one another or other pages. The main aim is to attempt to deceive search engines that place emphasis on the number of links in a website when determining relevancy. Link farms could be created manually but some are done by automated services and programs. Link farms are considered to be spamdexing and should be avoided at all costs. However, link farms are not to be confused with sensible link swapping, where reputable websites from the same community agree to cross-link to each other. See also *Citation*, *External link* and *Hyperlink*.

Link popularity – refers to a measure of how many other websites indexed by the same search engine have links to a given site.

Link spamdexing – a form of excess where many unrelated hyperlinks point to one webpage, creating the false impression that this webpage has content of high value and is related to all the incoming links. Often automated programs or systems are used to ensure that a link to the target webpage is inserted onto many outside webpages. These webpages (see also *Link farms*) often contain no more than hundreds or thousands of unrelated links and no useful content. This element of website visibility has been identified as the highest on the list of unwanted factors on a webpage which increase the chances of that webpage being blacklisted by search engines.

Listing – the process of getting a webpage to be included in the index of a search engine. This is required before a user can expect to see a certain webpage appear on the screen as part of a search engine result page.

Logical search – a search allowing the inclusion or exclusion of documents containing certain words through the use of operators such as AND, NOT, OR and NEAR. Research has proven that few searchers make use of the powerful but more complex features offered by logical searching. See also *Boolean operator*.

Meta search engine – meta search engines have no index and use the index of one or more other search engines (in parallel if more than one) to extract information. This leads to a wider range of possible answers but a higher chance of receiving more irrelevant answers to a user query.

Metadata – data about data. Metadata can be embedded in a webpage in the form of metatags which describe various aspects of that page, like a title for the webpage, a brief description of the content, etc. See also the various *Metatag* listings.

Metatag – a keyword inserted in the reserved section in the header of the HTML source document by the webpage author. There is a large number of possible metatags to use, but only a few have a direct bearing on website visibility. See also *DESCRIPTION*, *KEYWORDS* and *TITLE* *metatags*.

Metric – a measure of certain properties of webpages. See also *Hit, Page impression, Page view, Visitor*.

Model – a plan or description designed to represent abstract concepts in a way which a user can easily apply.

MSN – currently one of the top three search engines in the USA.

Natural results – see *Organic results*.

Navigation – the process an Internet user follows when finding his/her way through the Internet. It often involves making choices and clicking on links on a webpage to get to another webpage or section on the same webpage. In terms of website visibility, navigation links should be coded as plain text, to allow crawlers to interpret these links correctly, which would add to the visibility score.

Neighbourhood – in the context of this book the neighbourhood of a website refers to the collection of websites whose contents are similar or about the same topic. The most important positive element of a website in terms of visibility is the quantity and quality of hyperlinks between websites in the same neighbourhood.

Notepad – the name of a simple program supplied with the Windows operating system which is mostly used to create ASCII files. Therefore Notepad could also be used to create HTML files which could be displayed as webpages.

Operator – a focusing feature which can be included in a search query. This will either narrow the scope of the search by filtering answers (for example inclusion, exclusion, phrases, logical), or it could widen the scope of the search by including more answers (for example stemming).

Optimisation – see *Search engine optimisation*.

Organic results – refers to search engine results with websites which earned their place due to their contents and other elements of the website favoured by crawlers. Organic results are in contrast to paid results, where website rankings are earned through payment rather than content. It is also referred to as *Natural results*.

Outlinks – refers to hyperlinks on a website which link to websites other than the originating one. The destination websites of outlinks should be in the same neighbourhood as the originating website to increase website visibility.

Page impression – a measure of the number of visitors to a website, specifically the number of times a single webpage has been loaded. This count does not include other files, e.g. images, loaded with the webpage in question. Page impressions are considered to be a more accurate, although often much lower, indication of actual human visitors than hits. See also *Hit*, *Page view*, *Popularity measure*, *Visitor*.

Page rank – when used as two words, it refers to the placing of a webpage on a search engine result page. A higher ranking (a lower figure, i.e. 1st is better than 2nd), is considered to be better, since humans favour the first page of results. See also *PageRank*.

Page redirect – refers to the process whereby a user is redirected to another site when attempting to access a website. This process could be viewed as spamdexing because users visit a different webpage to the one that is viewed by search engine spiders.

Page view – the same as a *Page impression*. See also *Hit*, *Visitor*.

PageRank – when used as a single word, PageRank is the name of Google's link analysis algorithm which determines the ranking of webpages. This term is a wordplay on the surname of one of the original authors of Google, Larry Page. See also *Page rank*.

Paid inclusion (PI) – a search mechanism advertising practice where webpages are included in search engine indices in exchange for payment. This practice does not guarantee top rankings – only that the website will be indexed within a certain time period.

Paid placement (PP) – an advertising system where websites are guaranteed top rankings for certain keywords for a fee. Participating websites often bid for these rankings and the highest paying website receives the top rank whenever the keyword which has been bid on is used as a search query.

Paid submission – refers to the process whereby web designers pay certain fees to have their websites reviewed by directory editors more quickly than normal. It does not affect ranking or the chances of indexing websites.

Pay per click (PPC) – refers to a system which allows website owners to increase the traffic to their website. Owners bid on (a) keyword(s) or keyphrases and all websites having bid for a given keyword/phrase are displayed when it is used as a search query. However, the website with the highest bid for the relevant keyword/phrase will appear on top, the second highest bidder second from the top, etc.

Personal computer – a single computer which is cheap enough for the user not to have to share it with other users and which is capable of storing and executing programs on its own storage devices.

Phrase search – refers to a full text type of search for documents containing an exact sentence or phrase specified by a user. Normally the user has to enclose the search phrase in quotes to distinguish it from being separate keywords.

Popularity measures – different ways of measuring visits to a webpage, also called metrics. They measure these visits in radically different ways and some can give an inflated picture of popularity. See also *Hit*, *Page impression*, *Page view*, *Visitor*.

Portal – a centralised website which provides diversely sourced information in a unified fashion. Some search engines have grown into portals where a variety of other categories of information is provided, including weather, infotainment, news, stock prices, etc.

Practitioner – a person who is a specialist in a given field and works in industry. See also *Academic*.

Precision – the degree to which a search engine lists documents matching a query. The more matching documents the search engine lists, the higher the precision.

Programmer – see *Coder*.

Query – a word, phrase or a group of words entered into a search engine's search box, which represents the information required by the searcher. The relevance of the returned information depends to a large extent on the accuracy of the search query. Research has proven that many searchers are unable to specify an accurate search query or they use general single-word terms.

Ranking – the position a search engine allocates to a webpage in its sorted result list. A higher position (i.e. a lower figure, where 1st is better than 2nd) is considered to be better. The SEO industry revolves around achieving high rankings for their customers for given keywords or phrases.

Really Simple Syndication (RSS) feed – refers to a method of publishing frequently updated web content. Readers subscribe to RSS feeds such as news headlines, video or audio and any updated content from the source will then be sent to them automatically.

Recall – the degree to which a search engine returns all the matching webpages in its index. There may be 1,000 matching webpages, but a search engine may only find 800 of them. It would then list these 800 and have a recall of 80 per cent.

Refresh – the action of reloading a webpage from the server. If, for example, a user opens a news webpage and leaves that window open for the rest of the day, it might be worthwhile clicking on the 'Refresh' button from time to time to allow any updates to be downloaded from the news server to the browser.

Relevance – refers to how closely the search engine results appear to match the searcher's query as measured by the searcher.

Result page – see *Search engine result page (SERP)*.

Return on investment (ROI) – the ratio of money gained or lost on an investment relative to the amount of money invested, often expressed as a percentage. Website owners sometimes invest large amounts of money in website design and/or optimisation and would expect some return on this investment in terms of sales through the website.

Robot – see *Crawler*.

Robot.txt – refers to a file written and stored in the root directory of a website that restricts the search engine spiders from indexing certain pages of the website. This file is used to disallow certain spiders from seeing files that the website owner does not want them to see. A certain spider can also be prevented from viewing any of the webpages through this file.

ROBOTS metatag – a metatag which prescribes whether or not visiting crawlers should index the current webpage and follow hyperlinks from this same page.

Scutter – see *Crawler*.

Search box – refers to the box on a search engine screen in which the user has to type a search query to start the search process. Webpages other than search engines can also have a search box, the use of which often starts a search inside that webpage only.

Search engine – a service aimed at allowing users to find relevant information on the Internet in a short time. The term is often used to describe two different kinds of services: crawler-based search engines and human-powered directories. Although both provide essentially the same service, they gather their content in radically different ways. A search engine has four components although the user only interacts with the first: user interface, crawler/editor, algorithm and index file. Search services are normally free and companies generate income through advertising on search pages. See also *Directory*.

Search engine marketing (SEM) – a form of Internet marketing that seeks to promote websites by increasing their ranking in the search engine result pages. This type of marketing may manifest in a number of ways: through SEO, paid inclusion or paid placement.

Search engine optimisation (SEO) – a process involving changes to a website with the purpose of achieving higher ranking for that website on search engines. SEO is also called natural, organic or algorithmic optimisation, since no payment to the search engine is involved. Webpages having earned top rankings in natural search results have done so due to the relevance of their content and not through payment schemes. SEO is a complex process of fine-tuning many elements of a webpage – including rewriting content and hyperlinks, changing the website structure, adding image descriptions and manual submission to search engines, to name but a few. Certain elements of SEO, when taken too far, could reverse the process and reduce instead of increase website visibility. If important keywords are used too often in body text, for example, it could be construed as spamdexing by the visiting search engine crawlers, leading to the banning of the website.

Search engine result page (SERP) – refers to the result page produced by a search engine in response to a query submitted by a user. The search engine algorithm sorts the results on the SERP with what is perceived to be the most relevant answer first. If a relevant answer is present on the SERP the user is likely to click on the displayed link, thereby visiting the listed webpage. Research has proven that users seldom read results past the first SERP and very seldom past the third. This has given rise to the fierce competition (through the implementation of SEO and/or paid systems) for the coveted first few slots on a SERP.

Search engine submission – the process of registering data about a particular website in order to get the website indexed and promoted by that search engine, also known as search engine registration. Website owners should have their websites submitted manually rather than by using automated programs.

Search engine user – a general term describing an Internet user depending on search engines for information retrieval.

Searching – the process of attempting to find useful information on the Internet by correctly nominating keywords. The user chooses these keywords based on a perception of them being the best description of the information need.

Server – a computer which stores programs and/or data which is requested and used by users on other computers and which manages these requests in an orderly and timely fashion. A web server stores websites, but otherwise performs the same function as a standard server. Web servers are normally managed and maintained by commercial companies, since 100 per cent uptime and fast response is important. Furthermore, a high level of technical software and hardware expertise is required to manage a large number of websites in this way.

Server response – refers to the time it takes a server to service a request for a given website. Although a number of other factors play a role in the overall response time from the user's perspective, slow server response is generally blamed for long Internet downloads. When the server response time becomes excessive, a so-called timeout error could occur, which produces the same result as if the server was not working at all. This has serious consequences for both the user and the search engine crawler. For both these consumers the website they are trying to load will be inaccessible, which has serious consequences for its visibility.

Sitemap – a representation of the structure or architecture of a website, either as a series of simple text terms or as a hierarchy. A text-based sitemap should be provided on the homepage or as a separate webpage of a website. Apart from providing useful guidance to the human visitor, it provides a link to every webpage on the website, meaning that a visiting crawler has an easy way to index these webpages.

Spam – refers to the process of flooding a computer with (normally) useless information, sometimes in the form of e-mail messages, in an attempt to deactivate this computer or make productive work by the user difficult or impossible. Spam in a search engine context, called spamdexing, differs from traditional unsolicited e-mail spam. However, both types share the feature of being unwanted information forced onto an unwilling recipient. See also *Spamdexing*.

Spamdexing – the use of any search engine ranking technique which manipulates the quality of the results produced by the search engines. It is therefore an attempt to influence the sequence of results appearing on a search engine result page. Examples of spamdexing include excessive repetition of a keyword in a page, optimising a page for a keyword which is unrelated to the contents of the site and using invisible text. Most search engines will penalise a webpage which contains spamdexing. See also *Spam*.

Spider – see *Crawler*.

Splash page – refers to an image that appears on a screen, being the first thing the user sees while a program is loading. Splash pages often promote a product, service or company and may contain a button for the user bypass the viewing of the splash page. If the splash page contains only the image and no text, it offers the visiting crawler nothing to index and it will dramatically decrease its visibility.

Static page – a relatively simple webpage containing only so-called flat HTML, with no content that can change automatically. Static webpages are easy to create and easy for crawlers to index. However, they have limitations when complex websites are to be maintained, especially where a large database is involved (i.e. an airline booking system, online bank or bookshop). See also *Dynamic page* and *Dynamic URL*.

Stemming – refers to the ability to include the stem of a keyword in a search. For example, stemming allows a user to enter 'swimming' and obtain results also for the stem word 'swim'.

Stickiness – refers to the tendency of a webpage to keep customers on that page for a longer period of time, indicating that the page contains useful/relevant information. It is also sometimes measured as the number of webpages visited per session. Webpage designers aim to create websites with a high degree of stickiness. Ironically, search engine result pages have a low degree of stickiness, since users mostly navigate away from them very quickly.

Stop word – conjunctions, prepositions, articles and other words such as THE, AND, TO and A that often appear in documents yet alone may contain little meaning. Depending on the environment, any word can be nominated as a stop word. When searching within a collection of documents which covers assembler programming, for example, the (otherwise meaningful) word 'assembler' could be a stop word.

Stuffing – see *Keyword spamdexing*.

Terabyte – refers to a unit of computer data storage, abbreviated Tb, and equivalent to 1,000 Gigabytes (Gb) or 1,000,000,000,000 bytes. Technically the figure is 2^{40}, or 1,099,511,627,776 bytes, but the metric version is often accepted as being close enough for general use. One byte (b) is required to store one character.

Text spamdexing – a general term referring to the use of excessive words or phrases on a webpage in an attempt to artificially improve the ranking. See also *Spamdexing*.

Tiny text – see *Invisible text*.

TITLE metatag – an HTML tag used to define the text in the top line of a web browser, also used by many search engines as the title of search listings and for bookmark identification. Webpage designers should include a descriptive TITLE tag for every page, since it plays an important role in website visibility. See also *DESCRIPTION* and *KEYWORDS metatags* and *Metatag*.

Traffic – defined as the number of unique visitors to a single webpage but could also refer to the number of data packets generated by visitors to a website. Generally more traffic is better, since every visitor could be a potential client, assuming that a website has a commercial purpose. The purpose of both SEO and paid systems is to increase the visibility of a website and therefore the traffic in terms of human visitors.

Triangulation – refers to multiple research methods or information sources, in both cases used to increase the validity/reliability of research outcomes.

Trilogy – traditionally refers to a set of three connected works of art but in the context of this book it refers to the combination of a webpage, user and search engine. These three elements are closely linked and operate in synergy. If any one of the three is removed, the Internet as we know it will cease to exist.

Uniform resource locator (URL) – the address which identifies the location of a webpage or webpage element on the World Wide Web. For example, the URL of this book's website is *http://www.book-visibility.com*, which may often be shortened to just *www.book-visibility.com*.

Usability – in general this refers to the ease with which a human can employ a tool to achieve a specific goal. Specifically it refers to the degree of productivity or, alternatively, frustration which a user experiences when interacting with a webpage on the screen while attempting to complete a given task. In the context of this book, a website should be both usable and visible to achieve its goal.

User – generally refers to a human who is using an Internet service or a computer program. A distinction is generally made between non-expert users (often called end-users) and so-called power users. The latter are users who are capable of manipulating the advanced features of application programs to becoming more productive.

Video – in the context of this book refers to a video file, stored on a webpage, which can be played in a separate window by clicking on it. Search engines can generally not interpret the contents of a video on a webpage and descriptive text has to be included on the webpage if a crawler is to access and index a description of the video content.

Virtual library – refers to a collection of related information (also called a digital library) stored in a digital format and which can be accessed and queried through a computer interface.

Visibility – refers to the ease and effectiveness with which a search engine crawler can find and index a webpage. Webpage designers aim to design pages in such a way that they have high visibility to crawlers. Website visibility is a complex topic, and designing a highly visible website is a continuous process rather than a point to be aimed at. The target of visibility design (pleasing search engine algorithms) moves all the time, while competitors are also improving their websites. Other websites with similar content are continuously being updated in a constant drive to achieve the coveted few top spots for a given keyword search on search engine result pages.

Visible web – consists of all the webpages that are retrievable via search engine crawlers, also known as the indexable or surface web. See also *Invisible web*.

Visitor – in general refers to a human user who loads a certain webpage through his/her browser program. The more visitors a webpage draws, the more its content will become known. If the webpage is an online store, more visitors should equate to more sales and eventually more profits. A number of different classes of visitors are defined: first, repeat, singleton, unique and others. See also *Hit*, *Page view*, *Page impression*.

Web impact factor – refers to the status a given webpage has in the Internet community in terms of the number of hyperlinks from other authoritative webpages to this webpage. See also *Impact factor*.

Webpage – a single HTML document which is part of a website; it will commonly include text, graphics and links to other webpages. See also *Website*.

Website – a collection of connected webpages on the Internet containing related information and stored at a common URL. See also *Webpage*.

White hat – see *Black hat*.

Windows – a commonly used personal computer operating system whose main feature is the ability to execute different programs in separate frames, called windows, on the screen.

Wordpad – refers to a simplified word processing program, supplied as part of the Windows operating system when installed on a personal computer.

Yahoo! – one of the oldest directories on the Internet and currently ranked at number two in the world among search engines behind Google (in terms of searches done per day).

References

Aguillo, I.F., Granadino, B., Ortega, J.L. and Prieto, J.A. (2006) 'Scientific research activity and communication measured with cybermetrics indicators', *Journal of the American Society for Information Science and Technology*, 57(10): 1296–302.

Alimohammadi, D. (2004) 'Measurement of the presence of keywords and description meta-tags on a selected number of Iranian web sites', *Online Information Review*, 28(3): 220–3.

Ananzi (n.d.) *Ananzi Submissions*. See: *http://www.ananzi.co.za/Add_site/* (10 June 2008).

Anonymous (2002) *SEO Code of Ethics*. See: *http://www.searchengine ethics.com* (13 June 2008).

Anonymous (2006a) 'Search engine optimization', *Journal of Visual Communication in Medicine*, 29(1): 39–40.

Anonymous (2006b) *Does Google Index Flash?* See: *http://www.yourseo plan.com/google-flash.html* (24 June 2008).

Anonymous (2007) *6.4 HTML Frames*. See: *http://archive.cabinet office.gov.uk/e-government/resources/handbook/html/6-4.asp* (1 June 2008).

Anonymous (2008a) *Cybersquatting Cases on the Rise*, 28 March. See: *http://mybroadband.co.za/news/Internet/3314.html* (1 June 2008).

Anonymous (2008b) *Search Engine Optimization Standards and Spam Discussion*. See: *http://www.bruceclay.com/emergingstandards.htm* (03 June 2008).

Arnold, S.E. (2005) 'Relevance and the end of objective hits', *Online*, September/October: 16–21.

Ashley, M. (2007) *Search – The Killer App in Vista and Office 2007*. See: *http://www.networkworld.com/community/node/22148* (9 June 2008).

Baker, L. (2006) *Google Bans BMW for Search Spamming*. See: *http://www.searchenginejournal.com/bmw-booted-from-google-for-spamming/2886/* (28 June 2008).

Batelle, J. (2005) *Google Announces New Index Size, Shifts Focus from Counting.* See: *http://battellemedia.com/archives/001889.php* (2 June 2008).

BBC News (2006) *BMW given Google 'Death Penalty'.* See: *http://news.bbc.co.uk/2/hi/4685750.stm* (28 June 2008).

Bergman, M.K. (2001) 'The deep Web: surfacing hidden value', *Journal of Electronic Publishing*, 7(1). See: *http://hdl.handle.net/2027/spo .3336451.0007.104* (20 May 2008).

Binnedell, M. (2003) 'The WBPN Model: A Proposed Design Approach to Maximize Website Visibility to Search Engines'. Unpublished BTech mini-thesis. Cape Technikon, Cape Town, 10 December.

Bobnar, E. (2005) *Banned by Google? Dealing with a Google Ban.* See: *http://www.searchenginepromotionhelp.com/m/articles/search-engine-problems/google-ban-1.php* (14 June 2008).

Brin, S. and Page, L. (1998) 'The anatomy of a large-scale hypertextual web search engine', *WWW7 / Computer Networks*, 30(1–7): 107–17.

Brown, B.C. (2007) *The Ultimate Guide to Search Engine Marketing.* Ocala, FL: Atlantic Publishing.

Burke, M., Hornof, A., Nilsen, E. and Gorman, N. (2005) 'High-cost banner blindness: ads increase perceived workload, hinder visual search, and are forgotten', *ACM Transactions on Computer–Human Interaction (TOCHI)*, 12(4): 423–45.

BusinessLink (n.d.) *Search Engine Optimisation.* See: *http://www.e-future.ca/ alberta* (10 June 2008).

Ceaparu, I., Lazar, J., Bessiere, K., Robinson, J. and Shneiderman, B. (2004) 'Determining causes and severity of end-user frustration', *International Journal of Human–Computer Interaction*, 17(3): 333–56.

Chambers, R. (2005) *Search Engine Strategies: A Model to Improve Website Visibility for SMME Websites.* Masters thesis, Cape Peninsula University of Technology, November.

Chambers, R. and Weideman, M. (2005) 'Search engine visibility: a pilot study towards the design of a model for e-commerce websites', *Proceedings of the 7th Annual Conference on WWW Applications*, 29–31 August, Cape Town, South Africa. See: *http://www.zaw3.co.za* (28 June 2008).

Chellapilla, K. and Chickering, D.M. (2006) 'Improving cloaking detection using search query popularity and monetizability', *Proceedings of the 29th Annual International ACM SIGIR Conference on Research and Development in Information Retrieval*, 10 August, Seattle, USA. See: *http://airweb.cse.lehigh.edu/2006/chellapilla.pdf* (08 June 2008).

Cho, C.H. (2004) 'Why do people avoid advertising on the Internet?', *Journal of Advertising*, 33(4): 89–97.

Collins, D. (2006) *Frequently Asked Questions*. See: *http://www.reachpromotions.com/faq.html#doorway_pages* (24 June 2008).

CommerceNet/Nielsen Media (1997) *Search Engines' Most Popular Method of Surfing the Web*. See: *http://www.commerce.net/news/press/0416.html* (25 May 2008).

Csutoras, B. (2008). *From SEO to Social Media: Content Is Still King*. See: *http://searchengineland.com/080226-122341.php* (1 June 2008).

Cutts, M. (2005) Quoted by Turcotte. *Pictures from 2005 SES Search Engine Strategies Conference in New York*. See: *http://seoblog.backbonemedia.com/2005/03/pictures-from-2005-ses-search-engine.html* (3 June 2008).

Cutts, M., Moulton, R. and Carattini, K. (2007) *A Quick Word about Googlebombs*. See: *http://googlewebmastercentral.blogspot.com/2007/01/quick-word-about-googlebombs.html* (8 June 2008).

Dahm, T. 2000. *Search Engine Optimization Tips*. See: *http://www.webdevelopersjournal.com/articles/search_strategies_tips.html* (13 June 2008).

Dawson, A. and Hamilton, V. (2006) 'Optimising metadata to make high-value content more accessible to Google users', *Journal of Documentation*, 62(3): 307–27.

De Kunder, M. (2007) *Geschatte grootte van het geïndexeerde World Wide Web (Estimated Size of the Indexed World Wide Web)*. Masters thesis, Tilburg University, Tilburg. See: *http://www.dekunder.nl/Media/Scriptie%20Maurice%20de%20Kunder%20-%20Grootte%20geindexeerde%20web.pdf*.

Dunn, R. (2004) *The Top 10 Worst SEO Tactics*. See: *http://www.stepforth.com* (2 June 2008).

Elgin, B. (2005) *Google: A $50 Billion 'One-Trick Pony'?* See: *http://www.businessweek.com/technology/content/mar2005/tc2005033_5789_tc024.htm* (3 June 2008).

Enquiro (2008) *Enquiro Develops Google's Golden Triangle*. See: *http://www.enquiro.com/enquiro-defines-google-golden-triangle.asp* (9 June 2008).

Fishkin, R. and Pollard, J. (2007) *Search Engine Ranking Factors V2*. See: *http://www.seomoz.org/article/search-ranking-factors* (27 May 2008).

Fontaine, A.F. (2002) *E-Government Services and Computer and Internet Use in North Dakota*. Social Science Research Institute, University of North Dakota. See: *http://www.nd.gov/itd/planning/research/docs/citizen-it-report.pdf* (24 June 2008).

Franks, P. and Kunde, N. (2006) 'Why metadata matters', *Information Management Journal*, September/October: 55–61.

Gan, Q. and Suel, T. (2007) 'Improving web spam classifiers using link structure', *Proceedings of the 3rd International Workshop on Adversarial Information Retrieval on the Web*, ACM International Conference Proceeding Series, Vol. 215 Archive, Banff, Canada, pp. 17–20.

Gault, C. (2005) *Use of Flash Affects Search Engine Visibility for Five of the Ten Athletic Clubs Analyzed*. See: *http://www.webposition.com/aboutus/releases/01182005.asp* (8 June 2008).

George, D. (2005) *The ABC of SEO*. Morrisville, NC: Lulu Press.

Goldsborough, R. (2005) 'Get your site noticed without spamming', *Black Issues in Higher Education*, 21(26): 40.

Google (n.d.) *Why Does Google Remove Sites from the Google Index?* See: *http://www.google.com/support/webmasters/bin/answer.py?hl=en&answer=40052* (14 June 2008).

Hamdulay, Z. and Weideman, M. (2006) 'Search engine visibility: the effect of generic top-level domain choice', *Proceedings of the 8th Annual Conference on WWW Applications*, 5–8 September, Bloemfontein, South Africa. See: *http://www.zaw3.co.za* (28 June 2008).

Henzinger, M.R., Motwani, R. and Silverstein, C. (2002) 'Challenges in web search engines', *SIGIR Forum*, 36(2).

Hill, C. (2008) *How To Outrank Your SEO Competitors*. See: *http://searchenginewatch.com/showPage.html?page=3628461* (14 June 2008).

Institute for Human and Machine Cognition (2008) Program download. See: *http://cmap.ihmc.us* (downloaded 17 May 2008).

Introna, L. and Nissenbaum, H. (2000) 'Shaping the web: why the politics of search engines matters', *Information Society*, 16(3): 169–86.

iProspect (2006) *Search Engine User Behaviour Study*. See: *http://www.iprospect.com/about/whitepaper_seuserbehavior_apr06.htm* (20 May 2008).

Jackson, M. (2007) *Which Hat Should I Wear?* See: *http://searchenginewatch.com/showPage.html?page=3626787* (14 June 2008).

Jackson, M. (2008) *How to Tell If Your Domain Is Banned in a Search Engine?* See: *http://searchenginewatch.com/showPage.html?page=3629040* (14 June 2008).

Jansen, B.J. (2000) 'The effect of query complexity on Web searching results', *Information Research*, (6)1, October. See: *http://InformationR.net/ir/6-1/paper87.html* (15 August 2005).

Kay, R. (2007) 'Search engine optimization', *Computerworld*. See: *http://www.computerworld.com* (13 June 2008).

Köhne, J. (2006) *Optimizing a Large Dynamically Generated Website for Search Engine Crawling and Ranking*. MSc thesis, Delft University of Technology, Delft.

Kritzinger, W. (2007) *The Effect Webpage Body Keyword Location Has on Ranking in Search Engine Results: An Empirical Study*. Master's dissertation, Cape Peninsula University of Technology, November.

Kritzinger, W. and Weideman, M. (2004) 'The role keyword location plays in website visibility to search engines: an empirical study', *Proceedings of the 6th Annual Conference on WWW Applications*, 1–3 September, Johannesburg, South Africa. See: *http://www.zaw3.co.za* (28 June 2008).

Kritzinger, W. and Weideman, M. (2005) 'A study on the correct usage of webpage keywords to improve search engine ranking', *Proceedings of the 7th Annual Conference on WWW Applications*, 29–31 August, Cape Town, South Africa. See: *http://www.zaw3.co.za* (28 June 2008).

Kritzinger, W. and Weideman, M. (2007) 'Keyword placing in webpage body text to increase visibility to search engines', *South African Journal of Information Management*, 9(1). See: *http://www.sajim.co.za* (10 June 2008).

Kritzinger, W., Weideman, M. and Visser, E.B. (2007) 'Search engine ranking profile maintenance – a case study', *Proceedings of the 7th Annual Conference on WWW Applications*, 29–31 August, Cape Town, South Africa. See: *http://www.zaw3.co.za* (4 June 2008).

Li, D., Browne, G.J. and Wetherbe, J.C. (2006) 'Why do Internet users stick with a specific web site? A relationship perspective', *International Journal of Electronic Commerce*, 10(4): 105–41.

Machill, M., Neuberger, C. and Schindler, F. (2003) 'Transparency on the net: functions and deficiencies of Internet search engines', *Info – The Journal of Policy, Regulation and Strategy for Telecommunications*, 5(1): 52–74. See: *http:/www.emeraldinsight.com/1463-6697.htm* (10 June 2008).

Matthews, D. (2008) 'Google's new challenge: keyword spam'. See: *http://www.pcmag.com/article2/0,2817,2287888,00.asp#* (14 June 2008).

Mbikiwa, F. (2005) *Search Engine Exclusion Policies: Implications on Indexing E-commerce Websites*. Master's dissertation, Cape Peninsula University of Technology, November.

Mbikiwa, F. and Weideman, M. (2006) 'Implications of search engine spam on the visibility of South African e-commerce web sites', *South African Journal of Information Management*, 8(4). See: *http://www.sajim.co.za* (10 June 2008).

Miller, R.B. (1968) 'Response time in man–computer conversational transactions', *Proceedings of the AFIPS Fall Joint Computer Conference*, 33: 267–77 (8 June 2008).

Murray, M. (2008) *Fighting SEO Search Engine Optimization & ROI Tips*. See: *http://seo-experts-talk.blogspot.com/2008/05/fighting-seo-search-engine-optimization.html* (14 June 2008).

Nah, F.F.H. (2004) 'A study on tolerable waiting time: how long are Web users willing to wait?', *Behaviour and Information Technology*, 23(3): 153–63.

Neethling, R. (2008) 'User Profiles for Preferences of Search Engine Optimisation versus Paid Placement'. Unpublished MTech thesis, Cape Peninsula University of Technology, Cape Town.

Neethling, R. and Weideman, M. (2007) *Search Engine Optimisation or Paid Placement Systems: User Preferences*. Full research paper for the 9th annual Conference on WWW Applications, 4–7 September, Johannesburg, South Africa.

Ngindana, M. (2005) *Visibility of e-Commerce Websites to Search Engines: A Comparison between Text-Based and Graphic-Based Hyper-Links*. Master's dissertation, Cape Peninsula University of Technology, November.

Ngindana, M. and Weideman, M. (2004) 'Visibility to search engines: a comparison between text-based and graphics-based hyperlinks on e-commerce websites', *Proceedings of the 6th Annual Conference on WWW Applications*, 1–3 September, Johannesburg, South Africa. See: *http://www.zaw3.co.za* (28 June 2008).

Nielsen, J. (2000) *Flash: 99% Bad*. See: *http://www.useit.com/alertbox/20001029.html* (2 June 2008).

Nielsen, J. (2006) *F-Shaped Pattern for Reading Web Content*. See: *http://www.useit.com/alertbox/reading_pattern.html* (9 June 2008).

Nielsen, J. (2007) *Response Times: The Three Important Limits*. See: *http://www.useit.com/papers/responsetime.html* (8 June 2008).

Nobles, R. and O'Neil, S. (2000) *Maximize Web Site Traffic: Build Web Site Traffic Fast and Free by Optimizing Search Engine Placement*. Avon, MA: Adams Media Corporation.

Norman, D. (2004) *The Truth about Google's So-called 'Simplicity'*. See: *http://www.jnd.org/dn.mss/the_truth_about.html* (3 June 2008).

Noruzi, A. (2004) 'The Web impact factor: a critical review', *Electronic Library*, 24(4): 490–500.

Noruzi, A. (2005) 'Web impact factors for Iranian universities', *Webology*, 2(1). See: *http://www.webology.ir/2005/v2n1/a11.html* (9 June 2008).

Perkins, A. (2001) *The Classification of Search Engine Spam.* See: *http://www.silverdisc.co.uk/articles/spam-classification/* (10 June 2008).

Pi, S.S.H. (2006) *Online Publicity and Marketing in a Book Publishing House.* Master's thesis, Simon Fraser University, Burnaby, Canada. See: *http://ir.lib.sfu.ca:8080/retrieve/3674/etd2318.pdf* (31 May 2008).

Pouros, A. (2007) *Traffic Report.* See: *http://www.greenlightsearch.com/ Newslettertemplate/Newsletter0807/GLNLAUGUST07.html* (3 July 2008).

Powazek, D. (2006) *What Would Google Do?* See: *http://www .thinkvitamin.com/features/design/what-would-google-do* (3 June 2008).

Ramos, A. and Cota, S. (2004) *Insider's Guide to SEO.* Fremont, CA: Jain Publishing.

Rowlett, D. (2003) *Stop Search Engine Spam!* See: *http://www .internetmarketingwebsites.com/spam-review.htm* (13 June 2008).

Roy, S. (2001) *Frames and Search Engines.* See: *http://www.search engineguide.com/sumantra-roy/frames-and-search-engines.php* (13 June 2008).

Sack, J. (2005) 'HighWire Press: ten years of publisher-driven innovation', *Learned Publishing*, 18(2): 131–42.

Schwartz, B. (2007) *'Negative SEO' – Harming Your Competitors with SEO.* See: *http://searchengineland.com/070629-091438.php* (14 June 2008).

Sekhar, C. (2000) *Internet Marketing and Search Engine Positioning.* Nashville, TN: CS/Southern.

Sen, R. (2005) 'Optimal search engine marketing strategy', *International Journal of Electronic Commerce*, 10(1): 9–25.

Sherman, C. (2002) *Yahoo! Birth of a New Machine.* See: *http://searchenginewatch.com/searchday/article.php/3314171* (13 June 2008).

Sherman, C. (2007) *eTools.ch: A 'Swiss Army' Meta Search Engine.* See: *http://searchengineland.com/070330-131111.php* (19 May 2008).

Silverstein, C., Henzinger, M.R., Marais, H. and Moricz, M. (1999) 'Analysis of a very large web search engine query log', *SIGIR Forum*, 33(1): 6–12.

SIQSS (2000) *The Internet Study: More Detail.* Stanford Institute for the Quantitative Study of Society, Stanford University, CA. See: *http://www.stanford.edu/group/siqss/Press_Release/press_detail.html* (24 June 2008).

Smith, S. (2006) 'Searching outside the box: engines search out new business opportunities', *EContent*, 29(8): 32–6.

Spink, A. and Xu, J.L. (2000) 'Selected results from a large study of Web searching: the Excite study', *Information Research*, (6)1, October. See: *http://InformationR.net/ir/6-1/paper87.html* (26 May 2008).

Sullivan, D. (2000) *WebPosition Gold Review*. See: *http://www.searchenginewatch.com/sereport/print.php/34721_2165231* (27 March 2007).

Sullivan, D. (2001) *Desperately Seeking Search Engine Marketing Standards*. See: *http://searchenginewatch.com/sereport/article.php/2164371* (10 June 2008).

Sullivan, D. (2002a) *Google Bombs Aren't So Scary*. See: *http://searchenginewatch.com/showPage.html?page=2164611* (7 June 2008).

Sullivan, D. (2002b) *Death of a Meta Tag*. See: *http://searchenginewatch.com/showPage.html?page=2165061* (11 June 2008).

Sullivan, D. (2002c) *Search Engine Link Popularity*. See: *http://www.searchenginewatch.com/searchday/print.php/34711_2159711* (13 June 2005).

Sullivan, D. (2003) *Ending the Debate about Cloaking*. See: *http://www.searchenginewatch.com/sereport/print.php/34721_2165231* (2 June 2008).

Sullivan, D. (2006) *ComScore Media Metrix Search Engine Ratings*. See: *http://www.searchenginewatch.com/showPage.html?page=2156431* (3 June 2008).

Sullivan, D. (2007a) *Paid Search Advertising: Google AdWords, Yahoo Search Marketing & Microsoft adCenter*. See: *http://searchenginewatch.com/showPage.html?page=2167821* (12 June 2008).

Sullivan, D. (2007b) *YADAC: Yet Another Debate About Cloaking Happens Again*. See: *http://searchengineland.com/070304-231603.php* (28 June 2008).

Sullivan, D. (2008a) *Hitwise: Google Again Hits New High; Microsoft & Yahoo Again New Lows*. See: *http://searchengineland.com/080617-173543.php* (23 June 2008).

Sullivan, D. (2008b) *Google Now Fills Out Forms and Crawls Results*. See: *http://searchengineland.com/080411-140000.php* (24 June 2008).

Sung-Ryul Kim, S.R., Lee, I. and Park, K. (2004) 'A fast algorithm for the generalized k-keyword proximity problem given keyword offsets', *Information Processing Letters*, 91(3): 115–20.

Thelwall, M. (2001) 'Commercial web site links', *Internet Research: Electronic Networking Applications and Policy*, 11(2): 114–24.

Thelwall, M. (2007) 'Bibliometrics to Webometrics', *Journal of Information Science*, 34(4): 1–18.

Thurow, S. (2003a) *Search Engine Visibility*. Indianapolis, IN: New Riders.

Thurow, S. (2003b) *SEO Corner – JavaScript and Search Engine Visibility*. See: *http://www.webpronews.com/node/4414/print* (13 June 2008).

Vaughan, L. and Thelwall, M. (2004) 'Search engine coverage bias: evidence and possible causes', *Information Processing and Management: An International Journal*, 20(4): 693–707.

Vinson, J. (2007) *Killer Apps in Knowledge Management*. See: *http:// blog.jackvinson.com/archives/2007/01/17/killer_apps_in_knowledge_ management.html* (9 June 2008).

Visser, E.B. (2007) *Search Engine Optimisation Elements' Effect on Website Visibility: The Western Cape Real Estate SMME Sector*. Master's thesis, Cape Peninsula University of Technology, November.

Visser, E.B., Kritzinger, W. and Weideman, M. (2006) 'An empirical study on the implementation of the Chambers model: search engine optimisation elements and their effect on website visibility', *Proceedings of the 8th Annual Conference on WWW Applications*, 5–8 September, Bloemfontein, South Africa.

Voorbij, H.J. (1999) 'Searching scientific information on the Internet: a Dutch academic user survey', *Journal of the American Society for Information Science*, 50(7): 598–615.

Waganer, S. (2008) *Search Engine Optimization (SEO)*. See: *http://www .magnetiks.com/* (20 May 2008).

Wall, A. (2006) *How Do Flash Sites Rank Well?* See: *http://www .seobook.com/archives/001457.shtml* (12 June 2008).

Wallace, D. (2003) *Spamming Techniques That You Will Want to Avoid*. See: *http://www.searchrank.com/resources/art003.htm* (13 June 2008).

Wang, Y.M., Ma, M., Niu, Y. and Chen, H. (2007) 'Spam double-funnel: connecting web spammers with advertisers', *Proceedings of the 16th International Conference on World Wide Web*, Alberta, Canada, pp. 291–300.

Webb, C. (2007) *Banned From Google – How I Finally Got Listed*. See: *http://ckwebb.com/blogging/how-i-finally-got-my-website-listed-in- the-google-index/* (14 June 2008).

Weideman, M. (1999) 'An empirical study on Internet topic searching (using standalone Internet search engines) by undergraduate computer study students', *Proceedings of IRMA99, 1999*, 16–19 May, Hershey, USA, pp. 1044–5.

Weideman, M. (2001) *Internet Searching as a Study Aid for Information Technology and Information System Learners at a Tertiary Level*. PhD thesis, University of Cape Town, December.

Weideman, M. (2002a) 'Effective application of metadata in South African HEI websites to enhance visibility to search engines', *Proceedings of the 4th Annual Conference on WWW Applications*, 4–6 September, Bellville, South Africa. See: *http://www.zaw3.co.za* (10 June 2008).

Weideman, M. (2002b) 'FOIOTI: successful Internet searching for the average user', *Proceedings of the Annual Conference of the South African Institute of Computer Scientists and Information Technologists (SAICSIT)*, 16–18 September, Port Elizabeth, South Africa.

Weideman, M. (2003) 'Payment for increasing website exposure in search engine results – technical and ethical issues', *Proceedings of the 5th Annual Conference on WWW Applications*, 10–12 September, Durban, South Africa. See: *http://www.zaw3.co.za* (28 June 2008).

Weideman, M. (2004a) 'Ethical issues on content distribution to digital consumers via paid placements as opposed to website visibility in search engine results', *Proceedings of ETHICOMP 2004*, 14–16 April, Syros, Greece, Vol. 2, pp. 904–15.

Weideman, M. (2004b) 'Empirical evaluation of one of the relationships between the user, search engines, metadata and websites in three-letter .com websites', *South African Journal of Information Management*, 6(3), September. See: *http://www.sajim.co.za* (28 June 2008).

Weideman, M. (2004c) 'An interface to information retrieval from a postgraduate academic knowledge repository: open source vs freeware products', *Proceedings of the 6th Annual Conference on WWW Applications*, 1–3 September, Johannesburg, South Africa. See: *http://www.zaw3.co.za* (28 June 2008).

Weideman, M. (2005) 'FOIOTI: an implementation of the conceptualist approach to Internet searching', *South African Journal of Libraries and Information Science*, 71(1): 11–25.

Weideman, M. (2006) 'Crawler visibility and human usability of a government services website from a technomunity angle', *Proceedings of Community Informatics for Developing Countries: Understanding and Organising for a Participatory Future Information Society 2006*, 31 August – 2 September, Cape Town, South Africa, pp. 368–85.

Weideman, M. (2007) 'Use of ethical SEO methodologies to achieve top rankings in top search engines', *Proceedings of the Computer Science and IT Education Conference*, 16–18 November, University of Technology, Mauritius.

Weideman, M. (2008) *Case Study: XiCrypt Website Visibility to the English and German Speaking Worlds*. Invited Research Lecture, 5 May, Campus02 University, Graz, Austria.

Weideman, M. and Chambers, R. (2005) 'The application of best practice towards improving website visibility to search engines: a pilot study', *South African Journal of Information Management*, 7(4), December. See: *http://www.sajim.co.za* (23 June 2008).

Weideman, M. and Chambers, R. (2006) 'Improving website visibility and information retrieval of e-commerce ventures: a specification to please the crawlers', *Proceedings of E-society 2006*, 13–16 July, Dublin, Ireland, Vol. 2, pp. 285–9.

Weideman, M. and Haig-Smith, T. (2002) 'An investigation into search engines as a form of targeted advert delivery', *Proceedings of the Annual Conference of the South African Institute of Computer Scientists and Information Technologists (SAICSIT)*, 16–18 September, Port Elizabeth, South Africa, p. 258.

Weideman, M. and Kritzinger, W. (2003a) 'Search engine information retrieval: empirical research on the usage of metatags to enhance website visibility and ranking of e-commerce websites', *Proceedings of the 7th World Conference on Systemics, Cybernetics and Informatics*, 28–30 July, Orlando, Florida, Vol. 4, pp. 231–6.

Weideman, M. and Kritzinger, W. (2003b) 'Concept mapping vs. web page hyperlinks as an information retrieval interface – preferences of postgraduate culturally diverse learners', *Proceedings of the Annual Conference of the South African Institute of Computer Scientists and Information Technologists (SAICSIT)*, 17–19 September, Johannesburg, South Africa, pp. 69–82.

Weideman, M. and Ngindana, M.W. (2004) 'Website navigation architectures and their effect on website visibility – can search engines deliver on the promise?', *Proceedings of SAICSIT 2004 Conference: Fulfilling the Promise of ICT*, 5 October, Stellenbosch, South Africa, pp. 292–6.

Weideman, M. and Schwenke, F. (2006) 'The influence that JavaScript™ has on the visibility of a website to search engines – a pilot study', *Information Research*. See: *http://informationr.net/ir/11-4/paper268.html* (8 June 2008).

Weideman, M. and Strümpfer, C. (2004) 'The effect of search engine keyword choice and demographic features on Internet searching success', *Information Technology and Libraries*, 23(2): 58–65.

Whalen. J. (2000) *How to Optimize a Framed Site for High Rankings*. See: *http://www.webproguide.com/articles/How-to-Optimize-a-Framed-Site-for-High-Rankings/* (13 June 2008).

Wikipedia (2008a) *Spam (Monty Python)*. See: *http://en.wikipedia.org/wiki/Spam_%28Monty_Python%29* (18 May 2008).

Wikipedia (2008b) *Cybersquatting*. See: *http://en.wikipedia.org/wiki/Cybersquatting* (1 June 2008).

Wikipedia (2008c) *Usability*. See: *http://en.wikipedia.org/wiki/Usability* (28 June 2008).

Wikipedia (2008d) *Criticism of Adobe Flash*. See: *http://en.wikipedia.org/wiki/Cybersquatting* (1 June 2008).

Wikipedia (2008e) *Cost per Action*. See: *http://en.wikipedia.org/wiki/Pay_per_action* (1 June 2008).

Wikipedia (2008f) *Spamdexing*. See: *http://en.wikipedia.org/wiki/Spamdexing* (13 June 2008).

Wikipedia (2008g) *World Population*. See: *http://en.wikipedia.org/wiki/World_population* (28 June 2008).

Wilkinson, T.A. (2004) *Just Say No to SEO Spam*. See: *http://www.wedge.com/* (10 June 2008).

Wong, M. (2004) *Mike's Marketing Tools*. See: *http://www.Mikes-Marketing-Tools.com* (2 June 2008).

Woods, N.R. (2007) 'Initial interest confusion in Metatag cases: the move from confusion to diversion', *Berkeley Technology Law Journal*, 22: 393–418.

Yahoo! Answers (2008) *Anyone Else Irritated by the 'Flash' Adverts?* See: *http://answers.yahoo.com/question/index?qid=20080430220535AAVj5TC* (2 June 2008).

Yoo, C.Y. and Kim, K. (2005) 'Processing of animation in online banner advertising: the roles of cognitive and emotional responses', *Journal of Interactive Marketing*, 19(4): 18–34.

Zeeger, E. (2008) *Why Frames Are Bad for Search Engine Optimization*. See: *http://www.seomatrix.com/newsletter/archive/2006/SEO-Newsletter-July-2006/frames-bad-for-optimization.php* (13 June 2008).

Zhang, J. and Dimitroff, A. (2004) 'The impact of webpage content characteristics on webpage visibility in search engine results (Part I)', *Information Processing and Management*, 41: 665–90.

Index